Had there been a war, after all? There had been something, all right. Something. Something there was that turned us into a people who know we can't believe anybody anymore, including ourselves.

This was just about the saddest war's ending a man ever went to.

—Russell Baker, 1973

Contents

viii · Contents

Preface

> The cold war changed us. We used to be pretty much what we
> started out to be: a republic that expected normally to be at
> peace.
>
> —Daniel Patrick Moynihan[1]

THE COLD WAR has bequeathed America a number of legacies—a sense of permanent emergency; a consequent condition of continuous large-scale military preparation; covert military operations of a sort we never ran or sponsored before; the infectious attitude of secrecy, even dishonesty, toward the American people that such operations necessarily involve us in; the ruinous borrowing required to finance it all.[2]

This book is about another legacy of the Cold War—unfortunately it's about dishonesty too—the disappearance of the separation of powers, the system of checks and balances, as it applies to decisions to go to war. Contrary to the words and unmistakable purpose of the Constitution, contrary as well to reasonably consistent practice from the dawn of the republic to the mid-twentieth century, such decisions have been made throughout the Cold War period by the executive, without significant congressional participation (or judicial willingness to insist on such participation). It is common to style this shift a usurpation, but that oversimplifies to the point of misstatement. It's true our Cold War presidents generally wanted it that way, but Congress (and the courts) ceded the ground without a fight. In fact, and this is much of the message of this book, the legislative surrender was a self-interested one: Accountability is pretty frightening stuff.

A number of people helped me develop the ideas in this book. Among academic colleagues, Bill Van Alstyne, Jules Lobel, and Lori Damrosch were unusually generous and helpful, though overall I have probably profited most from the input of my students. (A pity such talented and distinctive young people get lost so soon in gargantuan law firms.) Several national security law classes at Stanford argued the ideas contained in this book with me to my great profit. (You will also find several of their papers quoted herein.) Earlier versions of chapters 2, 4, and 5 appeared in 1990 in the *Stanford Law Review* (where Matt Nosanchuk and Susan Pilcher proved helpful editors); an earlier version of the appendix (since seriously amended) appeared in a 1988 *Columbia Law Review* article (where Crystal Mayner played the same useful role). Stanford blessed me over the years I was working on this with a succession of unusually capable research assistants—Dan Bagatell, Nicole Cook, Ted Cooperstein, Jim Lico, Peter Savich, and Maria Tai Wolff—and Chrish Peel creatively commented on drafts of some of the chapters. For typing and retyping the manuscript I have only myself to thank—insidious development, word processors—but I couldn't have done so if my secretary, Cele Horn, hadn't taken over the management of much of the rest of my work. (Just as well: She's the better manager, I the better typist.) Finally, thanks are due to Carolyn Gunn, who helped me with just about everything over the past decade.

War and Responsibility

CHAPTER 1

The Constitutional Framework

> This system will not hurry us into war; it is calculated to guard
> against it. It will not be in the power of a single man, or a single
> body of men, to involve us in such distress; for the important
> power of declaring war is vested in the legislature at large . . . .
> —James Wilson[1]

> I didn't have to get permission from some old goat in the United
> States Congress to kick Saddam Hussein out of Kuwait.
> —George Bush[2]

ONE of the recurrent discoveries of academic writing about constitutional law—an all but certain ticket to tenure—is that from the standpoint of twentieth-century observers, the "original understanding" of the document's framers and ratifiers can be obscure to the point of inscrutability. Often this is true. In this case, however, it isn't. The power to declare war was constitutionally vested in Congress.[3] The debates, and early practice, establish that this meant that all wars, big or small,[4] "declared" in so many words or not—most weren't, even then[5]—had to be legislatively authorized.[6] Indeed, only one delegate to either the Philadelphia convention or any of the state ratifying conventions, Pierce Butler, is recorded as suggesting that authority to start a war be vested in the president. Elbridge Gerry, backed by others, responded that he "never expected to hear in a republic a motion to empower the Executive alone to declare war,"[7] and Butler subsequently disowned his earlier view.[8]

There were several reasons for the founders' determination to vest the decision to go to war in the legislative process. The one they mentioned most often is the most obvious, a determination not to let such decisions be taken easily. The founders assumed that peace would (and should) be the customary state of the new republic—James Madison characterized war as "among the greatest of national calamities"[9]—and sought to arrange the Constitution so as to assure that expectation.[10] Their assumption was not that Congress was any more expert on the subject of war than the executive—if anything they assumed the contrary—but rather that requiring its assent would reduce the number of occasions on which we would become thus involved. There were various statements by influential framers to the effect that executives tended to be more warlike than legislative bodies.

Madison's is typical: "The constitution supposes, what the History of all Governments demonstrates, that the Executive is the branch of power most interested in war, and most prone to it. It has accordingly with studied care, vested the question of war in the Legislature."[11] Patently the point was not to exclude the executive from the decision—if the president's not on board we're not going to have much of a war—but rather to "clog" the road to combat[12] by requiring the concurrence of a number of people of various points of view. Justice Story wrote in 1833, "[T]he power of declaring war is not only the highest sovereign prerogative; but . . . it is in its own nature and effects so critical and calamitous, that it requires the utmost deliberation, and the successive review of all the councils of the nation."[13] To invoke a more contemporary image, it takes more than one key to launch a missile: It should take quite a number to start a war.

Two other rationales that played a role can be highlighted by examining the (debated) decision to involve the House of Representatives in the decision to go to war. The House was certainly not included because of any perceived expertise: Indeed, because of its assumed lack thereof it was excluded from such foreign policy processes as the approval of treaties. Rather, authorization by the entire Congress was foreseeably calculated, for one thing, to slow the process down, to insure that there would be a pause, a "sober second thought," before the nation was plunged into anything as momentous as war.[14] Thus in defense of including the House, Story wrote that "[l]arge bodies necessarily move slowly; and where the co-operation of different bodies is required, the retardation of any measure must be proportionately increased."[15] (Occasionally there won't be time for such deliberation, but we shall see that that is something the framers foresaw and accommodated.)

The House was included for another reason as well, that it was conceived as "the people's house": Given the way the burdens of war get distributed, it was felt that the people's representatives should have a say. (It was felt further that the involvement of "the people's representatives" would increase the participation of the people themselves in the debate.[16]) The requirement of authorization by both houses of Congress was thus also calculated to increase the probability that the American people would support any war we entered into. The founders didn't need a Vietnam to teach them that wars unsupported by the people at large are unlikely to succeed. (Indeed, the difficulties of keeping the colonial troops in the field during the Revolution provided the beginnings of a similar lesson.)

This point applies a fortiori to the legislature. Unless Congress has unequivocally authorized a war at the outset, it is a good deal more likely later to undercut the effort,[17] leaving it in a condition that satisfies neither the allies we induced to rely on us, our troops who fought and sometimes died, nor for that matter anyone else except, conceivably, the enemy. Admiral

James Stockdale, who spent seven and a half years as a prisoner of war in Hanoi, put it well: "Our Constitution as written protected our fighting men from shedding blood in pointless exercises while a dissenting Congress strangled the effort. But what has evolved . . . affords them no such protection." Thus, he concludes, we cannot afford "to fight any more wars without a thoroughgoing national commitment in advance."[18] In fact this is a position often taken, understandably, by military men.[19] For example, General Alexander Haig testified at his confirmation hearing for the position of Secretary of State, "Heaven help us as a nation if we once again indulge in the expenditure of precious American blood without a clear demonstration of popular support for it. I think the legislature is the best manifestation of popular support."[20]

It is true that an early draft of the Constitution vested the power "to make war" in Congress, and this language was changed during the editing process to the power "to declare war." This change was made for two reasons.[21] The first was to make clear that once hostilities were congressionally authorized, the president, as "commander in chief," would assume tactical control (without constant congressional interference) of the way they were conducted. (Proponents of broad executive authority to involve the nation in military hostilities often rely on the constitutional designation of the president as "Commander in Chief of the Army and Navy of the United States," but the record is entirely clear that all this was meant to convey was command of the armed forces once Congress had authorized a war, that it did not carry authority to start one.[22]) The second reason for the change in language was to reserve to the president the power, without advance congressional authorization, to "repel sudden attacks."[23]

THE COUNTERARGUMENT FROM OBSOLESCENCE

> The need for Presidents to have that power [to use force abroad without congressional approval], particularly in the modern age, should be obvious to almost everyone.
>
> —Robert Bork[24]

The clarity of the Constitution on this question leaves two strategies open to advocates of executive authority to start wars—though it can be demonstrated quite rapidly that neither will work. The first is simply to assert that the Constitution does not fit today's world—that it is, in a word, obsolete. In fact this is a line that is rarely taken in so many words, as the conventions of constitutional discourse do not recognize it as a legitimate move. For good reason: The most archaic-sounding provisions of our founding document, their purposes intelligently unpacked, generate commands of complete contemporary relevance.[25] If there is a consensus that one of those commands has become unworkably burdensome—their point, of course, is to be at least somewhat burdensome[26]—the appropriate response is repeal by the constitutionally prescribed method, not a unilateral declaration by the burdened official that the provision no longer applies, at least not to him.[27]

In any event, the constitutional requirement that Congress express its formal approval before the president leads the nation into war is not remotely obsolete: The purposes that underlay it were rendered sufficiently transparent to permit their mapping onto contemporary conditions. Occasionally—though nowhere near as often as enthusiasts would have us believe[28]—military emergencies can develop faster than Congress can convene and react. That was also true, however, in the late eighteenth century—in fact it was probably truer then than it is today, given that (a) Congress was out of session most of the time and it took weeks, not hours, to round its members up, and (b) its members and committees did not have significant staffs. The founders understood this, though, and consequently reserved to the president authority to respond on his own to "sudden attacks" until there was time for Congress to convene and confer: In such situations the president could respond militarily and seek authorization simultaneously.[29]

It probably is the case, however, that enemy actions not actually amounting to attacks on the United States can more obviously threaten our national security now than they could when the Constitution was agreed to. This raises the question whether the reserved emergency presidential authority to "repel sudden attacks" should be (1) limited to actual attacks on United States territory[30] or (2) "functionally" extended to other situations where a clear danger to our national security has developed so unexpectedly, and immediate military response is so imperative, that advance congressional authorization to respond militarily simply cannot be awaited (though such authorization must be requested, at the latest, simultaneously with the issuance of the order dispatching the troops, our military response discontinued if such authorization is not promptly forthcoming).[31]

At first blush the language seems mildly helpful: "attack" might or might not mean "attack on the United States," but "sudden" does seem to suggest that time urgency is the point. This is building too much on too little, however, as the phrase appears not in the document but in Madison's notes on the debates. We therefore will make better progress by inquiring into the *purpose* of the reservation of authority to repel sudden attacks. One animating idea could have been that there would in the event of an attack on the United States inevitably be a consensus that a military response was in order, and thus a requirement of congressional approval would be a needless formality. If that was the idea, however, a limitation to actual attacks on U.S. territory seems highly questionable: The *preclusion* of such an attack by a preemptive strike seems likely to garner a similar consensus,[32] as for that matter would an American military response to, say, a Soviet invasion of Mexico or Canada. But then how about Guatemala, Great Britain, or Japan? Thus if we construe the reservation in "likely consensus" terms we confront two choices, each unacceptable. Either we limit it to actual attacks on the United States, which seems to undershoot the posited rationale and thus constitute a questionable approach to constitutional language, or we expand it to all cases where the executive believes that "all sensible people" would agree with his response, in which case we can be quite certain it would be invoked whenever the executive himself thought a military response appropriate. (The tendency of virtually everyone to assume that all rational people, properly advised, would agree with him is one I assume I need not annotate.[33])

The most natural alternative construction of the reservation would focus on the word "sudden" and assume the point was to give the president authority to respond without advance authorization when there has not been time to secure it (so long as he seeks it simultaneously and subsides if it is not promptly forthcoming). This path appears more promising. In the first place, it fits a general theory of emergency power entertained by some of the founders, that under emergency conditions the executive can properly act in excess of legislative authorization, so long as he makes swift and full disclosure to the legislature and subsides if they do not approve.[34] Second, it parallels a similar reservation of extraordinary military authority another section of Article I made in favor of the *states*: "No State shall, without the Consent of Congress . . . engage in War, unless actually invaded, *or* in such imminent Danger as will not admit of delay."[35] Finally, unlike the "most sensible persons would agree" rationale, "there wasn't time to secure advance authorization so we had to seek it simultaneously" seems susceptible to principled limitation[36] and thus may be given the sort of functional construction we are accustomed to according constitutional language. Thus although the point is arguable,[37] I am inclined to construe the president's reserved authority to go ahead and respond militarily (and seek congressional authorization simultaneously) as extending to genuine and serious threats to our national security beyond actual attacks on United States territory.

Thus construed, the constitutional command is certainly not obsolete: In fact other changes have made it more urgent than ever. In the nineteenth century—indeed, up until World War II—the nation took quite seriously the founders' fear of a "standing army": Thus in order to lead the nation into combat the president needed not only a declaration of war or comparable statement of authorization, but also statutory authority to raise an army and a congressional appropriation of the funds needed to support it. Now, of course, we do effectively have a standing army, which means that today the requirement of congressional authorization is all that stands in the way of unfettered executive discretion to commit it to combat.[38]

Another fact that might render the requirement of congressional authorization particularly important today is that at least for the present we have an all-volunteer army, thereby eliminating what might at certain periods in our history have been regarded as a further source of potential resistance to half-baked military schemes, namely draftees from all social classes (including politically influential ones) and their families and friends.[39] I won't linger long on this one, however. This "check" was probably never terribly significant: I know I didn't emerge from basic training programmed for independent thinking. (For the moment at least it seems to be professional soldiers who provide the most reliable brake on the ill-conceived military schemes of amateurs,[40] though obviously not so reliable that we should continue to tolerate the exclusion of Congress from the process.) Worth more attention is the fact that we have spent much of the late twentieth century in an era of "divided government" (president from one party, Congress from the other). Thank God it didn't happen, but as of, say, February 1992, the risk that the executive might start a war to demonstrate toughness and "leadership" in perilous political times (when, for example, the economy refuses to "jump-start" in time for an upcoming election) seemed anything but remote.[41]

As far as the need to bring the American people on board is concerned, another change—actually in this case a return to the earlier traditions of the republic—seems relevant. We now have a citizenry more willing than those of prior decades to take on the administration on questions of foreign policy, particularly questions of war and peace. That this change too (at least assuming, as I do, that national unity behind authorized wars is generally a desirable goal[42]) has increased the importance of the congressional authorization requirement was noted well in a student paper I received in the spring of 1991:

> [T]his writer must enter a personal note . . . . The congressional process that led to the authorization of January 12, 1991, had a significant bearing on my own attitude towards the war once it began. I was highly doubtful of the march to war, agreeing (as did congressional opponents of the war resolution) that the Iraqis ought to be ejected from Kuwait, but believing that sanctions and blockade were a wiser course, and that war was both hazardous and not necessary. Had President Bush gone to war by fiat, without authority from Congress . . . I believe I would have marched against it. But the war was in fact duly authorized, and I therefore believed it best to reserve my own doubts and not actively oppose a war which was entered into in a constitutional manner.[43]

Another change of conditions repeatedly pressed by proponents of unencumbered presidential power is that the possible consequences of war are more serious now than they were in the eighteenth century. But this one too turns out on a moment's reflection to argue the other way—*in favor of* the original conclusion that "no one man should hold the power of bringing this oppression upon us."[44] The fact that we can all be blown to kingdom come only reinforces the need, where there is time, for a "sober second thought" before war is entered into, and a collective judgment that it should be.

Of course, if he asked, the president probably would usually receive rather readily the support of both Congress and the American people when he decided to have a war. (Admittedly this is somewhat hard to judge, as of late congressional and popular opinion has generally not been permitted to register until the war is under way, at which point support notoriously increases.) From childhood we Americans are programmed to fall in when the bugle sounds, a fact that has caused no small percentage of my friends to ask me why, if approval is a foregone conclusion, I'm wasting my time worrying about increasing participation in such decisions. Is there any reason to suppose, given their respective performances, that Congress will prove wiser on issues of war and peace than the president? Actually I think our history does support, if slightly, the founders' judgment that Congress (if only because it is necessarily more deliberate) tends to be more responsible in this area than the executive.[45] To answer the question on its own (comparative) terms, however, is to miss the point.[46] The constitutional strategy was to require more than one set of keys to open the Pandora's box of war. As usual, Alexander Bickel said it well: "Singly, either the President or Congress can fall into bad errors . . . . So they can together too, but that is somewhat less likely, and in any event, together they are all we've got."[47]

THE COUNTERARGUMENT FROM PRACTICE

The other argument that we can ignore the original demand of the Constitution here—this one is made more explicitly—is an argument from post-ratification practice, that the behavior of various presidents, and the acquiescence of various congresses, during the 200 years since the document was adopted have in essence amended it, effectively eliminating the requirement of congressional authorization. The most obvious answer here is one the Supreme Court has given many times, that past violations are only that—violations—and cannot change the meaning of the Constitution: "That an unconstitutional action has been taken before surely does not render that same action any less unconstitutional at a later date."[48] Though that's got to be generally right, it may oversimplify somewhat, unduly assimilating constitutional provisions of relevantly different types. If, for example, the question before the Court were whether a certain action was appropriately classified as within the "legislative power" or the "executive power"[49]—*and* there were no more precise provision suggesting an answer—one would rightly expect the judges to be interested in how various presidents and congresses, most particularly *early* presidents and congresses,[50] had by action and acquiescence effectively classified it. Our question, however, does not present a case of one or more vague documentary vessels that must receive their meaning from subsequent experience. In language and recorded purpose the War Clause made an unmistakable point that needed no further gloss: Acts of war must be authorized by Congress.[51] In cases like this the Court is quite right: Usurpation isn't precedent, it's usurpation.

Assume this were not so, however, and that on some oddly repotted "adverse possession" theory,[52] post-ratification practice in violation of the Constitution could change it, still the argument could not work in this context. At the very least we would require "a systematic, unbroken, executive practice, long pursued to the knowledge of the Congress and never before questioned,"[53] a pattern that on every count is manifestly lacking here. Of course real life is never entirely neat and clean, but the original constitutional understanding was quite consistently honored from the framing until 1950.[54] And when certain presidents did play a little fast and loose with congressional prerogatives—Polk at the start of the Mexican War; Wilson and Roosevelt, respectively, in the events leading up to the First and Second World Wars—they obscured or covered up the actual facts, pledging public fealty to the constitutional need for congressional authorization of military action.[55] It is therefore impossible to build the occasional nonconforming presidential actions of this period into an argument that they had gradually altered the constitutional plan. Shifts of constitutional power, to the extent they are possible at all, must be accomplished in the open.

> In the case of executive wars, none of the conditions for the establishment of constitutional power by usage is present. The Constitution is not ambiguous. No contemporaneous congressional interpretation attributes a power of initiating war to the President. The early Presidents, and indeed everyone in the country until the year 1950, denied that the President possessed such a power. There is no sustained body of usage to support such a claim. It can only be audacity or desperation that leads the champions of recent presidential usurpations to state that "history had legitimated the practice of presidential war-making."[56]

Korea

In 1950 this long-standing legislative-executive consensus shattered.[57] As it sent American troops into Korea the Truman Administration, speaking most capaciously through Secretary of State Dean Acheson, not only claimed unprecedented unilateral authority to commit our troops to combat (and keep them there long after there was opportunity for congressional consideration) but even went so far as to suggest that Congress lacked authority to stop it![58]

The waters were muddied by certain semiattractive rationalizations: that our actions were taken in *defense* of South Korea (which was at least initially true, but constitutionally irrelevant[59]) and that authorization by the United Nations Security Council could take the place of authorization by the United States Congress (which understandably appealed to those hoping we had entered a new era of world government, but violated the American Constitution and the explicit terms on which Congress had approved our U.N. membership[60]). The fallacy of both these defenses led soon to the recurrent assertions of the Truman Administration—now a part of our national treasury of graveyard humor—that Korea wasn't really a war but rather a "police action,"[61] and its adoption of a constitutional reading that had from the dawn of the republic been recognized as erroneous,[62] that the Commander in Chief Clause encompassed the authority not simply to manage wars approved by Congress but the right to start them unilaterally as well: "The President, as Commander in Chief of the Armed Forces of the United States, has full control over the use thereof."[63]

There was some grumbling on the constitutional front over Korea, though from the perspective of 1993 it seems remarkably limited. Apparently there was only one lawsuit challenging the President's audacious claim, and it was dismissed on standing grounds[64] (which isn't terribly surprising, given that 1950 was some years in advance of the Warren era's judicial power revolution). Those in Congress who understood and were offended by the administration's claim that the power to decide on war was its alone, notably Senator Robert Taft of Ohio, had to soft-pedal the point lest they appear critical of the war on the merits and thus "soft on Communism."[65] (Taft in particular was angling for the 1952 Republican nomination.) What's more, this initial separation-of-powers problem was soon eclipsed by another—the "civilian control of the military" issue raised by General MacArthur's defiance of administration policy—on which those concerned with questions of process in this area were forced to side *with* Truman. Finally, before the war was over Congress had voted draft extensions and special appropriations,[66] which by some people's lights constituted sufficient authorization and thus rendered rhetorical the quarrel over whether it had been lawfully begun. Even assuming that view of the legal situation to have been correct,[67] however, rhetorical revolutions can have serious consequences, and this one persists, at least in the attitude of the executive, to the present day.[68]

In terms of public and congressional willingness to question the legality of executive-initiated war, Vietnam was very different. Throughout that later war its opponents, in and out of court, continually hammered the theme that it had not been constitutionally authorized. Chapter 2 will evaluate this claim.

CHAPTER 2

Vietnam: The (Troubled) Constitutionality of the War They Told Us About

Once I loved my country because of the birds and butterflies
Because of the days of escaping from school.
But now I love my country because in each handful of soil
You are there, beloved.
>—Poem by soldier in National Liberation Front
whose fiancée, also a guerrilla, had been
killed in the south[1]

What is there to have pangs of conscience at night about with
Vietnam?
>—Henry Kissinger, 1976[2]

I PROPOSE to break this subject down into several parts: the overall constitutional legality[3] of the American war in Vietnam that was begun, in earnest, in 1964 and 1965; the legality of the American ground incursion into Cambodia in 1970; the legal relevance of the repeal of the Tonkin Gulf Resolution in January of 1971; and the legality of our government's continued bombing of Cambodia between the final withdrawal of our troops on April 1, 1973, and August 15 of the same year.

From these discussions two common themes will emerge. First, as the constitutional requirement of congressional authorization has historically been understood, Congress does indeed appear (years of denial and doubletalk notwithstanding) to have authorized each of these phases of the war. Second, that weak-kneed "appear" will turn out not to be standard academic waffling, but instead will be seen to result from Congress's penchant for studied ambiguity in this area. Throughout the Indochina war—as in connection with various lesser conflicts since[4]—a majority in Congress showed itself to be consistently unwilling to end the fighting, in fact quite willing (until the very end) to continue to fuel it, but at the same time quite resourceful in scattering the landscape with rationalizations whereby it could continue to claim that it wasn't really *its* war.

The Constitutionality of the Vietnam War, 1964–1973

> "Now tell us all about the war,
> And what they killed each other for."
> —Robert Southey, *The Battle of Blenheim*[5]

President Truman sent a few American soldiers to Vietnam, but it wasn't until the Kennedy Administration that anything serious started to happen.[6] (At the end of the Eisenhower Administration, we had 685 military advisers there.) Under Kennedy, some of our advisers began to play peripheral combat roles, and at the time of his assassination there were about 16,000 American troops in Vietnam.[7] On August 2, 1964, North Vietnamese patrol boats may have attacked the *Maddox*, an American destroyer in the Gulf of Tonkin. A second incident, supposedly involving an attack on the destroyer *Turner Joy*, was reported two days later. On August 5, twelve hours after this second episode, U.S. warplanes retaliated by bombing four North Vietnamese patrol boat bases and a large oil storage depot. On August 7, Congress passed the Southeast Asia Resolution (more commonly known as the Tonkin Gulf Resolution), which on its face gave the president broad powers to defend against aggression in the area.

The rest, unfortunately, is history. Operation Rolling Thunder, involving the sustained American bombing of North Vietnam, began on February 24, 1965, and on March 6, two Marine battalions, the first full-fledged American combat troops in Vietnam, landed to defend Danang Air Field. Thousands of other American troops, Army and Marine Corps, followed, and by year's end we had 184,000 men in Vietnam. By inauguration day 1969, there were 536,000. By the time we were done, the American war in Indochina had become the longest in our history, the second most expensive monetarily, and the fourth most costly in American lives.[8] We dropped about four times the tonnage of bombs used in all of World War II, and over a million Vietnamese soldiers died.[9]

Defenders of the Vietnam War's constitutionality claimed that the required congressional authorization could be found in some combination of (a) the Southeast Asia Collective Defense (SEATO) Treaty of 1954; (b) the Tonkin Gulf Resolution of August 7, 1964; and (c) various pieces of congressional legislation supporting the war, notably defense appropriation acts and extensions of the draft. I shall deal with these in turn.

The SEATO Treaty

The SEATO Treaty was signed at Manila on September 8, 1954, and approved by the Senate on February 19, 1955. Article IV, paragraph 1, provided:

> Each party recognizes that aggression by means of armed attack in the treaty area against any of the Parties or against any State or territory which the Parties by unanimous agreement may hereafter designate, would endanger its own peace and safety, and agrees that it will in that event act to meet the common danger in accordance with its constitutional processes.[10]

By protocol signed and ratified at the same time, the parties "unanimously designate[d] for the purposes of Article IV of the Treaty the States of Cambodia and Laos and the free territory under the jurisdiction of the State of Vietnam."[11] Understandably, the State Department and other defenders of the war's constitutionality cited the Treaty and its accompanying protocol as authorization for the war.

There is a debate over whether a treaty can ever constitute a congressional authorization of armed hostilities.[12] During the war, many commentators argued that it could not, as the House of Representatives is not involved in the treaty process. As Professor Wormuth put it, "If this is [permissible], the President and the Senate might make a treaty with Liberia, let us say, and then embark upon a war with any country in the world. This is to substitute Liberia for our House of Representatives."[13] Well, almost. Under the Constitution, treaties must be approved by a two-thirds vote of the Senate,[14] which means, in Wormuth's example, that Liberia *and sixteen Senators* are being substituted for the House. Even that, however, is troubling—or at least it could be in eras when the Senate is more "hawkish" than the House.

The problem with the argument is that it proves too much. From the beginning, virtually all the players in our constitutional system have recognized the possibility of self-executing treaties—that is, treaties that can take effect as domestic law without the subsequent passage of an implementing statute by the entire Congress.[15] Every such treaty has the effect of excluding the House of Representatives from the legislative process. Indeed, in the 1920 case of *Missouri v. Holland*,[16] the Supreme Court held that a treaty could regulate subjects that could not otherwise be regulated by the federal government. Were such a treaty self-executing, it would have the effect not simply of eliminating the House of Representatives from the process, but also of bypassing the process of constitutional amendment ordinarily required to broaden the domain of federal constitutional power. In such a case, to revert to Professor Wormuth's figure, Liberia[17] would be taking the place of two-thirds of the House of Representatives, and the legislatures of three-quarters of the states as well! Compared with *Holland*, our case seems almost tame—at least as tame as any case involving war can be.

The answer has been given that treaties authorizing war are different from other treaties because, at the Constitutional Convention, the possibility of vesting the war power in the combination of the Senate and the president was suggested and rejected.[18] Tempting as the conclusion may be, however, this argument cannot work. For surely the judgment here made explicit at the convention, that the power in question should not be vested solely in the Senate but had to be shared with the House of Representatives, underlay *every* congressional power listed in Article I, section 8. A point of the entire exercise was to create a bicameral system, and distinctions of constitutional magnitude should not be permitted to hang on whether the framers actually said, "The commerce power? Well, we don't want it to be vested in the Senate alone, so we'll put it here in Article I, section 8, along with all the others." In fact, if you think about it, the argument turns out to be somewhat perverse. The fact that the war power was discussed in these terms demonstrates that some of the framers were thinking about vesting it in the Senate alone. Presumably those powers not thus mentioned received little or no such consideration.[19]

Still the question whether a treaty should be able in theory to serve as a constitutionally acceptable authorization of a war is not entirely free from doubt: There are at least a couple of other not implausible (though in my opinion not quite convincing) arguments against the proposition that it should that I shall take the liberty of relegating to an endnote.[20] I do so because in practice it is virtually unthinkable that a treaty would be ratified that would at the same time (a) be self-executing in the sense that it required no further action on the part of Congress and (b) satisfied what I shall later in this chapter argue to be about the only formal requirement of a congressional combat authorization imposed by the Declaration of War Clause, namely that it indicate who the enemy is to be.[21] Of course from time to time we ratify mutual defense treaties obligating the United States to come to the defense of the other signatories in case of attack by (unnamed) other nations, but naturally in such situations we will want to reserve to ourselves the right to find out more about the nature of the attack (notably but not exclusively who the attacker is and how clear and unjustified the "attack" in question was) before actually committing troops.[22] Thus we will invariably commit ourselves, as indeed we have, to defend our cosignatories (and they us) "in accord with [our] constitutional processes."[23] The constitutional processes of the United States require congressional authorization. The sharp-eyed among you will have noted that this was the form of the obligation to which we agreed in the SEATO Treaty. Thus whether or not a treaty could ever constitutionally stand in for a declaration of war, by its terms the SEATO Treaty could not.

The Tonkin Gulf Resolution

The Southeast Asia (Tonkin Gulf) Resolution was passed by the House on August 6, 1964, the Senate on August 7, and signed by President Johnson three days later. It provided, in full:

Whereas naval units of the Communist regime in Vietnam, in violation of the principles of the Charter of the United Nations and of international law, have deliberately and repeatedly attacked United States naval vessels lawfully present in international waters, and have thereby created a serious threat to international peace; and

Whereas these attacks are part of a deliberate and systematic campaign of aggression that the Communist regime in North Vietnam has been waging against its neighbors and the nations joined with them in the collective defense of their freedom; and

Whereas the United States is assisting the peoples of southeast Asia to protect their freedom and has no territorial, military or political ambitions in that area, but desires only that these peoples should be left in peace to work out their own destinies in their own way: Now, therefore, be it

Resolved by the Senate and the House of Representatives of the United States of America in Congress assembled, That the Congress approves and supports the determination of the President, as Commander in Chief, *to take all necessary measures to repel any armed attack against the forces of the United States and to prevent further aggression.*

Sec. 2.   The United States regards as vital to its national interests and to world peace the maintenance of international peace and security in southeast Asia. Consonant with the Constitution of the United States and the Charter of the United Nations and in accordance with its obligations under the Southeast Asia Collective Defense Treaty, the United States is, therefore, prepared, as the President determines, *to take all necessary steps, including the use of armed force, to assist any member or protocol state of the Southeast Asia Collective Defense Treaty requesting assistance in defence of its freedom.*

Sec. 3.   This resolution shall expire when the President shall determine that the peace and security of the area is reasonably assured by international conditions created by action of the United Nations or otherwise, except that it may be terminated earlier by concurrent resolution of the Congress.[24]

On its face, this certainly was broad enough to authorize the subsequent actions President Johnson took in Vietnam.[25] Numerous Senators and Congressmen, scrambling for cover, later denied that they had understood this. Particularly disillusioning over the years was the performance of Senator J. William Fulbright, Chair of the Foreign Relations Committee. Despite the fact that he had acted as the administration's floor manager for the Resolution—we shall hear from him in that capacity presently—Fulbright later claimed that he had been "unaware of the significance of the measure," that its passage "must stand as the only instance in the nation's history in which Congress authorized war without knowing that it was doing so."[26] Senator Richard Russell, who also grew to rue the Resolution, was perhaps more candid when he said, in 1966, "Personally, I would be ashamed to say that I did not realize what I was voting for when I voted for that joint resolution. It is only one page in length; it is clear; it is explicit. It contains a very great grant of power."[27] Or as Senator Norris Cotton put it, "We can all read."[28]

LEGISLATIVE HISTORY

Not surprisingly, the legislative history[29] of the Resolution confirms that those members of Congress who had read it understood it at the time of the vote (though a number subsequently "forgot"). Since the House of Representatives hardly discussed the Resolution at all, I shall concentrate on the Senate debate, which took place on August 6 and 7. President Johnson's transmittal message was phrased in terms as broad as the Resolution itself, describing it as stating "the resolve and support of the Congress for action to deal appropriately with attacks against our Armed Forces and to defend freedom and preserve peace in southeast Asia in accordance with the obligations of the United States under the Southeast Asia Treaty."[30] On the first day of the debate, Senator Jacob Javits stated that "We who support the joint resolution do so with full knowledge of its seriousness and with the understanding that we are voting a resolution which means life or the loss of it for who knows how many hundreds or thousands? Who knows what destruction and despair this action may bring in the name of freedom?"[31]

Senator Daniel Brewster asked if the resolution contained any language "which would authorize or recommend or approve the landing of large American armies in Vietnam or in China." Senator Fulbright responded, "There is nothing in the resolution, as I read it, that contemplates it. I agree with the Senator that that is the last thing we would want to do. However, the language of the resolution would not prevent it. It would authorize whatever the Commander in Chief feels is necessary."[32] Senator Gaylord Nelson also was troubled by the Resolution's broad language, and he asked Fulbright:

> Am I to understand that it is the sense of Congress that we are saying to the executive branch: "If it becomes necessary to prevent further aggression, we agree now, in advance, that you may land as many divisions as deemed necessary, and engage in a direct military assault on North Vietnam if it becomes the judgment of the Executive, the Commander in Chief, that this is the only way to prevent further aggression"?

Fulbright responded, "I do not know how to answer the Senator's question and give him an absolute assurance that large numbers of troops would not be put ashore. I would deplore it. And I hope the conditions do not justify it now." Nelson indicated that he did "not think, however, that Congress should leave the impression that it consents to a radical change in our mission or objective in South Vietnam." Fulbright answered:

[I]t seems to me that the joint resolution would be consistent with what we have been doing. We have been assisting the countries in southeast Asia in pursuance of the treaty. But in all frankness I cannot say to the Senator that I think the joint resolution would in any way be a deterrent, a prohibition, a limitation, or an expansion of the President's power to use the Armed Forces in a different way or more extensively than he is now using them.[33]

A colloquy with Senator John Sherman Cooper indicated that the Resolution was intended to constitute the "constitutional processes" contemplated by the SEATO treaty:

MR. COOPER: Does the Senator consider that in enacting this resolution we are satisfying that requirement of article IV of the Southeast Asia Collective Defense Treaty? In other words, are we now giving the President in advance authority to take whatever action he may deem necessary respecting South Vietnam and its defense, or with respect to the defense of any other country included in the treaty?

MR. FULBRIGHT: I think that is correct.

MR. COOPER: Then, looking ahead, if the President decided that it was necessary to use such force as could lead into war, we will give that authority by this resolution?

MR. FULBRIGHT: That is the way I would interpret it. If a situation later developed in which we thought the approval should be withdrawn, it could be withdrawn by concurrent resolution. That is the reason for the third section.[34]

On August 7, the second and final day of the Senate debate, Senator Nelson offered an amendment that responded to his concern about possible escalation. It provided: "Our continuing policy is to limit our role to the provision of aid, training assistance, and military advice, and it is the sense of Congress that, except when provoked to a greater response, we should continue to attempt to avoid a direct military involvement in the southeast Asian conflict." Fulbright refused to accept the amendment, indicating:

I do not object to it as a statement of policy. I believe it is an accurate reflection of what I believe is the President's policy, judging from his own statements. That does not mean that as a practical matter I can accept the amendment. It would delay matters to do so. It would cause confusion and require a conference, and present us with all the other difficulties that are involved in this kind of legislative action.[35]

Summing up the debate on the Resolution, Fulbright indicated his pleasure in reporting that the House had passed it unanimously, and his hope that the Senate would "approach that unanimity, if possible." Concerning the broad power being granted to the president, Fulbright reminded the Senate that "[w]e always have a reserve power, when we see that the President has made a mistake. We can always later impeach him, if we like."[36]

Senator Wayne Morse spoke last—he had spoken several times before—indicating his belief that "within the next century, future generations will look with dismay and great disappointment upon a Congress which is now about to make such a historic mistake."[37]

Ninety senators were present and voting. Eighty-eight voted "aye," and the ten absentees were all recorded in the affirmative. Only Morse and Ernest Gruening voted "nay": Each was defeated for reelection the next time he ran. The Resolution had earlier passed the House of Representatives by a vote of 416–0.[38]

ARGUMENTS THAT THE RESOLUTION SHOULDN'T HAVE COUNTED

One reason we were told we shouldn't take the Resolution seriously was that "it was passed with great speed and in the heat of emotion that resulted from the reported attack on American naval vessels in the Tonkin Gulf."[39] And so it was. The problems with this as a legal excuse are obvious, however. Most legislation would be at risk were inattention a nullifying factor. The critics constantly held up the official "declaration of war" as the way it *should* be done. However, declarations of war were often enacted with unusual haste and emotion:[40] Think for a moment about the reaction to Pearl Harbor. The conditions under which the Tonkin Gulf Resolution were enacted were indeed a scandal—forty minutes of discussion in the House, eight hours and forty minutes in the Senate (before a chamber that was generally less than one-third full)[41]—but while that may bear on whether its perpetrators should have been returned to office, it is hard to make it count legally.

The second attempt to nullify the Resolution was that the administration had lied to Congress about the details of the incidents in the Gulf. "I confess," Senator Fulbright said later, "I was hoodwinked and taken in by the President of the United States, the Secretary of State, and the Chief of Staff and the Secretary of Defense who told us about certain alleged events that I do not believe occurred."[42] From this he reasoned, "Insofar as the consent of this body is said to derive from the Gulf of Tonkin Resolution, it can only be said that the resolution, like any other contract based on misrepresentation, in my opinion, is null and void."[43]

It is true that the administration misled Congress about what happened in the Tonkin Gulf. The facts of the "attacks" will probably never be fully known, but their general contours are by now moderately clear. The supposed second attack, on the *Turner Joy*, almost certainly never took place, the report resulting instead from freak weather effects on radar and overeager sonarmen.[44] There is a higher probability that the first attack actually took place,[45] but if so, it inflicted nothing more than a single one-inch bullet hole in the *Maddox*,[46] and at all events was the result of provocation. The *Maddox* was part of a coordinated operation in which high-speed boats manned by South Vietnamese commandos raided the North Vietnamese coast, and American destroyers equipped with specialized electronic gear gathered information on North Vietnam's radar systems, and were engaged more generally in a show of force.[47] (Then Under Secretary of State George Ball indicated some years later that our destroyers were also there in part to provoke a response that would pave the way for a bombing campaign.[48] In any event the reason we were able to retaliate so fast was that our bombing targets had been picked months in advance, as part of a general "scenario" for war against North Vietnam.[49]) The administration was well aware of the doubts about the attack on the *Turner Joy*, and obviously was aware of the mission of both ships, but concerning both, largely in the person of Secretary of Defense Robert McNamara, it flagrantly misled the Congress.[50]

The administration's behavior was outrageous. However, it too is difficult to make count legally. A source in the Pentagon had called Senator Morse with a tip that the *Maddox* was an intelligence ship, not (as the administration claimed) on "routine patrol," and that its mission was associated with the South Vietnamese raids.[51] Even Morse (perhaps because the election campaign against Barry Goldwater was in progress) appears to have held back a little—at least he didn't ask the committee to call his informant as a witness—but he was forthcoming enough about his information, and asked enough knowledgeable and embarrassing questions, to make it clear to anyone actually interested in what had happened that further investigation was needed.[52] No one, it turned out, was interested.

The main reason they weren't probably was that most members of Congress didn't think what had happened in the Gulf was really to the point. As Congressman Dante Fascell, then a member and later Chair of the Foreign Affairs Committee, put it some years later:

> My own impression of what happened at that time was that most everybody said, well, the President wants this power and he needs to have it. It had relatively little to do with the so-called incident. I don't know why so much stress has been made on whether or not there was an incident or whether or not the President was deceitful or whatever . . . . The President needed the authority. Who cared about the facts of the so-called incident that would trigger this authority? So the resolution was just hammered right on through by everybody.[53]

As for those who did care, it would seem it was their duty to investigate further. The excuse later given for not having done so was that there was time pressure, that the administration had said it needed the Resolution right away.[54] But it didn't (except for the election): No further significant military action was taken for six months. It was *Congress's job* not simply to insist on getting the facts straight before giving the president a functional declaration of war, but also to decide for itself just how great an emergency there was.[55] That's why we have separate branches. That's why the war power is vested in Congress.

Another set of attempts to nullify the Resolution lay in the general claim that Congress "hadn't meant" to authorize the sorts of things that President Johnson later did in its name. There were several variants of this claim. The most restricted was to the effect that the Resolution had been passed in response to the naval incidents in the gulf and really was intended only to approve the President's defense of our ships and his retaliatory acts against the patrol boat bases and the oil storage depot and, perhaps, to approve similar limited responses to similar future provocations.[56] In light of the legislative history we have traversed, this account is plainly infirm. Floor manager Fulbright, and others, had indeed said several times that they *hoped* we wouldn't get into a real war, but invariably in the context of an explicit recognition that the Resolution opened up that possibility. Section 1 of the Resolution had granted the president authority to take all necessary measures "to prevent further aggression." "Aggression" only against our forces, perhaps? Astonishingly, Fulbright suggested just this construction in 1967: "We were approving the response to an attack upon our armed services, and the prevention of further aggression, which would well be read in the context of the time as meaning further attacks upon our armed forces."[57] This would have been an odd use of the word "aggression" under any conditions. Beyond that, section 1 gave the president authority to take necessary measures "to repel any armed attack against the forces of the United States *and* to prevent further aggression." It is unlikely that both phrases would have been included to refer to the same thing. The suggested construction is also rebutted by the Preamble's reference to the "deliberate and systematic campaign of aggression that the Communist regime in North Vietnam has been waging against its neighbors" and some quite explicit references during the debates:

> MR. MILLER: It is left open. It does not say aggression against whom. It is broad enough so that it could mean aggression against the United States, or aggression against the South Vietnamese Government, which I would suggest certainly fits in with the President's determination—
>
> MR. FULBRIGHT: I believe that both are included in that phrase.
>
> MR. MILLER: I would hope so.
>
> MR. FULBRIGHT: I would so take it.[58]

The second variant of this legislative intent argument went that if Congress had known how things were going to turn out, it might not have enacted the Resolution. Thus in 1967 Senator Charles Percy opined, "I don't know whether or not that resolution would have been approved, if it had been expressed that some years hence it would have involved the commitment of 540,000 American forces abroad."[59] Senator Fulbright added, "The intent of the Congress at that time was not to have things develop as they have . . . ."[60] No one disputes that: Indeed I would have hoped it was clear (rather than an "I don't know") that Congress would not have gone along if it had been able to foresee the tragedy that ensued. However, as an argument against the proposition that Congress had authorized the war, this too is invalid. There are many things Congress might not have authorized had it foreseen their effects—prohibition seems a conspicuous example—but we don't conclude from regrettable outcomes that the law didn't authorize what its plain language and legislative history tell us it did. We conclude that Congress made a mistake. Presumably Japan wouldn't have bombed Pearl Harbor had its leaders foreseen Hiroshima and Nagasaki—but that doesn't mean they didn't intend to do it.

Another rendition of the "we didn't mean it" argument appeared in a 1967 Report of the Foreign Relations Committee:

> [I]n the case of the Gulf of Tonkin Resolution, there was a discrepancy between the language of the resolution and the *intent* of Congress. Although the language of the resolution lends itself to the interpretation that Congress was consenting in advance to a full-scale war in Asia should the President think it necessary, that was not the *expectation* of Congress at the time. In adopting the resolution Congress was closer to believing that it was helping to *prevent* a large-scale war by taking a firm stand than that it was laying the legal basis for the conduct of such a war.[61]

This intertwines two errors. First, there is the attempt to equate a failure of expectation with a lack of relevant legislative intent, here made disarmingly explicit. Only the latter is legally relevant—and it is to be found in the operative document (which in this case is unambiguous) and, where necessary, in the legislative history (which in this case entirely corroborates the document). As for the second argument, that by authorizing military action Congress was actually trying to prevent a wider war, the appropriate responses are "Of course" and "So what?" I would hope that it is essentially *always* Congress's intention in authorizing military action to reduce the threat of a wider war. When it works, that's great. When it doesn't, however, that doesn't render the authorization inoperative. We can't have it both ways.

This last variant was refined even further, to the claim that Congress meant the Resolution as a sort of bluff, expecting the North Vietnamese to back down in the face of it. Senator Charles Mathias subsequently put it this way:

> What we were familiar with was a pattern or practice that had existed since the end of World War II, whereby the United States, by merely passing a resolution of the Congress, could bring about certain dramatic events in the world . . . . [I]n the context of what had gone before, we were saying, "Well, we'll sign this blank check, but we don't have any expectation that it will ever have to be used. All you'll have to do is wave it in front of your creditors and they'll all go away."[62]

To his credit, Mathias was not attempting to use this to nullify the Resolution—that would, again, confuse what was expected with what was authorized. When the only way of making a credible threat is actually to load a gun and hand it to your partner, there's no getting around it: You have to load the gun and hand it to your partner. It is in the nature of such a "bluff" that the gun may end up being used. (However, should your partner then go on a rampage, you don't have to go on handing him ammunition for nine years.)

If only by quoting him, I have been pretty hard on Senator Fulbright throughout this section. During the war he styled himself one of its foremost critics, to the point of making many of us admirers at the time, and there is no doubt his ventilation of the issues helped America rethink the war. Yet this was not the last time he voted with the administration forces, only to claim later that he had been duped and thus his vote should not be taken to represent what he really thought.[63] That said, however, it should be reported that George Reedy, President Johnson's press secretary at the time, has recalled that the Senator "had very definite assurances from Johnson that the Tonkin Gulf Resolution was not going to be used for anything other than the Tonkin Gulf incident itself."[64] Whatever rehabilitating effect this revelation may have on one's opinion of Fulbright,[65] it too cannot influence the legal status of the Resolution. Even had some secret protocol existed between the President and the entire membership of Congress, to the effect that the Resolution didn't mean what it said, it would have been of no legal effect. The laws of the United States are not private deals between the legislators who enact them and the presidents who sign them, subject to whatever secret restrictive covenants they may have attached. In any event the entire Congress was surely not party to any such "deal" in this case: Senator Fulbright's statements to the Senate as administration floor manager are entirely inconsistent with the existence of any such protocol. His elucidation of the meaning of the Resolution made it clear that while he, like others, hoped the United States wouldn't get involved in a land war in Vietnam, that possibility was within the authorization of the Resolution.

THE DELEGATION DOCTRINE (AND RELATED IMPLICATIONS
OF THE DECLARATION OF WAR CLAUSE)

The breadth of the Tonkin Gulf Resolution generated attacks under the (long moribund) delegation doctrine,[66] the argument being that the Resolution failed to provide sufficiently precise directions to the executive and thus could not qualify as valid legislation.[67] (Note the shift in the attack here: The Resolution is now assumed to have authorized what Johnson and Nixon did, and attacked on the ground that it authorized too much, or at least too vaguely.)

A conspicuous barrier to this argument was presented by *United States v. Curtiss-Wright Export Co.,*[68] decided in 1936, which came very close to indicating that the delegation doctrine simply does not apply in the foreign affairs area. (And this was back when the doctrine otherwise meant something: In fact 1935 was its year.[69]) It is true that *Curtiss-Wright* is not an opinion that readily commands intellectual respect: One need only read Articles I and II of the Constitution to recognize how wrong Justice Sutherland was about the opinion's featured dicta that (1) most of the federal government's foreign affairs powers are unstated in the Constitution and thus must be inherent, and (2) most such powers are assigned to the president rather than Congress.[70] Nor did the feature of the opinion with which we're concerned here, that the delegation doctrine must be considerably weaker in the international than in the domestic area, make sense either:[71] The point of the doctrine, that important policy choices are to be made by Congress, is no less implicated in international cases,[72] and could hardly be more implicated than it is with respect to the choice that is the subject of this book, whether or not to go to war.[73] But sensible or not, the Court unmistakably said the delegation doctrine applies less forcefully to foreign affairs cases, and in 1965, in *Zemel v. Rusk*, the Court, in an opinion by Chief Justice Warren, cited this aspect of *Curtiss-Wright* with approval.[74]

It is true that the *Zemel* opinion almost immediately softened its endorsement.[75] But even granting that *Curtiss-Wright* doesn't mean "that the delegation doctrine has *no* application to international relations [but rather] that it does not have *equal* application,"[76] that is more than enough to take it out of play. For the hard fact is that since the late New Deal, even with regard to domestic legislation, the delegation doctrine has been virtually nonexistent: "Since that time Congress has quite commonly by statute said to administrative officials, 'Find the problems in this area and solve them,' and the Court, when the question has even been raised, has upheld the delegation."[77] The real problem, therefore, isn't that the delegation doctrine doesn't apply to international cases, or even that it applies more weakly, but rather that it isn't clear that the doctrine any longer exists at all. The bottom line must therefore be that the Tonkin Gulf Resolution could not have been held at the time, and cannot now responsibly be said, to violate the delegation doctrine unless one postulates a general doctrine significantly stronger than any the Supreme Court (or the academy) has been willing to recognize since the 1930s.[78]

A few of us have advocated the general revival of the delegation doctrine,[79] but frankly, we don't seem to have many takers. Most of those who argued at the time for the doctrine's application to the Tonkin Gulf Resolution hadn't had much to say for it before, and haven't since either for that matter. Absent a strong feeling that the president is abusing his discretion with regard to some matter about which they care deeply, most people are perfectly prepared to live in a world where Congress doesn't really get involved in the job of governing. Thus it will probably take "another Vietnam" to get the delegation doctrine back on many people's agendas, at which time, I fear (though I'm bound to admit with some justice) it is unlikely to fare any better than it did last time.

The general demise of the delegation doctrine aside, there is another reason the attack on the Tonkin Gulf Resolution seems bound to fail. It comes into focus when one examines the sort of document the Constitution indicates is the paradigmatic combat authorization, the declaration of war, which typically was almost entirely nondirective. A declaration of war didn't tell the president how to fight the enemy, or how vigorously, or even when to begin: All it did was declare that we were at war with one or more enemies and leave the "how" up to him. Indeed, had it done more than that it would at least have flirted with unconstitutionality, as it was the point of the Commander in Chief Clause to keep Congress out of day-to-day combat decisions once it had authorized the war in question.[80]

We're on a good track here, however—looking not to some general (and no longer viable) "delegation doctrine," but rather to the specific constitutional provision in issue to see what *it* might suggest about the requisite degree of specificity. Article I, section 8 provides that "The Congress shall have Power . . . To declare War, grant Letters of Marque and Reprisal, and make Rules concerning Captures on Land and Water." In a recent article,[81] J. Gregory Sidak has argued (at least tentatively[82]) that congressional combat authorizations must actually be labeled "declarations of war." This is manifestly out of accord with the specific intentions of the founders—most eighteenth-century wars were not "declared" in so many words, a fact of which the founders took specific and approving note[83]—but nonetheless possesses some attractiveness as a twentieth century device for forcing Congress to reassume its constitutional responsibilities in this area.[84] If the only authorizations that count must be actually entitled "declarations of war," it will become difficult for Congress to play "we didn't mean it."

Unfortunately unexamined by Sidak is either (1) the fact that documents most commentators seem inclined to count as historic "declarations of war" have varied so widely in form that it's not at all clear what ought to count as one,[85] or (2) the oft-asserted costs of imposing such a requirement, notably the possibility that in certain situations calling an authorization a "declaration of war" might overstate our resolve, unduly hardening domestic attitudes[86] and perhaps even bringing in additional enemies against us.[87] It seems to me the latter can be handled quite readily by a careful delineation of our goals,[88] and as for the former, if the Court stood ready to impose a requirement that authorizations be labeled "declarations" I suppose there's no reason it couldn't go on to dictate the exact wording it meant to require.[89] The real problem with Sidak's suggestion is that given the flatly contrary history it would be justifiable only if it constituted the only effective way the War Clause's underlying purposes could be effectively served under current conditions, and there has been no showing by Sidak (or anyone else) that those purposes could not be served equally well by reverting to a regime of serious enforcement of a less straightjacketed requirement that *is* historically precedented, namely that there be *some* clear advance congressional authorization, however labeled, of acts of war. (It also is undoubtedly the case that courts are much more likely to revert to this unquestionably legitimate tradition than they are to accept Sidak's more radical suggestion.)

But if the label put on the authorization should not be constitutionally determinative, it *is* important constitutionally to insist that the authorizing document functionally resemble in pertinent respects the traditional declaration of war to which the document refers. One thing we've seen this doesn't mean is that the congressional authorization has to tell the president how and when to fight: In fact it would probably be unconstitutional if it did so.[90] It does mean something that is at least potentially important, though, that the authorization ordinarily be specific in terms of who it is we're prepared to go to war against—that is, that it not be a wholesale delegation of authority to the president to make war against whomever he regards as a suitable foe. Unlike most of the provisions of Article I, section 8, the War Clause speaks of a "declaration"—signaling a specific designation—not in terms that comfortably encompass a grant of general legislative discretion to the executive. Like "Letters of Marque [or] Reprisal" (and unlike a "rule concerning Capture") a "Declaration of War" includes the element of specificity: Whatever historical variation there may have been in declarations of war, "Go to war against whomever you want" would not have counted. The War Clause means only two things, but they are something: that Congress is to decide whether we go to war, *and* whom we go to war against.[91]

This will become relevant to some issues we will consider later,[92] but it does not appear to disqualify the Tonkin Gulf Resolution as a suitably specific combat authorization. The Resolution's preamble referred to the "campaign of aggression that the Communist regime in North Vietnam has been waging against its neighbors." (No other country, aside from the United States, was mentioned anywhere in the Resolution.) The enemy thus *was* specified, and the Resolution cannot be disqualified on the ground that the authorization was wholesale. In the relevant constitutional respects it was, as Under Secretary of State Nicholas Katzenbach testified, the "functional equivalent of the constitutional obligation expressed in the provision of the Constitution with respect to declaring war."[93]

Appropriations Acts and Selective Service Extensions

Throughout the course of the war, hundreds of billions of dollars were appropriated to support it, and the draft was repeatedly extended.[94] Supporters understandably cited these measures as further congressional authorization.

The law generally pertaining to authorization by appropriation is about what first-order common sense suggests it should be. If there is no reason to infer that Congress knew what the agency or program in question was about, the fact that it was buried in an appropriations measure is typically not taken to constitute authorization of it. If the program was conspicuous, it is.[95] Indeed, assuming sufficient notice of what was going on, appropriations may in some ways constitute unusual evidence of approval, in that typically Congress acts twice—once to authorize the expenditure and again to appropriate the money.

In this case, it would be an understatement to say that the program for which Congress was appropriating funds (and extending the draft) was conspicuous. In May of 1965 Congress enacted a special appropriation of $700 million for "military activities in southeast Asia."[96] The President's message requesting this appropriation had begun:

> I ask the Congress to appropriate at the earliest possible moment an additional $700 million to meet mounting military requirements in Vietnam.
>
> This is not a routine appropriation. For each Member of Congress who supports this request is also voting to persist in our effort to halt Communist aggression in South Vietnam. Each is saying that the Congress and the President stand united before the world in joint determination that the independence of South Vietnam shall be preserved and Communist attack will not succeed.[97]

A few members of Congress stated for the record that in voting for the appropriation they did not intend to be voting for the war. Senator Albert Gore (Sr.), to take but one example, indicated that by his vote he did not intend "to approve an escalation of the war or to approve the sending of combat troops into South Vietnam."[98] However, Operation Rolling Thunder was well under way, we had had combat troops in Vietnam for two months, and the appropriation was $700 million for military activities in Vietnam: What exactly did Gore and his similarly exculpatory colleagues think they *were* voting for? As one court put it, they "talked like doves before voting with the hawks."[99] The requested measure passed the House 408 to 7 and the Senate 88 to 3 (five of the Senate absentees indicating that if present they would vote in favor).[100] An additional $1.7 billion, also for "military activities in southeast Asia," was appropriated in September of the same year. It too was hardly hidden, appearing as a separate title of the Defense Department's annual appropriation act.[101]

Four months later, in his 1966 State of the Union Address, President Johnson predicted that "special Vietnam expenditures for the next fiscal year" would rise by $5.8 billion.[102] And sure enough, on March 1, 1966, Congress approved a $4.8 billion supplemental military appropriation by votes of 393 to 4 and 93 to 2 (the five absent senators indicating, you guessed it, that they would have voted yes).[103] Senator Gruening's amendment to limit the president's authority to send draftees to Vietnam was defeated in the Senate, 94 to 2.[104] Senator Morse also added a motion, to repeal the Tonkin Gulf Resolution. Just before the vote the White House announced that the President regarded this as a test vote, that those who opposed the war should vote with Morse. A grand total of four people did; the motion was tabled 92 to 5.[105]

Over the next seven years the debate heated up and the rationalizations proliferated, but when it came time to vote the same basic story line prevailed. As Stanley Karnow's history of the war reports:

> During the seven-year span from July 1966 through July 1973, Congress recorded one hundred and thirteen votes on proposals related to the war. But its first limitation on U.S. military activities in Southeast Asia was not imposed until 1969—a restriction on American troop deployments in [Thailand] and Laos— and it directed its full opposition to a continued commitment in the region only in August 1973, when it voted to stop all bombing throughout Indochina. By then, the U.S. combat forces had been withdrawn and the American prisoners of war held in Hanoi had come home; the argument that "our boys" needed support had lost its validity.[106]

ARGUMENTS THAT THE APPROPRIATIONS AND DRAFT EXTENSIONS
SHOULDN'T HAVE COUNTED

A number of members of Congress were visibly uncomfortable with the evident inference to be drawn from their continued funding of the war. Some dealt with this by unvarnished denial. Senator Joseph Clark announced, "I wish to make it very clear indeed that my votes, both against the Morse amendment and for the [appropriation], do not indicate an endorsement of the policy which I fear the administration is following."[107] The prevailing attempt to rationalize this paradox was the one the quotation from Karnow suggests, that repeated appropriations and draft extensions were needed to "support our boys in the field". During the March 1966 hearings on supplemental appropriations, Senator Morse, attempting to pull the plug, noted that "the only check, one of the best checks we have, is to say we are not going to finance it. If the President can't get the finances, then he has to change his policy." Senator Russell Long gave an impassioned version of the stock response: "I would just like to ask you, do you plan to send those boys off over there without giving them whatever it takes for them to fight and defend themselves and to win? [Shouldn't we] give them whatever help it takes to see that they are not cut off and surrounded and decimated as those people were at Dienbienphu?"[108] Senator George McGovern, quoting Senator Russell, elaborated: "It involves more the throwing of a rope to a man in the water. We may have cause to question how he got there, but he is there, he is a human being, he is our friend and a member of our family . . . ."[109]

This was said so often I assume it convinced some constituents, and it must have been internalized by the men who said it as well. However, it doesn't make sense. The image conjured up—of our troops on the front line suddenly left defenseless—is misleading. Congress could have phrased its funds cut-off as a phase-out, providing for the protection of the troops as they were withdrawn. (This was the device attempted by some members of Congress as the war wound down, as in, for example, Senator McGovern's own ill-fated McGovern-Hatfield Amendment.[110]) True, the president could veto such a measure (though McGovern-Hatfield never got that far) and there might not be the two-thirds majority needed to override. However, a simple refusal to appropriate funds can't be vetoed. And the president is not going to be so callous (or politically stupid) as to leave the troops on the battlefield defenseless, waiting to be slaughtered: Instead he will withdraw them (and protect them while doing so). Sometimes wars need to be fought, and if Congress agrees it should say so. But if their principal goal is really to minimize the chance that the boys on the line will be killed, they should shut the war down.

Sometimes, admittedly, this can get complicated. The president might, for example, have other Defense Department funds on which to draw, funds whose use had not been specified very precisely by Congress. (And if Congress then tried to say they couldn't be used for a particular military action, *that* measure could be vetoed.[111]) But as we've seen, that doesn't describe Vietnam, at least not in the early years. President Johnson needed large and repeated special appropriations to escalate the war to the level of approximately half a million men;[112] he asked for those special appropriations; he received them by near-unanimous votes. Anyone who really wanted the troops withdrawn need only have voted no: They wouldn't have been left there to die. Instead, as we have seen, attempts even modestly to qualify the early appropriations measures went down in flames. What "problem" there is, I would suggest, stems not from anything unusual about appropriations measures, but rather from congressional dread of being seen as either—I'm not sure which is perceived as worse—chicken or unAmerican. Congress is reluctant, *by whatever means*, to refuse to fight a war the president has indicated he wants, particularly (though I think this factor may also tend to be overrated) one he has already begun. Never, for example, was invocation of the concurrent resolution provision of the

Tonkin Gulf Resolution, withdrawing authorization for the war (then without the possibility of a presidential veto[113]) even considered in Congress until 1971, at which point an attempt to do so was defeated in favor of a package extending the war.[114]

A variation on this theme—this one to the effect that we must continue to pursue the war in order to support those boys *who have already died*—found expression in the World War I classic *In Flanders Fields*, whose final stanza reads:

> Take up our quarrel with the foe;
> To you from failing hands we throw
> The torch; be yours to hold it high.
> If ye break faith with us who die
> We shall not sleep, though poppies grow
> In Flanders fields.[115]

This may be moving—it was written by a man who was killed after four years of service on the western front—but it suffers from what our economist friends would call a "sunk costs" fallacy (admittedly a macabre figure in this context). There may, sometimes, be good reasons for prolonging a war, but it won't do a thing for those who have already died. It will only insure that there will be more of them.

Least reputable of all was the excuse that appropriations had to be voted "to support the president." During the debate on the Tonkin Gulf Resolution, Senator George Aiken indicated that he was "apprehensive" about President Johnson's decision to escalate, but "I feel that I, as an American citizen, can do no less than support the President in his capacity as leader of our Nation."[116] Senator Russell sounded the same theme: "I think this is the greatest mistake this country's ever made. I could not be more opposed to it . . . but . . . if he does it I will never raise my voice."[117] Aiken and Russell were principled men. However, the principle they expressed here, that Congress must support the president right or wrong, is flatly unacceptable. It was Congress's duty to exercise independent judgment. That's why we have separate branches. That's why the war power is vested in Congress.

THE AMERICAN GROUND INCURSION INTO CAMBODIA, 1970

On March 18, 1970, while Cambodian President Norodom Sihanouk was abroad, he was deposed by the Cambodian Parliament and replaced by Marshal Lon Nol. On April 30, American and South Vietnamese troops crossed the border and attacked Communist sanctuaries in Cambodia. At its peak the operation would involve 32,000 American troops. The administration had not consulted any congressional committees before taking this action, and instead apparently confided in only one member of Congress, Senator John Stennis of Mississippi, Chair of the Armed Services Committee.[118] After the incursion the Senate began considering in earnest the Cooper-Church Amendment, forbidding American troops in Cambodia—a modified version became law the following January—and on May 8, in a surprise move, President Nixon announced at a press conference that all American troops would be removed from Cambodia by June 30, 1970, which they were.

The Cambodian incursion caused a firestorm here at home.[119] (The shootings at Kent State, for example, occurred four days later.) The incursion's *legality* was attacked with equal vigor: Some even went so far as to argue that it represented the high-water mark, in all our history, of congressionally unauthorized military adventurousness.[120] On analysis, however, the Cambodian operation also appears to have been constitutionally authorized.

Even if we were to regard the operation as one designed to shore up the Lon Nol regime against internal and North Vietnamese Communist threats—and it was that in part—the authorization seems adequate, though barely. Patently the consultation with Stennis did not count as congressional approval of anything. Neither had any pre-1970 appropriations act mentioned Cambodia. As for the Tonkin Gulf Resolution, section 2 authorized the president to use armed force to assist only those protocol states "requesting assistance in defense of [their] freedom" against the North Vietnamese, and it is not entirely clear that Cambodia should be counted as having made such a request. On April 14, it is true, Lon Nol had made a general plea for outside help against the Communists,[121] and he cooperated with the Americans once we were there and reportedly even wept when he learned we were planning to leave.[122] However, he hadn't been consistent about his desire for assistance,[123] and his chagrin at our departure seems to have stemmed largely from a sense of being betrayed by the perilous position into which we had put his people and in which we were planning to leave them.[124] Beyond that, even if the charges are untrue that the CIA was complicit in the coup and thus substantially responsible for Lon Nol's place as the leader of his country, we certainly made no secret of the fact that we would welcome such a shift, and facilitated it in various collateral ways.[125] Cambodia's "request for assistance" thus seems a slim reed on which to base the legality of our intervention: Defenders of the incursion had better look for something sturdier.

It appears to exist. Section 1 of the Resolution, unlike section 2, did not depend on a request from the country in question: It simply empowered the president to resist aggression. At this point one might be tempted to press the delegation objection, since there was no legislative history (comparable to the Miller-Fulbright interchange on South Vietnam[126]) indicating that

Cambodia would be among the countries to which we would be lending our assistance. However, declarations of war don't typically specify allies: They specify enemies. (We certainly stood ready during World War II to come to the assistance of anyone attacked by the Axis powers.) The Resolution's preamble—by adverting to the "campaign of aggression that the Communist regime in North Vietnam has been waging against its neighbors"—not only designated the enemy but also described with fair precision the likely set of nations we would be assisting. "Neighbors" is plural, and at this time North Vietnamese troops were assisting the Viet Cong and Khmer Rouge in pushing Lon Nol's forces back into the Cambodian interior.

Beyond all that, however, probably the principal reason we went into Cambodia was to protect our troops in South Vietnam and otherwise to assist with our defense of that country—not simply by destroying Communist sanctuaries being used to further the assault on South Vietnam, but also to demonstrate to North Vietnam that President Nixon was prepared to take steps President Johnson had been unwilling to, thus inducing Hanoi to negotiate. The defense of South Vietnam, we have seen, was a project that had been congressionally authorized by the Tonkin Gulf Resolution and other statutory provisions as well. (There is no doubt that Cambodian sanctuaries were in fact being used as bases for Communist moves into Vietnam.) Thus viewed, it is difficult to understand the theory on which the president needed additional statutory authorization for the drive—any more, for example, than Franklin Roosevelt needed special congressional permission for our landings in French North Africa (at the time a neutral territory) or on various Pacific islands with which we, similarly, were not at war.[127]

THE REPEAL OF THE TONKIN GULF RESOLUTION, 1971

Congress repealed the Tonkin Gulf Resolution on January 12, 1971. Some observers concluded that it had thereby withdrawn the authority for the American war in Indochina.[128] You will not be surprised to learn that it was not that simple. Congress threw so many anchors to windward, leeward, and every other whichward that by the time it got through it was difficult to determine what, if any, course it intended to chart.

The movement for repeal was born of a desire to end the war, and many who voted for it undoubtedly hoped that it would contribute to that result. The Nixon forces were slick, however.[129] Having originally opposed repeal, the administration subsequently decided to support it, asserting that the Resolution wasn't essential to the president's authority. (You might suppose that doesn't amount to a reason to support repeal, but if your long-range goal is to aggrandize executive power, it does.[130]) Thus it was actu-

ally administration spokesman Robert Dole's version of the repeal provision that ended up being enacted, to the scant notice of the press or
public.[131]

There is a danger in reading the repeal as anything other than a withdrawal of authorization: We don't want to set a precedent to the effect that
a measure's opponents can effectively nullify it simply by announcing their
support and turning its legislative history inside out. On the other hand, a
rule to the effect that measures must be construed as carrying their "original" meaning would plainly be unworkable. The inquiry, here as always,
must be first into the measure's language—in isolation the repeal of the
Resolution could bear either construction—and then, if necessary, into
context. And here it is context that is fatal to the conclusion that the repeal
was intended by most of its supporters as a withdrawal of the war's authorization.

The repeal was part of a package that included a modified version of the
Cooper-Church Amendment, prohibiting the reintroduction of American
ground troops into Cambodia.[132] If, however, the entire war were being
"deauthorized" there would have been no need for such a narrower prohibition. The McGovern-Hatfield Amendment, requiring a total troop withdrawal from Indochina by December 31, 1971, had been defeated in the
Senate by a vote of 55 to 39 on September 1, 1970.[133] On June 16, 1971, the
Senate again defeated McGovern-Hatfield, 55 to 42, as did the House the
next day, 237 to 147.[134]

But maybe I am applying a double standard here—exalting intention
over enacted language in a way I seemed hesitant to do regarding the *adoption* of the Tonkin Gulf Resolution. As Professor Van Alstyne argued, "It
matters not at all . . . that members of Congress may not themselves have
intended the consequence of their affirmative vote for outright repeal, any
more than careless misapprehension of the significance of one's vote can
alter the consequence of other acts of Congress."[135] And indeed it would
not have mattered, had the Tonkin Gulf Resolution stood as of 1971 as the
only congressional authorization for the war: When the only authorization
goes, the war goes, irrespective of what people think they are up to. However, by 1971 the situation was far from that: Congress had by then, by a
number of appropriations measures, quite pointedly reiterated its authorization of the war. Moreover, and not surprisingly under the circumstances,
it continued after its repeal of the Tonkin Gulf Resolution to appropriate
funds for military activities in Southeast Asia, and to extend the draft.[136]

Tantalizing as the repeal must thus have seemed to those wishing to
mount a legal attack on the war, it unfortunately was just more of Congress's playing Pontius Pilate. To a legislature unwilling either to stop the
war or to take responsibility for it, the prospect of getting that incriminating
Tonkin Gulf Resolution off the books must have seemed a godsend: "The

... debate made evident a Senate consensus that repeal ... would 'wipe the slate clean' of any residual congressional authority for the Vietnam war and leave the President relying exclusively upon his powers as Commander in Chief."[137] And to an executive interested in increasing presidential power—in attempting to set a precedent to the effect that troops can be deployed without congressional authorization—it must have seemed so too (particularly when the president in question could claim that this unpopular war wasn't really his, but his predecessor's). The repeal had it all: Congress could hide and the President could aggrandize. What few people at either end of Pennsylvania Avenue appear to have intended was that it would actually end the war.

The Continued Bombing of Cambodia, 1973

Our ground forces came out of Cambodia on June 30, 1970, but our bombing of Communist sanctuaries in that country continued. At least so long as American forces remained in Vietnam (and Congress did not forbid it) such bombing could be, and was, rationalized on the theory that it was protecting our troops and otherwise helping us defend South Vietnam. However, on January 27, 1973, the Paris cease-fire agreements had been signed; on March 29 the last American troops left Vietnam; and on April 1 our last known prisoners of war were released.[138] Nonetheless, the bombing of Cambodia continued until August 14, 1973.

This too inspired outrage here at home, and again, the argument was made that the administration was behaving illegally, that its actions exceeded congressional authorization. This argument convinced United States District Judge Orrin Judd of the Eastern District of New York. In the case of *Holtzman v. Schlesinger*, Judge Judd entered an order on July 25 enjoining further bombing as of July 27.[139] The Court of Appeals for the Second Circuit immediately stayed the order pending appeal. There followed an embarrassing minuet in which Justice Marshall refused to vacate the stay; Justice Douglas (located by counsel in Goose Prairie, Washington) did so; and Justice Marshall, having consulted with the rest of the Court, reinstated it.[140] The circuit court heard argument on August 8, and reversed the District Court by a 2 to 1 vote the same day. The bombing was stopped (pursuant to congressional direction) before the case reached the Supreme Court.

By now you will not be surprised by my conclusion: As the test of congressional authorization stood then,[141] a careful analyst would have to conclude that the 1973 bombing of Cambodia was authorized—although, as usual, with maximum congressional obfuscation. Indeed we shall see that by this time the obfuscation had achieved the status of a high art form, rendering the statutory construction issues here the equal of any to be found in the Internal Revenue Code. It will help if we break the arguments that the bombing was unauthorized into two broad categories—arguments that Congress had never done anything to authorize it in the first place, and arguments that certain congressional prohibitions had outlawed it.

Was There Authorization to Begin With?

THE PARIS PEACE AGREEMENTS

At one point the administration justified the continued bombing as part of the enforcement of the Paris cease-fire agreements. It appeared to have two theories—that North Vietnam and Sihanouk's government-in-exile were violating the provision for a cease-fire in *Cambodia*,[142] and that North Vietnam was continuing to use Cambodia as a staging area to move troops into *South Vietnam* in violation of the agreements.[143]

The law of executive agreements is troubled. It is sometimes asserted that such agreements can simply replace treaties, that anything a treaty can do can be done by executive agreement.[144] That, however, simply cannot be right, lest the constitutional safeguard of approval by two-thirds of the Senate be rendered a complete nullity. More discriminating critics have opined that executive agreements can replace treaties, but only sometimes, specifically when they are appendant to an unquestionably executive power.[145] Indeed, armistice agreements are generally adduced as the paradigm case here, appendant as they seem to be to the president's authority as commander in chief.[146] On the other hand, every commentator of whom I am aware,[147] as well as the State Department,[148] is clear that executive agreements (unlike treaties, some would say[149]) cannot constitute the authorization for military action by the president. For if the president could make an agreement authorizing the use of force without even the concurrence of the Senate, and then turn around and implement that agreement, he would have become a virtual law unto himself: The bootstrap would be too clearly visible.

This combination of positions may pull us up short, however, as it appears to mean that the president is powerless (without further congressional authorization) to respond to the erstwhile enemy's violation of an armistice or cease-fire. That seems clearly wrong, but the contrary position also seems questionable. (The threat from that direction, though in practical terms it may not be a great danger, would be that the president would put all sorts of only tangentially related terms into the armistice agreement and then claim "bootstrap" authority to use force to implement them.) The temptation is thus to break armistice enforcement actions down, in terms of whether the violation being combatted constitutes a resumption of the war the armistice ended on the one hand, or violation of a more extraneous term on the other.[150]

That suggests a more direct and logical line of analysis, however. We were right the first time: Executive agreements *can't* give presidents authority to initiate military actions. Any authority they have in this area must be derived from somewhere else. However, the commander in chief can respond to an enemy's resumption of a war *under whatever authority he was exercising in pursuing the war in the first place.* (Plainly Congress will neither explicitly nor by fair implication have terminated that authority as of the armistice. On the contrary, it will have wanted the president to retain the very authority to combat cease-fire violations we are talking about.)

Thus the Paris peace agreements could not by themselves have provided the authorization for the administration's subsequent bombing of Cambodia. Authority must be found, if at all, in Congress's earlier authorizations of the Vietnamese and Cambodian campaigns.

THE PRESIDENT'S PRE-ARMISTICE AUTHORITY

When our ground troops came out of Cambodia in June of 1970, the authorization picture was as follows. (1) Certainly Congress had not authorized the president to protect the Lon Nol government against indigenous resistance. (2) Though the point is arguable, the Tonkin Gulf Resolution had probably authorized the protection of the Lon Nol government from North Vietnamese aggression. (3) More clearly, moves against the sanctuaries to protect our troops in South Vietnam (and otherwise to defend South Vietnam against North Vietnamese aggression) had been authorized under both the Resolution and various appropriations acts.

As of 1973, the Tonkin Gulf Resolution had been off the books for two years. However, the bombing had been quite constant and (since 1970[151]) entirely open. (As the ground troops came out, President Nixon announced that the United States would continue to conduct air interdiction missions to prevent supplies and personnel from being moved through Cambodia toward South Vietnam.[152]) Congress was well aware that the bombing had three purposes—to protect our troops in Vietnam; more generally to protect South Vietnam from North Vietnamese infiltration; and to protect the Lon Nol government from both the North Vietnamese and the indigenous Communist Khmer Rouge. In full knowledge of all this, congressional appropriations for Indochina continued apace from 1970 to 1973. We have noted that appropriations acts could not constitute authorization for the Cambodian ground incursion in 1970 because there had been no prior notice to Congress that the funds might be thus used. But they could constitute authorization for the 1970–1973 bombing, respecting which notice was conspicuous.

As of April 1, 1973, all relevant American troops[153] were out of Indochina, so the first of these three rationales could no longer apply. How-

ever—unless Congress took some affirmative action to disqualify them—
the other two rationales, protection of South Vietnam from North Vietnamese infiltration, and protection of the Cambodian government from the
North Vietnamese and the Khmer Rouge, were still applicable. It is thus
necessary to inquire into the arguments that Congress had affirmatively
prohibited the bombing.

Did Congress Prohibit the Bombing?

THE FULBRIGHT PROVISO

This proviso made its first appearance in the War Forces-Military Procurement Act of 1971, signed by President Nixon on October 7, 1970.[154] It
stated:

> [N]othing [herein] shall be construed as authorizing the use of any such funds to
> support Vietnamese or other free world forces in actions designed to provide
> military support and assistance to the Government of Cambodia or Laos; *Pro-*
> *vided further*, That nothing contained in this section shall be construed to prohibit
> support of actions required to ensure the safe and orderly withdrawal or disen-
> gagement of U.S. Forces from Southeast Asia, or to aid in the release of Ameri-
> cans held as prisoners of war.[155]

On its face, this appears to be the usual congressional equivocation: It says
it isn't "authorizing" certain uses of military force, but on the other hand it
doesn't say it's prohibiting them either. However, Congress may have out-
foxed itself this time and actually done something. For when the only possible authorization for a given action is continuing appropriations, a cessation of appropriations necessarily amounts to a prohibition. (The Fulbright
Proviso was repeated in all subsequent military authorization and appropriations acts between October 1970 and the bombing campaign under
discussion.[156])

The reference to "forces" should certainly be read to include bombing
crews: Congress knew how to restrict its prohibitions to ground troops
when that was what it wanted.[157] The Fulbright Proviso has thus conventionally been read to have meant that American forces could not bomb
Cambodia except to protect our troops or prisoners of war.[158] Once the
troops and POWs were out, the syllogism ran, authorization to bomb Cambodia was withdrawn. Therefore, those defending the bombing campaign
did so by arguing that the Fulbright Proviso had effectively been
repealed.[159]

In fact "other free world forces" should probably not be read to include
American forces of any sort. Before we return to that question, however, it
will be helpful to analyze the debate as it in fact unfolded—that is, on the

assumption that American bombing was outlawed except to protect our troops—as it will serve to illuminate not only some interesting issues of statutory construction but also, further, the theme of congressional obfuscation that permeates the events reported in this chapter.

THE COOPER-CHURCH AMENDMENT

This amendment, attached to a supplementary foreign assistance authorization, was signed by the President on January 12, 1971. It provided, in part: "In line with the expressed intention of the President of the United States, none of the funds authorized or appropriated pursuant to this or any other Act may be used to finance the introduction of United States ground combat troops into Cambodia, or to provide United States advisers to or for Cambodian military forces in Cambodia."[160] This doesn't seem to evidence any intention to repeal the postulated earlier command that American forces were to be used in Cambodia only to protect the withdrawal of our troops from Vietnam. Rather, it adds another prohibition, on American ground troops in Cambodia, thus apparently preventing ground troops from being used for any purpose in Cambodia and permitting bombers to be used there only to protect our troops in Vietnam.

THE FOREIGN ASSISTANCE ACT OF 1971

This act, approved by the President on February 7, 1972, placed a ceiling on the amount of money that could be spent "in, to, for, or on behalf of Cambodia."[161] It went on to provide, however, that this ceiling "shall not apply with respect to the obligation of funds to carry out combat air operations over Cambodia."[162] It also capped the number of United States government personnel, civilian and military, who could be present in Cambodia, "excluding such members while actually engaged in air operations in or over Cambodia which originate outside Cambodia."[163]

By excluding bombing operations over Cambodia from the financial and personnel ceilings, Congress was plainly authorizing such bombing. The question remains, however, whether it meant thereby to repeal the Fulbright Proviso—which, on its "received" reading, limited the bombing of Cambodia to the protection of American forces. This issue seems more difficult than that presented by Cooper-Church, because instead of saying that something else was *not* allowed, Congress indicated in this act that bombing *was* allowed (without recognizing any differences among the purposes for which such bombing might be effected).

It is true that the Senate Report on this law indicated that the exceptions for Cambodian bombing operations were inserted "because of the view of some Committee members that monetary limitations on air operations in Cambodia might jeopardize the continuing withdrawal of U.S. Forces from

Vietnam."[164] However, that language was not included in the law, and indeed the Senate Report itself (in the very same paragraph) indicated that the "exception covers *all* United States and South Vietnamese combat air operations."[165] Thus, out of a concern for the safety of our troops, Congress permitted the bombing to continue, but did not indicate that it would be permitted only for that purpose. On the other hand the Fulbright Proviso (on its received reading) *had* drawn that distinction. Could it be that Congress was trying to confuse us about exactly what it had authorized—or maybe it was just confused itself?

The prickly question whether the Foreign Assistance Act of 1971 implicitly repealed the Fulbright Proviso fortunately need not be answered, because as I have indicated the Proviso was reenacted several times after the passage of the Foreign Assistance Act, for example in the Military Procurement Act of 1973 (enacted September 26, 1972)[166] and the Department of Defense Appropriation Act of 1973 (enacted October 26, 1972).[167] The Proviso was therefore still in effect as of the 1973 Cambodian bombing operations.

THE MODIFIED EAGLETON AMENDMENT OF JULY 1, 1973

In June, 1973 the two houses of Congress agreed on an amendment introduced by Senator Thomas Eagleton, and attached it to a general appropriations bill (which included funds for, among other things, the continued operation of the Social Security Administration). This original Eagleton Amendment simply cut off the bombing in Cambodia: "None of the funds herein appropriated under this Act or heretofore appropriated under any other Act may be expended to support directly or indirectly combat activities in, over or from off the shores of Cambodia, or in or over Laos by United States Forces."[168] The President vetoed the bill, and the House voted 241 to 173 to override—a majority, but thirty-five votes short of the required two-thirds.[169]

The amendment then was attached to a bill to continue the existing ceiling on public debt, a measure necessary to the expenditure of government funds for any purpose.[170] However, Senator Fulbright was still fearful that President Nixon would veto it, and undertook to make a deal. After conferences with White House officials, he introduced, on June 29, 1973, the following modified version of the amendment: "Notwithstanding any other provision of law, on or after August 15, 1973, no funds herein, heretofore or hereafter appropriated may be obligated or expended to finance the involvement of United States military forces in hostilities in or over or from off the shores of North Vietnam, South Vietnam, Laos, or Cambodia."[171] Senator Fulbright did his best to obscure the obvious implication of the August 15 provision:

> MR. EAGLETON: . . . I want to inquire as to what this resolution includes . . . .
> Does it permit continued bombing between now and August 15?
>
> MR. FULBRIGHT: As I have said, I do not regard him as having the right to do this.
> He has the power to do it . . . . I do not want my statement to be taken to mean
> that I approve of it or think that it is constitutional or legal for him to do it. He
> can do it. He has done it. Do I make myself clear?
>
> MR. EAGLETON: In a way yes, and in a way no . . . . [T]he President will exercise
> a power to bomb in Indochina within the next 45 days, is that correct? A power
> that will now be sanctioned by our action?
>
> MR. FULBRIGHT: The President has the power to do a lot of things of which I do
> not approve.[172]

However, the statutory language was just too clear this time—telling your kids to be home by midnight gives them permission to stay out until then—as even Fulbright acknowledged in his less cagey moments:

> MR. EAGLETON: In the light of the legislative history, meaning the statement of
> former Secretary of Defense Richardson that we will continue the bombing
> unless the funds are cut off, will we with the adoption of this resolution permit
> the bombing of Cambodia for the next 45 days? That is the question I pose to
> the Senator from Arkansas.
>
> MR. FULBRIGHT: Until August 15.[173]

Not surprisingly, Senator Eagleton, along with several other members of Congress, including Representative Holtzman, ended up voting against the reconstituted Eagleton Amendment (which Eagleton's book refers to as the Fulbright Amendment[174]) on the ground that it indefensibly gave the president six weeks of extra bombing. Nonetheless it was adopted by the Senate, 64 to 26, and the House of Representatives, 266 to 75.[175]

Even if Ms. Holtzman wasn't the ideal plaintiff, she did prevail in district court. How could that be, in light of the modified Eagleton Amendment? Judge Judd gave three reasons why it shouldn't count: I'll deal with two of them now and save the third for later. First, he said Congress had agreed to the August 15 date "merely in order to avoid the veto which had met their earlier efforts."[176] However, the legislative process provided by the Constitution includes presentation to the president, and Congress often must compromise to get a law past his veto: It's cheating to reconstruct laws to mean what they *would* have said had Congress not had to worry about the president.

Judge Judd's second argument was that Congress compromised "[i]n order to avoid a constitutional crisis that would have resulted in a temporary shutdown of vital federal activities (including issuance of monthly Social Security checks), due to lack of funds for the next fiscal year."[177] However, it was *Congress's* ploy to attach the amendment to a general appropriations bill and then to a bill to raise the ceiling on the national debt: Plainly it thought the President would thus be coerced into signing it. That one works both ways, though, and the members of Congress soon came to realize that if they persisted in not appropriating funds for social security and so forth, *they* would feel some political heat.[178] Again, laws are a product of the entire legislative process: Congress challenged President Nixon to a game of chicken, and ended up having to compromise.

Where does all this leave us so far as the authorization of the 1973 bombing of Cambodia is concerned? Well, initially, in quite a mess, because every time Congress authorized the bombing, a number of those voting for the measure said that wasn't what they meant. Fighting our way through the smoke, however, our conclusions—still on the assumption that the Fulbright Proviso applied to American forces—now appear to be this: The bombing was illegal from April 1, 1973 (the date on which the last known American prisoner of war was released) until July 1 of the same year. This is because the Fulbright Proviso, which had been briefly repealed by the Foreign Assistance Act of 1971, had been reinstated (several times) prior to April 1, 1973, rendering the bombing illegal as of the release of our last prisoner of war. However, the Fulbright Proviso was repealed (for good) by the passage of the modified Eagleton Amendment. Thus the bombing was legal from July 1, 1973 (the day on which the President approved the modified Eagleton Amendment) through August 14 of the same year (when, pursuant to the Amendment, the President terminated the bombing).

ANOTHER LOOK AT THE FULBRIGHT PROVISO

Following the literature, we passed too quickly over a couple of points that should be made respecting the Fulbright Proviso. First (still on our postulated reading), it had an undistributed middle, which to my knowledge has not been previously noted. It provided that we *could* bomb Cambodia to support our troops or prisoners of war, but *could not* do so to support the Lon Nol government. There is some space between those two mandates, however: The Proviso had nothing to say one way or the other about bombing Cambodia in order to protect South Vietnam from North Vietnamese infiltration. That is a rationale that survived the withdrawal of our troops and prisoners of war. Since prior to the enactment of the Fulbright Proviso funds had repeatedly been provided for the bombing in full knowledge that this was one of its purposes, it would seem, assuming this *continued* to be one of its purposes, that authorization for the bombing survived.

The question framed by the Proviso thus appears to be to what extent the post-troop withdrawal bombing of Cambodia was designed to interdict

North Vietnamese infiltration into South Vietnam, and to what extent it was designed to support the Lon Nol government. The former would be legal, the latter illegal. In certain unguarded moments the administration spoke only of the protection of the Lon Nol government, but as the controversy heated up it began to speak in terms of both purposes. Its behavior in the *Holtzman* case reflected this ambivalence. The administration's offer of proof in district court apparently spoke only of Cambodian affairs:

> Defendants stated on oral argument that if summary judgment is denied, they would propose to offer testimony from Secretary of State Rogers, Secretary of Defense Schlesinger, and Dr. Kissinger concerning the necessity for the air operations and the importance of continuing bombing in Cambodia because of continuing confidential negotiations for a Cambodian cease-fire. No other offer of proof has been made on behalf of the defendants.[179]

However, an affidavit Rogers filed in the court of appeals after the district court's decision also mentioned (if secondarily) the possible undermining of "the cease-fire agreements presently in effect in Viet-Nam and Laos"[180]—presumably by North Vietnamese infiltration through Cambodia. He didn't exactly elaborate it that way—one didn't have to be a member of Congress to wax ambiguous about Indochina—and it is a little tricky to square with the mention of Laos.[181] On the other hand, at least as regards Vietnam, it is at least plausible: There really *was* a Ho Chi Minh trail, and the administration's interest in propping up the Saigon regime surely didn't disappear with the withdrawal of our troops.[182]

One trying to figure out the purpose of bombing raids, however,[183] is better advised to consider where the bombs are being dropped than to attempt to decipher the statements of public officials. Approached thus, the present inquiry turns out to be susceptible to surprisingly discrete analysis. The military's own figures for the first two and a half weeks of April 1973 (that is, the relevant period immediately following the release of our last prisoner of war) disclose that only about 20 percent of our air strikes on Cambodia were sited such that they could reasonably be regarded as interdiction of the flow of personnel and supplies to South Vietnam, whereas about 80 percent were in locations that could only be construed as in support of the Lon Nol government's forces.[184] Thus, on the received reading of the Fulbright Proviso, about four-fifths of the post-troop withdrawal bombing of Cambodia would seem to have been illegal. How one might react to such a picture of fractionalized legality is not, however, a question we need to face, as there is another point to be made respecting the Proviso to which we need to return, one that seems dispositive.

It seems mildly breathtaking in light of the literature, but some further attention to context demonstrates that the Fulbright Proviso wasn't intended to control the use of American forces in the first place. It provided that it should not be "construed as authorizing the use of any such funds to support Vietnamese or other free world forces in actions designed to provide military support and assistance to the Government of Cambodia or Laos." The received assumption has been that "other free world forces" included American troops, and certainly in some contexts such language might mean that. However, other sections of the appropriations acts to which the Fulbright Proviso was attached—including the first one—differentiated between "free world forces" and "Armed Forces of the United States," and at one point during the debates Senator Fulbright characterized the Proviso as operative in respect to "South Vietnamese or other foreign military operations in support of the Cambodian or Laotian Governments."[185] Indeed, on reflection, it would have been quite odd for an American statute to designate Vietnamese forces by name and then to include our own troops only under a follow-up, catch-all expression. This more careful reading explains much that was mysterious in Congress's behavior, suggesting it was less obfuscatory than it might have appeared at first. It demonstrates, for example, that the interplay between the Fulbright Proviso and the Foreign Assistance Act of 1971 was not the ping pong game it appeared to be, and also explains why Senator Fulbright did not, during the debates on the modified Eagleton Amendment, cite "his own" Proviso in support of the proposition that the president already lacked authority to bomb Cambodia.

THE ARGUMENT THAT IT IS UNFAIR TO REQUIRE A TWO-THIRDS
VOTE TO TERMINATE HOSTILITIES

It is now time to consider Judge Judd's third argument: "It cannot be the rule that the President needs a vote of only one-third plus one of either House to conduct a war, but this would be the consequence of holding that Congress must override a Presidential veto in order to terminate hostilities which it has not authorized."[186] When you parse this, it turns out to be overdetermined. Hostilities that Congress "has not authorized" don't need *any* kind of a vote to render them illegal: They are that already. And indeed Judge Judd, relying on the Fulbright Proviso, was proceeding on the assumption that the bombing of Cambodia was not authorized at the outset of the legislative-executive byplay over the Eagleton Amendment. Further analysis, however—in particular a more careful reading of the Fulbright Proviso—has suggested the opposite conclusion. That doesn't render the quotation from Judge Judd's opinion irrelevant, though. On the contrary, it gives life to what on his assumptions was irrelevant rhetoric. For it conjures up a disturbing spectre, that of a Congress unable to get us out of *authorized* combat by a simple majority vote. Of this the legislative-executive byplay over the Eagleton Amendment provided at least an arguable example.

Abstractly it may not be clear why this should bother us, as it seems the way it's always supposed to work: Having authorized a legislative program, Congress can ordinarily then repeal it only with the cooperation of the president or by a two-thirds vote of each house. It is true we are talking about war, a subject of unusual moment. However, nothing in Article I, section 8, seems to differentiate a war from any other legislatively authorized program in terms of the votes needed to get us in or out.[187]

Beyond that, at least during certain phases of a war, a bare majority of both houses of Congress *can* get us out, just as they can extricate us from any program requiring ongoing appropriations, by refusing to supply further funds.[188] Such a refusal cannot be vetoed. Now admittedly it may not be that simple, where the president has access to sufficient other funds that Congress did not have the foresight to designate so as to preclude the use he now proposes to make of them: A post-appropriation prohibition *can* be vetoed. One should not too hastily assume that that is generally likely to be the situation, however, nor is it clear it was the situation even near the end of the war in Indochina. A congressional reduction of appropriations by the amount it figured the Cambodian bombing campaign to be costing would have been at least difficult to "make up" by shifting funds from elsewhere in the defense budget. (This was, for one thing, a general period of rapid growth in the Soviets' strategic and conventional forces worldwide, growth with which we felt it necessary to try to keep up: A diversion of funds from other defense programs, to cover a congressionally created "Cambodian shortfall," would thus have required more than a simple stroke of the pen. At the very least such a shortfall would have caused the president to think twice about whether the Cambodian campaign was worth it.) But assume he *was* able and willing to take funds from elsewhere in the budget to cover Cambodia:[189] There was still a "veto-proof" countermove available to Congress, namely attaching its bombing prohibition to something the president really needed or wanted, such as a politically popular benefit program or a bill raising the ceiling on the national debt. In fact Congress tried both these gambits—only to break down when it turned out that the President was more willing than they to run the political risk of being blamed for the cessation of other government services.

Thus a majority of Congress *could* have halted the bombing of Cambodia before August 15. They just didn't have the President's willfulness (or political courage, depending on your sympathies). But still there's something haunting about Judge Judd's point. It flows, I think, from the fact that although a neutral commentator must conclude on balance that Congress did indeed authorize the bombing, the authorization was tongue-and-groove, proceeding more by notice and acquiescence than by anything resembling a straight in-or-out vote on whether we ought to be bombing (or for that matter doing anything in) Cambodia. Then came the Eagleton Amendment, which *did* propose a straight in-or-out vote; both houses voted "out"; and yet the bombing continued. Yes, a bare majority of both houses could have halted the bombing, but only at political risk to its members. We never clearly voted to get in, Congress felt, and yet a clear vote to get out wasn't good enough—some sort of extra effort was required, be it an override or an act of political courage. "We slid into this war," they must have been thinking. "Under the circumstances you'd think a clear 'no' vote could get us out without asking us to put our careers on the line."

It sounds as if there may be something here, but what do we do about it? It surely should not become the legal test that "clearly authorized" wars need a two-thirds vote (or the concurrence of the president) to end them, whereas "ambiguously authorized" wars can be ended by a mere majority vote of each house. (Actually I suppose one could carry this line of "analysis" even further and argue that such a war should be terminable by a majority vote of *one* house, since such a majority could have blocked entry in the first place.)

The better way out of the dilemma, and this will be the burden of the next chapter, would be to change, or clarify, the law so as to provide that "ambiguous authorizations" don't count in the first place. The nation shouldn't be permitted to "slide into" war: An unambiguous in-or-out vote should be required at the outset. And where the authorization *has* been unambiguous (as it would have to be under the suggested approach) it seems entirely reasonable to expect disengagement to be, if not exactly difficult, then not entirely easy—for the sake of those allies who have depended on us, the general stability of our foreign policy, and, not least, the morale of our troops in the field. (Barriers to exit also function ex ante as barriers to entry: Thus to the extent getting out of a war is not entirely easy, getting into one should not be either.[190]) Once the presence of American troops has received the required unambiguous authorization, they should be supported to the hilt, all the way up to the point that a contrary consensus has developed—a consensus sufficient (a) to carry the president along; (b) to override his veto by a two-thirds vote of both houses; or (c) to inspire an act of political courage on the part of the congressional majority, such as firmly fastening its disengagement directive to something it knows the president and public want.

Having survived the legal maze, where have we ended up regarding the 1973 bombing of Cambodia? Still in something of a mess, because every time Congress authorized the bombing a number of its members said that they weren't. However, as best we can make out (given contemporaneously accepted notions of "authorization") Congress probably *did* authorize the bombing of Cambodia from mid-1970 on. With tolerably full knowledge of what was going on Congress continued to fund the bombing (along with the rest of the war) and never, not even in the Fulbright Proviso, moved to cut it off until it legislated a completion date of August 15, 1973—at which time the bombing in fact did stop, and with it the active military involvement of the United States in Indochina.[191]

CHAPTER 3

Inducing Congress to Face Up to Its Constitutional Responsibilities

> I have announced time and time and time again I will never be guilty of any kind of action that can be interpreted as war until the Congress, which has the Constitutional authority, says so . . . and I am not going to order any troops into anything that can be interpreted as war, until Congress directs it.
>
> —President Dwight D. Eisenhower (1956)[1]

> [S]ince the United States has given up declaring war and started sending armies forward . . . without a national consensus behind them, things have not gone well.
>
> —Vice Admiral (ret.) James Bond Stockdale (1988)[2]

THUS CONGRESS did authorize the war in Vietnam—at least its public aspects,[3] at least as the law of authorization stood at the time.[4] But it did so backhandedly, generally without anything resembling serious consideration of the consequences of its actions, and where possible so ambiguously that when things went wrong it could continue to claim mere bystander status. Who, us? This isn't *our* war. It's Johnson's war. Or maybe Nixon's.

Most people today acknowledge this, but many are inclined to respond "So what?" If Congress doesn't want to take its constitutional role seriously, but prefers instead to yield its decision authority to the president, why should the rest of us worry about it? The answer is that the prerogatives of congressmen aren't what's at stake here. What is at stake—and was so understood by the framers—is the judgment that no single individual should be able to take the nation into war and thereby risk the lives of all of us, especially our young people.[5] We saw in chapter 1 (and our study of Vietnam has underscored the conclusion) how this rationale, and others underlying the requirement that wars be deliberately authorized by the legislative process, are anything but obsolete. This chapter examines strategies for endowing that requirement with renewed life.

THE EXPERIENCE SINCE VIETNAM

There was a brief reflective moment near the end of the war in Indochina when Congress looked itself in the mirror and saw what wasn't there. Since 1950, it realized, it had been dodging its constitutional duty to make the decision whether to commit American troops to combat. Instead it had been laying back, neither disapproving presidential military ventures nor forthrightly approving them, instead letting the president use troops wherever and whenever he wanted and waiting to see how the war in question played politically. It therefore decided it could not count on itself to decide such issues unless forced to, and enacted, over President Nixon's veto, the War Powers Resolution of 1973.

The Resolution's core[6] resides in sections 4(a)(1) and 5(b). The former requires the president to report to Congress within forty-eight hours of introducing United States forces "into hostilities or into situations where imminent involvement in hostilities is clearly indicated by the circumstances." Section 5(b) then provides:

> Within sixty calendar days after [such] a report is submitted or is required to be submitted . . . whichever is earlier, the President shall terminate any use of United States Armed Forces with respect to which such report was submitted (or required to be submitted), unless the Congress (1) has declared war or has enacted a specific authorization for such use of United States Armed Forces, (2) has extended by law such sixty-day period, or (3) is physically unable to meet as a result of an armed attack upon the United States.

In operation the sixty-day period is likely to be expanded to ninety, as the Resolution grants an additional thirty days upon presidential certification (which I assume could almost universally be made in good faith) that "unavoidable military necessity respecting the safety of United States Armed Forces" requires it. Section 8(a) elaborates on what constitutes a "specific authorization": It provides that authority to commit troops shall not be inferred from any law that does not specifically refer to the War Powers Resolution, or from any treaty not separately implemented by a law incorporating such a reference.

Like the Gramm-Rudman-Hollings Budget Control Act of 1985[7] and other recent "framework" legislation,[8] the War Powers Resolution is designed to force a decision regarding matters that Congress has in the past shown itself unwilling to face up to. Unlike Gramm-Rudman-Hollings, however, it does not push the tough decisions onto somebody else (such as the Comptroller General) but rather provides that once the Resolution is triggered by the commitment of troops, Congress itself has sixty days to make the critical decision on war and peace.

However, "post-Watergate congressional bravado had a way of sputtering out in the face of crisis,"[9] and thanks to a combination of presidential defiance, congressional irresolution, and judicial abstention, the War Powers Resolution has not worked. Repeatedly—as in the final stages of the war in Indochina, the botched 1980 attempt to free our hostages in Iran, the tragic 1982–1983 commitment of our troops to Lebanon, the 1983 invasion of Grenada, the Gulf of Sidra incident of March 1986, the bombing of Tripoli a month later, the 1987–1988 Persian Gulf naval war against Iran, and the 1989 invasion of Panama—the president filed either no report at all or a vague statement pointedly refusing to identify itself as a Section 4(a)(1) "hostilities" report (with the result that the sixty-day clock was not deemed to have been started).[10]

Despite this pattern of presidential evasion "successive Congresses have been unwilling either to tighten obvious loopholes in the relevant legislation or even to enforce existing requirements."[11] Thus Congress has managed an official response only once—in connection with the Lebanon crisis—when after much hemming and hawing it negotiated with the White House a "compromise" recognizing the applicability of the War Powers Resolution (which recognition President Reagan immediately repudiated[12]) and extending the period the troops could remain in Lebanon for eighteen months.[13] Generally it has left it at simply hemming and hawing, sidetracking resolutions to start the sixty-day clock with incomprehensible "points of order,"[14] passing resolutions to similar but not identical effect in the two houses and then being "unable" to reconcile them until the war was over,[15] or more often, just doing nothing. Of course this is just a reversion to pre-Resolution form—letting the president initiate military action while retaining for Congress the option (depending on how the war went) of pointing with pride or viewing with alarm. Thus in 1988 former Senator Thomas Eagleton testified:

> Finally . . . I came to the conclusion that Congress really didn't want to be in on the decisionmaking process as to when, how, and where to go to war. I came to the conclusion that Congress didn't really want to have its fingerprints on sensitive matters pertaining to putting our Armed Forces into hostilities. I came to the conclusion that Congress preferred the right of retrospective criticism to the right of anticipatory, participatory judgment.[16]

Desert Storm

By now you may be wondering whether I am aware of our recent famous victory, 1991's Operation Desert Storm against Iraq, in particular the fact that it was authorized in advance by Congress, in pointed compliance with the War Powers Resolution.[17] The subhead is a big clue: I am. And although I was personally skeptical that the operation would do more good than harm, this procedural development (in context a virtual innovation) was certainly encouraging. What's more, the debates preceding the votes in both houses, though truncated by the eleventh-hour nature of the President's request, were among the most responsible within memory.

However, it would be a clear mistake to conclude from the Desert Storm authorization that from here on we can count on the president and Congress to do their constitutional duties.[18] The situation was unique in a number of critical respects. By the time of the Resolution the President had massed over 400,000 troops in the area—the same order of magnitude as Vietnam at its peak—together with concomitant numbers of ships, planes, and tanks: There was no doubt that there was going to be a war, and a big one at that.[19] In addition, so many months of preparation had passed that every Tom, Dick, and Harriet—regular columnists, guest columnists,[20] "friends of the court"[21]—had rehashed every angle of the proposed war so often that the correct constitutional conclusion had actually had a chance to become embedded in the public's consciousness: There being no colorable claim that there had not been time for debate, Congress had to authorize this war explicitly and in advance. Indeed, in *Dellums v. Bush*,[22] Judge Harold Greene of the United States District Court for the District of Columbia, though he refused to enter an injunction on what I regard as an erroneous "ripeness" ground,[23] had issued a powerful opinion indicating that if President Bush went ahead with the war without congressional authorization he would be violating the Constitution (which opinion thus was effectively a nonappealable declaratory judgment, and had precisely the effect the challengers had been hoping for). In light of numerous judicial (in)actions in recent similar cases, to say nothing of the trend line of recent judicial appointments, one would be foolhardy to bet on finding Greene or someone like him on the bench the next time a similar action is brought.

Even all that probably wouldn't have been enough to move Congress to act, though. Recall how it had reacted to President Bush's earlier assertion[24] that the War Powers Resolution was inapplicable because there was no "imminent danger of hostilities"—by going home for a two-month recess. "They didn't want to vote to authorize Bush to use force, and they also didn't want to vote against what he said was current policy. They were worried that he would call them into session and were relieved that he didn't."[25] Up until the end the administration indicated repeatedly that it didn't need and had no plans to seek congressional authorization[26]—it lobbied hard for the endorsement of the U.N. Security Council while treating that of Congress as optional[27]—and still Congress didn't move. What turned it around was President Bush's eventual *request* that Congress vote their "support." By that request he deprived them of the usual option of waiting until the war was over before deciding whether to approve of it.

Well, then, is that the answer: that from now on we can count on the president to ask permission before going to war? Plainly not. In addition to the special factors of scale and time noted above, President Bush reportedly agreed to seek congressional endorsement only after he had received quite firm assurances that he would get it. That suggests that such requests are unlikely to be made where assurances of agreement cannot be given—that is, in cases where there is a chance Congress might actually act as the counterweight the Constitution intended. What's more, despite the assurances, the vote turned out to be quite close, at least in the Senate, a development that might convince future presidents not to request one unless the congressional support promises to be overwhelming.

Also, one of the main reasons Bush finally decided to request authorization had nothing to do with domestic political considerations, let alone constitutional niceties—his desire further to tighten the screws on Saddam Hussein, to convince him to withdraw from Kuwait without the necessity of our using military force. The likelihood of such a request's being made in the more usual case, where we harbor no serious hope of succeeding by threat alone, seems substantially less. Finally, although it did not turn out that way, all indications going in were that this war would be protracted, the kind President Bush was intelligent enough to realize was in unusual need of consensus backing of a sort congressional authorization could help build. That suggests that at least one of the "lessons of Vietnam" had been learned. The downside is that the likelihood that the precedent will be followed in our now more common predictably "quickie" wars is diminished.

And even if the president *could* be counted on (as he plainly cannot) to request authorization before sending our troops into combat situations, Desert Storm provides no assurance that Congress would respond as nonevasively in the future as it did this time. By continually stating that he did not need congressional authorization, President Bush strongly implied that he would invade whether he got it or not. (Having induced the Security Council to set a deadline for Saddam Hussein to get out of Kuwait, he would have been embarrassed internationally if he *hadn't* invaded.) This obviously influenced Congress, which didn't want to appear irrelevant.[28] It is true that at least in terms of relative body counts, Desert Storm turned out to be closer to a turkey shoot than the "mother of all battles" promised by Saddam. That might be taken to suggest that the next time the president requests a vote of congressional support, there will be a virtual stampede to give it to him (particularly among Democrats seeking to reestablish their machismo). In terms of the constitutional goal of assuring the independent judgment of Congress, that would hardly be a happy outcome. However, the prediction probably underestimates Congress's sophistication on the subject of self-preservation. The euphoria soon fades after even the most "splendid little wars" (such as the Spanish-American War, for which, indeed, that phrase was coined[29])—a fact the aftermath of Desert Storm would have taught its members if they didn't know it already. They presumably are also aware that the war against Iraq was special in certain ways—visible terrain without serious air cover, to name only the most obvious[30]—ways that destroy the simplistic inference that just because from our perspective it turned out to resemble a video game, the next one is certain to do so too. The likely congressional reaction thus seems not the simple-minded one of rushing to approve whatever war the president comes up with next, but rather a return to the tradition of evasion, a resolve of still greater doggedness in resisting suggestions—even, in the unlikely event it again comes to it, a suggestion by the president—that casting a vote on whether Americans are to die might be part of their job. The next war might be another Desert Storm or it might not: better to keep your options open and claim vindication either way.

Developments since Desert Storm seal the folly of concluding that it represents the procedural wave of the future: At least as of January 1993 the President and Congress had reverted entirely to form. President Bush had ordered (and begun to enforce) "no fly" zones over Iraq, an action not remotely authorized by the Desert Storm Resolution, which was limited to the expulsion of Iraqi forces from Kuwait;[31] he had sent troops into Somalia (the congressional leadership dutifully if illogically indicating that there couldn't be a significant danger of hostilities because we were just delivering food); and there was talk of military intervention in Bosnia. As to none of these had there been conspicuous indication on anyone's part that Congress might have a role to play under either the Constitution or the War Powers Resolution: In particular, President-elect Clinton, who may have unusual incentives to earn his military spurs, had not been heard to that effect. Desert Storm, it appears, was sui generis.

CAN ANYBODY HERE FIX THIS THING?

That Congress has lost its intended constitutional position in deciding on war and peace is hardly a new discovery. The usual suggestion, however, has taken the form of a halftime pep-talk imploring that body to pull up its socks and reclaim its rightful authority.[32] That would be terrific, but unfortunately it seems unlikely to happen. Decisions on war and peace are tough, and more to the point they're politically risky. Since 1950 Congress has seen little advantage in making them, either without or within the framework of the War Powers Resolution. Sure our post-1973 presidents have been clever in sending up pieces of paper that refuse to acknowledge that they're 4(a)(1) "hostilities" reports. But it wouldn't have taken a rocket scientist to come up with the counterploy of construing them all, unless otherwise labeled, as 4(a)(1) reports, and deeming the sixty-day clock as having been started accordingly—rather than haggling endlessly, and without conclusion, about whether *Congress* should somehow start the clock (a procedure, incidentally, not apparently contemplated by the Resolution[33]). So it's unlikely to have been a failure of wit, and more likely has been one of will: Once the clock is started Congress will actually have to make a decision. Ulysses tried, genuinely I think, to tie himself to the mast in 1973, but the knots were loose, and he was soon back to his old ways of avoiding responsibility. It would be great if he could mend them, but unless the character of the institution undergoes a radical change, it's hard to see what the incentive is likely to be.[34]

The president, then? We shouldn't scoff *too* fast at this one. There are clear political advantages to the executive in spreading the responsibility for such risky decisions. If the war goes well, it is the president, not Congress, who will get to play the hero in the parades and political cartoons. If it goes badly, the blame can be spread around: Misery loves bedfellows. In fact that was pretty much the way it worked for the century and a half prior to 1950. Naturally the president generally (though not invariably) had been the point man in involving us in wars, but until the latter half of the twentieth century presidents were pretty scrupulous about insuring that Congress had enlisted before marching the troops off to battle.[35] Presidents may have maneuvered Congress and the nation generally toward that goal—Franklin Roosevelt before the Second World War is probably the classic example here[36]—but that's what we expect presidents to do with respect to all sorts of legislative programs: lead, even maneuver, but don't impose them unilaterally.

That changed in 1950—insofar as ideas can be pinpointed, this one appears to have been Dean Acheson's[37]—and as is the wont of bureaucrats, executive officials have been reflexively guarding the turf thus claimed ever since. But 1950 wasn't *that* long ago, and even since 1950 the experience hasn't been monochromatic: Desert Storm isn't the only deviation. In many ways the Tonkin Gulf Resolution of 1964 was a reversion to the pre-1950 pattern: We have seen that it was presented to the Congress and voted on as what it said it was, an authorization to wage war against North Vietnam.

That's an example that may cut the wrong way, however. We have also seen that despite the Tonkin Gulf Resolution most members of Congress felt no compunction whatever about disclaiming responsibility for the war and blaming it entirely on the President. As Lyndon Johnson put it with characteristic color, "I said early in my Presidency that if I wanted Congress with me on the landing of Vietnam, I'd have to have them with me on the take off. And I did just that. But I failed to reckon with one thing: the parachute. I got them on the takeoff, but a lot of them bailed out before the end of the flight."[38]

Beyond the reasonable doubts that Congress would ever actually be willing to take its allotment of the blame, however, a presidential move back in the direction of sharing responsibility in this area would buck a strong general tide of post–World War II history. During that period a tacit deal has existed between the executive and legislative branches, not just with respect to foreign policy but more generally, to the effect that the president will take the responsibility (well, most of it) so long as he can make the decisions, and Congress will forego actual policy-making authority so long as it doesn't have to be held accountable (and can scold the president when things go wrong).[39] No matter what the advantages, let alone the constitutional proprieties, it would be surprising if we soon found a president willing, unprodded, to make a significant move back toward the original arrangement. Candidates may sometimes talk that way; presidents seldom do, at least not since Eisenhower.

Judicial "Remand" as a Corrective for Legislative Evasion

I certainly don't mean to recommend that judges decide what wars we should and shouldn't fight—not because I think they'd necessarily do it worse than anybody else, but rather (to risk sounding naive) because it simply isn't their job. Because of their lifetime tenure, and to a more limited (and decreasing) degree the mode of their selection,[40] the judiciary is the most politically insulated branch of our government. But if the courts' relative insulation from the democratic process suggests that it's no business of theirs to decide what wars we fight, it does situate them uniquely well to police malfunctions in that process,[41] including the one with which we are here concerned, which essentially amounts to a conspiracy between the executive and legislative branches to enhance their own political fortunes at the expense of the interests of the people at large (now more than ever, its least advantaged segments).

Thus courts have no business deciding when we get involved in combat, but they have every business insisting that the officials the Constitution entrusts with that decision be the ones who make it.[42] The general idea here—we will get to specific legal rubrics presently—would be that when someone adversely affected by a president's decision to start a war (paradigmatically but not necessarily a member of the armed forces ordered to the theatre of operations) came to court challenging its legality, the court would ask whether Congress had authorized it, and if it hadn't, rule the war unconstitutional unless and until such authorization was forthcoming (almost certainly refraining from issuing an actual withdrawal order long enough to give Congress a reasonable time to consider the issue).

Such a general judicial power, nay duty, to invalidate decisions made by a government official or agency other than the one to which they were

entrusted by the document, is constitutionally unproblematic.[43] It has become moderately fashionable to assert, however—normally under the general heading of the "political question doctrine"—that there is something
special about cases involving "foreign affairs" that renders such an ordinarily routine judicial exercise improper. In such wholesale form, however,
this is just that—assertion—unsupported by Supreme Court precedent[44]
and affirmatively refuted by the language of the Constitution, which lists
among the heads of federal judicial jurisdiction cases arising under treaties,
cases affecting ambassadors and other public ministers and consuls, cases
in admiralty or maritime jurisdiction, and cases to which the United States
and/or foreign nations are parties—and indicates further that treaties shall
be the supreme law of the land "and the Judges in every State shall be
bound thereby."[45] It thus comes as no surprise to learn that the Supreme
Court has routinely decided "foreign affairs" and "national security" cases
throughout our history,[46] and more specifically has from the outset decided
numerous cases involving the "war power,"[47] in particular the question
whether Congress had sufficiently authorized a military action the president was conducting.[48] It was Chief Justice John Marshall, in the mother of
all landmarks *Marbury v. Madison*,[49] who originally indicated that courts
might decline to decide certain questions on the ground they were "political." It was the same Chief Justice Marshall, writing for the Court just one
year later in *Little v. Barreme*,[50] who invalidated the seizure of a foreign
ship during the naval war with France, *even though the seizure was on the
President's order*, on the ground that the President had thereby exceeded
the authorization granted him by Congress—without so much as a moment's pause to inquire whether *this* might not be one of those political
questions to which he had alluded in *Marbury*.[51]

The "political question doctrine" is a little like the "Holy Roman
Empire"—not simply because it's doubtful that it even exists any more (at
least at the Supreme Court level), but also because it's not clear that any of
the label's words was ever applicable. It certainly never had anything to do
with whether the question presented was "political" in any ordinary sense
of that term: "[T]he presence of constitutional issues with significant political overtones does not automatically invoke the political question doctrine. Resolution of litigation challenging the constitutional authority of
one of the three branches cannot be evaded by courts because the issues
have political implications . . . .[52] Nor was it ever a "doctrine": Even in its
heyday it was nothing more than a congeries of excuses for not deciding
issues otherwise properly before the court.[53] Most of these excuses have
been eliminated by the Supreme Court,[54] though a couple may remain and
warrant consideration.

It is sometimes said that a question is "political" if there is "a lack of
judicially discoverable and manageable standards for resolving it."[55] The

Court has come generally to recognize, however, that if the issue is otherwise properly before it—that is, if it raises a question under the Constitution or laws of the United States—its first duty is to try to *fashion* manageable standards. Thus manageability is certainly a consideration, but primarily at the stage of devising principles and remedies as opposed to the stage of determining whether to decide the issue at all.[56] If the question presented in our case were whether the war in question was a good thing, whether its benefits outweighed its costs, we would all presumably respond that that is not a question a court should decide. Some might be tempted to say that this is because such a question cannot be rendered amenable to judicial evaluation.[57] We needn't debate that characterization, however, as there is an incontrovertible basis for treating the question as nonjusticiable: The Constitution commits it elsewhere. It commits it to the legislative process, and the problem is that Congress has been refusing to decide it. That emphatically does not mean that we should turn the question over to the courts. They should, however, be enlisted in inducing Congress to answer it.[58]

A different strain of the political question doctrine—generally wrapped in the rhetoric of "potentially embarrassing confrontation"—is more prudential, residing in the judgment that the courts should not weaken their standing by issuing orders that are likely to be disobeyed. That the president will disobey an order of the Supreme Court seems less likely in 1993 than it might have 100 years ago. President Truman did, after all, remove the National Guard from the steel mills when ordered to do so in the middle of the Korean War, and even more dramatically, President Nixon complied with the Court's order to make public tape recordings he had to know would mean the end of his presidency. The Court is aware of this trend, and has altered the political question "doctrine" accordingly: In ordering the House of Representatives to reverse itself and seat Congressman Adam Clayton Powell, it dealt with the possibility of legislative disobedience by citing *itself* to the effect that disobedience is unthinkable![59] However, we need not linger on this point, for as we shall see, judicial enforcement of the requirement of congressional authorization of wars should not generate a direct confrontation between the Court and the president. Intelligently framed, the Court's decision will merely "remand" the issue of authorization to Congress. Either Congress will approve the war in question, thereby serving the values of the Constitution (and the War Powers Resolution), or it will disapprove it, rendering itself the Court's ally in the unlikely event the president still proves recalcitrant.

I mentioned above that a serviceperson under orders to report to the combat zone would be the paradigmatic plaintiff in a suit challenging a presidential war.[60] Paradigmatic perhaps, but often less than adequate. An officer bringing such a suit would risk sacrificing his career by doing so, and expecting enlisted personnel to do so demands a kind of independence and skepticism about superior orders it is a central point of basic training to eliminate. This factor is likely to attenuate as we depend (at least as to wars we anticipate will be protracted[61]) less on regular forces and more on re-servists. However, a suit brought by a serviceman ordered to the theatre of operations is also likely to come too late to do much good in compelling congressional consideration of the war in question.

In moments of rhetorical excess, I know I have talked as if no one in Congress cares about the president's assumption of the war power. This is an exaggeration: A number of members of Congress have demonstrated that they do care, and my point really is that they are a distinct minority. Thus in virtually every one of our recent presidential wars a number of congressional plaintiffs have stepped up and filed suit.[62] And while it is true that the prerogatives of congressmen are not to the ultimate point—trying to keep the nation out of ill-considered wars is—their prerogatives (specif-ically their right to vote on questions of war and peace) do give them an interest that is differentiated from that of the rest of us. Moreover, they are likely to be better informed than the general public about what is going on, and therefore well situated to get to court quickly when the president is failing in his duty to seek congressional authorization.

Sensibly enough, therefore,[63] this turns out to be the sort of situation in which the courts have been prepared to grant standing to members of Con-gress. We are not talking here about a member of Congress's seeking in court information that in some general way bears upon her general right to function as an effective legislator[64] or complaining that the president has wronged her by misinterpreting a statute for which she had voted.[65] Instead, as has been true in the cases in which members of Congress *have* been granted standing, she will be complaining about the preclusion of a specific vote (here on the merits of the war in question) by a presidential violation of law (here the refusal to file a 4(a)(1) report or otherwise to seek the congressional authorization the Constitution requires).

> To be cognizable for standing purposes, the alleged diminution in congressional influence must amount to a disenfranchisement, a complete nullification or with-drawal of a voting opportunity; and the plaintiff must point to an objective stan-dard in the Constitution, statutes or congressional house rules, by which disen-franchisement can be shown.[66]

A possible additional hurdle to challenges brought by congressional plaintiffs—likely to be included under the rubric of "ripeness"[67]—surfaced in Judge Harold Greene's otherwise admirable 1991 decision in *Dellums v. Bush*,[68] involving a lawsuit brought by fifty-four members of Congress to enjoin the President from sending American troops into Kuwait without congressional authorization (which authorization, of course, was ultimately forthcoming). Judge Greene's opinion was forthright and powerful in its indications (a) that the Constitution places unambiguously in the legislative process authority to decide whether the nation goes to war; (b) that whether the required congressional authorization has been obtained is not a "political question" that courts should refuse to decide; and (c) that the congressional plaintiffs had standing to bring the challenge.

The lawsuit ran aground, however, on a fourth finding by Judge Greene, that unless and until the plaintiffs could get a majority of their colleagues to join their challenge, the case was not "ripe" for decision.[69] He appeared to believe that his ripeness holding followed directly from the fact that it takes a majority vote in Congress to authorize a war: "[T]he majority of [Congress] under the Constitution is the only one competent to declare war, and therefore also the one with the ability to seek an order from the courts to prevent anyone else, *i.e.*, the Executive, from in effect declaring war."[70] The only problem is it isn't a "therefore": In fact allegations that the wrong government official or body has taken the action complained of are most commonly brought by someone other than the official or body whose authority was usurped.[71]

But maybe Greene just worded it the wrong way around. If it takes a majority of Congress to declare a war, it also takes a majority to block one.[72] Greene's point, I guess, was thus that because it would take a majority to vote down a presidentially requested declaration of war on the floor of Congress, it should take a similar majority to bring suit to block a presidentially announced decision to go to war unilaterally. On first reading this version may flow a little more easily, but on analysis it too proves to be a non sequitur. In the first place, Greene's language at several points suggests that the sort of majority he meant to require is a majority of both houses of Congress.[73] Since it would take a majority of just *one* house to block a declaration of war, however, it would seem to follow, on our reconstruction of Greene's logic, that such a one-house majority should also be able to sue.

While that confusion may raise questions about the coherence of Judge Greene's rationale, it is unlikely often to make a real world difference. There are, however, more fundamental respects in which Greene's "ripeness" qualms misunderstand the point of the War Clause, especially as it bears on the political structure of late twentieth-century America. Most obviously, requiring the president to follow the constitutionally prescribed procedures—one might suppose that even a single person who will be disadvantaged by the war should be able to insist on *that*—is not the same thing as telling him he can't go to war.

But even assuming it were the same—that everyone who wanted to see Congress play its constitutionally mandated role felt that way only because she opposed the war on its merits—the fact that a majority can block a war by refusing to vote yes still should not imply a power on the part of the president to go forward unless a majority can organize itself to vote (or sue) no.[74] The framers were explicit in their understanding that if Congress did not approve of the executive's pursuance of a given war, it could end it by refusing it further funding.[75] But they also understood that once the president had committed "our boys" to the battlefield, it would become emotionally and politically difficult to vote to cut off their "support." The Constitution requires a congressional declaration of war—it does not say the president can commit troops to combat unless Congress takes steps to stop him—and there is every indication that this choice was deliberate.

As we have seen, this original decision has taken on additional validity today. The late twentieth century is in general an era of comparatively unassertive congresses (perhaps one would better say congresses comparatively unprepared to put their votes where their misgivings are). As a sizeable political science literature has documented, congressmen today have found the most comfortable road to survival—and do they ever survive—to lie in combining a maximum of individual services for constituents, and other interest groups seen as critical to reelection, with a minimum of actual legislative policy-making.[76]

The New York Times' editorial of December 16, 1990 summarized the administration's position thus: "Congress knows how to say no, officials argue, and if it fails to do so . . . that's tantamount to a declaration of war."[77] We have seen, however, that this never was, and today it assuredly is not, a symmetrical situation. The fact that a majority of Congress can take action to stop a war if it can organize itself to do so is not remotely a functional substitute for the constitutional requirement that wars are not to be begun without Congress's affirmative approval.

Actually the framers didn't want it to be symmetrical—but the asymmetry they sought was the exact opposite of that created by the combination of the administration's assertions that it doesn't need authorization and Judge Greene's decision. George Mason said he was "for clogging rather than facilitating war; but for facilitating peace," and Oliver Ellsworth defended the requirement of congressional authorization by saying that "It should be more easy to get out of war, than into it."[78] Unfortunately Greene's "ripeness" ruling—that it should take one or another sort of "declaration of peace," some affirmative action by a majority of Congress to keep the country out of war—puts the shoe on the other foot.

Thus Congressman Dellums and his fifty-three fellow plaintiffs did not purport to be speaking for a majority of their colleagues. While President Bush was the nominal, and certainly a proper, defendant, he was only part of the story. The suit was aimed in reality not simply at the executive branch but at the "silent majority" (well, maybe not exactly silent) of the plaintiffs' colleagues as well, the majority who were proving most reluctant actually to cast a vote on the question whether, and subject to what limitations, the invasion should proceed. Though professional courtesy[79] may have precluded its being put just this way, it was a suit that said "The president's unilateral actions, and the unwillingness of a majority of our congressional colleagues to be forced on the record one way or the other, is depriving the fifty-four of us of a right the Constitution guarantees us, that of voting on wars before the president starts them." It makes no sense in a suit thus conceived for the judge to say he'll listen as soon as the plaintiffs can get a majority of their colleagues to join them.[80] A central point, without which the suit would have been unnecessary,[81] was that the very majority the judge wished to see signed up as plaintiffs were striving mightily to avoid having to take a stand on the issue one way or the other.

But whether or not a minority of congressional plaintiffs are granted standing to challenge presidential wars—and I believe I have removed any reason for supposing they shouldn't[82]—*some* entirely uncontroversial plaintiffs (such as service personnel) are likely to be available to bring suit.[83] It also seems clear that if Congress is to be induced to do its job in this area, the courts will have to become involved. It is thus time briefly to consider the relative advantages and disadvantages of the various legal rubrics under which they might.

Suing under the Existing War Powers Resolution

The War Powers Resolution provides that unless Congress has authorized the hostilities in question, the president is to terminate them within sixty days after a 4(a)(1) report "is submitted *or is required to be submitted* . . . whichever is earlier." The language I have italicized would seem to provide a peg on which to hang a lawsuit seeking to correct a presidential refusal to file such a report and thus start the clock. It is true that in such a case the court would have to determine whether there exist "hostilities" or a situation "where imminent involvement in hostilities is clearly indicated by the circumstances." Certainly this is not a question that will generate automatic answers—legal questions rarely do—and it is not one respecting which judges are particularly expert. This, however, is the way our legal system habitually works. Judges and lawyers generally are not experts on *any* substantive area. Instead they make their decisions (in a variety of areas on which others are more expert than they) by listening to the relevant facts, and where necessary the opinions of experts, and coming to a decision.

> Is it really more difficult to determine whether a group of soldiers, performing certain tasks in the midst of a civil war, are likely to get shot at, than to ascertain the probable economic impact of a given merger? Is there a basic difference between deciding whether a witness is lying when he or she testifies that certain

military personnel have not participated in combat missions than when he or she testifies that a certain employer never mentioned race in considering applicants for a job? Is the task of judging the credibility of a colonel who claims that he never gave advice on specific military operations to a given foreign government inherently less tractable than that of deciding whether one company intended to get a free ride on the goodwill of another company in adopting a certain trademark?[84]

Indeed, courts are routinely called upon, without incident, to decide insurance cases in which the existence or nonexistence of hostilities must be judicially determined for purposes of giving effect to a war risk clause.[85]

It would thus seem to make perfectly good sense for a court to entertain a lawsuit under the existing War Powers Resolution when the president has wrongfully refused to start the clock, giving Congress twenty additional days to authorize the war if it finds sixty days have passed since hostilities became imminent.[86] There are, however, a couple of reasons we should not too quickly assume this to be our salvation. The first is that the Resolution makes no reference to any such lawsuit. That objection doesn't seem very serious, though. The Resolution's reference to the (clock-starting) moment at which a 4(a)(1) report "is submitted or is required to be submitted" plainly envisions someone other than the president's determining that the clock should have been started when he has wrongfully failed to do so. Since there is no legislative history indicating that that someone is to be Congress either, and Congress has shown every disinclination to volunteer for the job, the courts are the most natural nominees. (Determining what is "required" by an existing statute is in our system normally the job of the judiciary,[87] and not simply an unaccustomed, but even an arguably unconstitutional,[88] one for Congress.) When the language of the law in question comfortably bears a given construction, and that construction is the only one capable of serving the law's purposes (here determining that the clock has been started and thereby forcing Congress to perform its deliberative duty) uncontroversial canons of statutory interpretation decree the adoption of that construction.

The other problem with bringing suit under the existing War Powers Resolution is more psychological and more serious, that in the twenty years since its enactment the Resolution has developed a bad aura, so bad in fact that most (though not all) courts have proved willing to invoke quite tortured "justiciability" doctrines to avoid enforcing it.[89] "Perhaps not since the Volstead Act ushered in the Prohibition Era has a federal law been talked about more and respected less than the War Powers Resolution of 1973."[90] In fact the Resolution is often blithely dismissed, in toto, as "unconstitutional." Most often this is just the unreflective epithet of a politician in full flight of political attack—such as Senator Helms's pronouncement in the course of a 1988 floor debate that "once the War Powers Act hits the Supreme Court of the United States, they are going to throw it out just like a tub of lard."[91]

Sometimes, however—though most academic analysis comes down the other way—this "overall unconstitutionality" position has been endorsed by more thoughtful commentators.[92] Although we shall see that the most flagrantly unconstitutional aspect of the Resolution is its grant of sixty (actually ninety) free days to the president to fight any war he wants,[93] the attacks have almost invariably argued that the Resolution unconstitutionally *limits* the executive. Such arguments take one of two invalid forms. The first is to note, correctly, that section 5(c) of the Resolution, permitting Congress to abort a war before the sixty-day clock has run by concurrent resolution, would probably be invalidated under the Supreme Court's 1983 decision in *INS v. Chadha*,[94] and irresponsibly[95] to infer from the unconstitutionality of that unimportant section that the entire Resolution must therefore be unconstitutional.[96]

The other "scholarly" attack has proceeded by drumbeat reiteration of the notion that foreign affairs just aren't any of Congress's business.[97] As we have seen, such assertions bear no relation to the language or purposes of the founding document, or the first century and a half of our history. The position taken by the Truman Administration respecting Korea ruptured this long-standing consensus, but the next president, Dwight Eisenhower, was quite deferential to Congress respecting the use of U.S. troops.[98] President Johnson's 1965 invasion of the Dominican Republic, though much more limited than Korea, was a reversion to Truman's form. But even if we were to concede 1950 through 1973, twenty-three years of deviance are hardly sufficient so clearly to have redefined the constitutional arrangement as to render unconstitutional the War Powers Resolution's attempt to return to the prior understanding.[99] The Constitution grants Congress authority to "make all laws which shall be necessary and proper for carrying into Execution the foregoing [congressional] Powers, *and all other Powers vested by this Constitution in the Government of the United States, or in any Department or Officer thereof.*"[100] The central executive-limiting provisions of the War Powers Resolution give concrete contemporary meaning to the constitutional understanding written into the document and consistently honored for a century and a half thereafter, and are plainly constitutional.[101]

Yet the bad aura persists. The situation is not helped by the fact that even general supporters of the Resolution admit it has significant flaws.[102] (For one thing, the Resolution that finally emerged was a compromise between significantly different House and Senate versions, and the pages of the law reviews still ring with articles by former staffers stridently denouncing the ruination of their handiwork by the injection of elements of the other house's version.[103]) Unfortunately this provides more grist for the mill of those who scream unconstitutionality—people able or willing to distinguish policy objections from constitutional defects are increasingly a rarity even within academia—and the charge continues to feed upon itself.

One important reason the undifferentiated allegations of unconstitutionality continue unabated is that the Supreme Court has yet to decide a case involving the War Powers Resolution. If it did, I am convinced, it would readily perceive the emptiness of the attacks and uphold the executive-limiting aspects of the Resolution (save, probably, section 5(c)), thus performing a great service of legitimation. As a former State Department Legal Adviser wrote in response to an earlier article of mine:

> [T]his is a situation where judicial settlement would work. I don't think there would be much resistance from the executive branch if the Court were to say "This is OK." In the absence of such a pronouncement, however, the President and his lawyers feel like they might be giving something away. The most important thing to be adjudicated, therefore, . . . is whether the whole scheme is constitutional. Once that was established, I think the machinery would run fairly smoothly—but I don't think Congress would override the President too often.[104]

To date the Supreme Court has not been presented with such a case, however, and given the prevalent aura it seems unlikely it will in the foreseeable future. For it is probably partly because of all the loose allegations of "unconstitutionality" that lower courts, understandably wishing to avoid the daunting task of attacking such an allegation head on, have repeatedly resorted to highly questionable "justiciability" grounds for dismissal of challenges brought pursuant to the Resolution. And by the time such questionable dismissals could make their way up to the Supreme Court (itself also undoubtedly not anxious to face the broad constitutional issue) the "Andy Warhol war" in issue—fifteen minutes of fighting, followed by fifteen minutes of fame—is likely to be over, thus mooting the case.

Amending the War Powers Resolution

The appendix to this book analyzes the War Powers Resolution in detail, going so far as to write a new one. A few of the changes suggested there are sufficiently central to deserve mention here, however. We should, for one thing, get rid of the probably unconstitutional (and almost certainly useless) section 5(c), so that it can no longer be used as a fulcrum for the fallacious inference that because it is unconstitutional the whole Resolution must be. We should also make clear that the prescribed procedure when the president has wrongfully refused to file a 4(a)(1) hostilities report is to have a court entertain a lawsuit to that effect, give Congress a reasonable opportunity to authorize the war, and if it doesn't, rule it illegal. The cases are clear that the various "justiciability" dodges lower courts have been using to avoid suits under the Resolution can be eliminated by statute:[105] They should be.

As noted, the existing Resolution indicates that once the president has committed troops to hostilities, he has forty-eight hours to report that fact to Congress, which then must approve his action within sixty days (extendable by the president to ninety) or the troops are to be withdrawn. Now occasionally it *is* necessary that the authorization follow the commencement of hostilities: The founders recognized that by reserving to the president authority to repel sudden attacks, authority I personally am prepared to construe more broadly than many commentators, as extending to any sudden and serious threat to the nation's security.[106] Unmistakably, however, the founders' presumption was that this was to be the exceptional case, that ordinarily wars had to be authorized in advance.

The existing Resolution stands this presumption on its head, granting the president the universal option of committing the troops first and seeking authorization later—an inversion that given the momentum of war would (even assuming compliance) most often prove of dispositive import. (There is little evidence that this effect was conscious, but it *does* constitute another method of effectively passing the buck to the president.) At this point it is likely to be suggested that this is the twentieth century and thus military response must *inevitably* be so swift as to preclude advance authorization, but that is nonsense: Particularly given the passing of the Cold War,[107] we are likely increasingly to encounter situations more resembling Desert Shield/Desert Storm in that it will take weeks, even months, to get the needed troops and equipment into position.[108]

The statute I propose in the appendix restores the original and constitutionally mandated presumption, requiring that congressional authorization precede military action on our part unless there are compelling military reasons precluding it, in which case the president may request authorization from Congress contemporaneously with his order commencing military action. (In some cases the advance authorization will most sensibly be conditional—"Unless Iraq clears out of Kuwait by January 15, 1991, the President is hereby granted specific authorization, within the meaning of section 5(b) of the War Powers Resolution, to . . . ."—but such declarations are substantially in accord with the Constitution's purposes[109] and precedented historically.[110] The central point, however, is that post-commencement authorization, though sometimes inevitable, must be the exception and not, as it is under the existing Resolution, a universally available—and thus very likely, assuming compliance at all, a universally elected—option.)

Another change proposed in the appendix that warrants mention here is my suggestion that the sixty/ninety-day "free period" of presidential war—now universally available, though under my proposed statute available only when advance authorization was not possible—be shortened to twenty days. A free period of combat of any length is defensible only as a contemporary iteration of the reserved executive authority to respond to emergencies—that is, to the extent it coincides with a reasonable estimate of the time it should take Congress to decide whether to authorize the war the president felt national security required him to start unilaterally. Viewed otherwise, as a simple delegation of authority to fight any war the president can wrap up in under ninety days, the period amounts—especially in this period of "walkover wars"—to yet another device by which Congress can duck responsibility for such decisions, and mightily offends not only whatever vestiges of the delegation doctrine remain, but the central point of the provision assigning the decision on war and peace (crucially including the decision whom to wage war against) to the legislative process.[111] Ninety days, however—and sixty days just as clearly—is an indefensibly lengthy estimate of how long it should take Congress to decide whether the president's "emergency" response should be made more permanent.

There is, of course, a massive problem with the entire idea of amending the War Powers Resolution so as to compel timely congressional consideration of whether we should go to war, and that is that we have seen no inclination, in fact we have seen every disinclination, on the part of recent congresses to play anything beyond a critic's role in such decisions. However, stepping up and taking responsibility on the question whether to fight a particular war for which the president is beating the drums, and binding oneself in advance and outside any particular context to do so, are at least potentially different matters. In fact the latter is precisely what Congress tried in all apparent good faith to do in 1973 (unfortunately not adequately planning on presidential resistance). Admittedly Congress has since learned some things about itself it didn't know even in 1973, but the general effort remains one that in theory might still seem attractive.

The problem is it doesn't seem to. I made many of the suggestions in the appendix in a moderately conspicuous article published in 1988,[112] and others have made somewhat similar efforts to stiffen Congress's back,[113] with the same result (deafening silence). Indeed, when Congress gets to talking about amendment it soon becomes clear that the options most members find attractive are (1) overt repeal and (2) disguised repeal[114]—in any event *somehow* getting the embarrassing monkey of accountability off

their backs. Thus as attractive an option as this might be from the standpoint of the good of the country, it is not at present an attractive option for
Congress. It thus seems not to be in the cards, at least for the foreseeable
future.

Suing Directly under the Constitution

Or one could sue "directly under the Constitution,"[115] seeking a declaratory
judgment (and perhaps an injunction) to the effect that the war in question
is illegal on the ground that it hasn't been congressionally authorized. That,
indeed, was the form of *Dellums v. Bush*, whose complaint didn't even
mention the War Powers Resolution. The chief advantage of this tactic is
that it avoids the Resolution's (unjustified) bad aura.[116] (No one dares bad-
mouth the Constitution, at least not in so many words.[117])

Admittedly the Constitution doesn't give the sort of specific guidance
the Resolution does on the question of what should count as a valid congressional authorization, but this doesn't seem like a serious problem. It is
true the Resolution provides that authorizations must be "specific," but any
intelligent application of the Declaration of War Clause would yield that
result anyway. And as far as the Resolution's more specific interpretive
instructions are concerned, it would seem they should be followed even in
a suit brought "under" the Constitution rather than the Resolution: The
question even in a "purely constitutional" case is whether Congress has
authorized the war in question, and surely Congress is entitled to tell us
how to construe its enactments, which instructions should be heeded unless
and until Congress repeals them.[118]

Similarly, while the War Powers Resolution is quite specific about the
sort of conflict that requires congressional authorization—"hostilities or
. . . situations where imminent involvement in hostilities is clearly indicated by the circumstances"—the Constitution's simple reference to "war"
seems so brief as to leave room for many quibbles (some real, others so-
phistical) about what it comprises. Whenever a court has to decide whether
the institution constitutionally vested with authority to create an x has done
so, however, it must first decide whether an x in fact has been created.
"War" is a lot less obscure than many other constitutional concepts. Nonetheless, if that were all there were to the constitutional provision, this might
indeed be a problem in some cases (though by no means all of those in
which the executive branch seeks to make it one[119]). In any event that's not
all there is to the provision, which grants Congress power to "declare War,
grant letters of Marque and Reprisal, and make Rules concerning Captures
on Land and Water."[120] A letter of marque or reprisal was a grant of governmental permission, sometimes to a government employee but more often to
a private party, to engage in what amounted to one or more acts of war

against agents of another country (typically by the seizure of ships, though by no means universally: Some letters of marque and reprisal were "land-based"). Thus the framers and ratifiers of the Constitution provided that all acts of armed combat performed on behalf of the United States—*even if they didn't amount to "war"*—had to be authorized by Congress.[121] It therefore needn't be a "war": Congress must authorize all combat engaged in on behalf of the United States. This one therefore shouldn't be a serious problem either.

Assuming, therefore, that the War Powers Resolution is not amended for the better, my own inclination would be—at least in a case where the president has already initiated combat—to sue for violations of both the War Powers Resolution and the Constitution. Though courts seem somehow to keep missing the point, the former count may render the inquiry marginally more amenable to judicial resolution, and it would be an enormous service to get such a count to the Supreme Court and thereby—I am as confident as one can be in these changing judicial times[122]—to get the central executive-limiting sections of the Resolution authoritatively legitimated. The constitutional count should be included, however, in case the allergy of most lower courts to the Resolution retains its resistance to rational inoculation. Where the fighting has not yet started, however—as was the case in *Dellums v. Bush*—I'd do just what Dellums' lawyer did, however, and omit the War Powers Resolution count. Including it might serve only to remind the executive's lawyers and the court that at least as currently phrased[123] the Resolution gives the president an effective ninety free days of fighting.[124]

This chapter's main message, however, is that no matter what benefits such a step would bring not only to both Congress's and the president's[125] long-run institutional positions but also to our constitutional system as a whole, under current conditions it seems unlikely that either of them will, on its own motion, take serious steps to enforce either the War Powers Resolution or the Constitution's War Clause.[126] The assistance of the courts thus appears to have become essential if Congress is to be induced to discharge its constitutional responsibilities in this area. (Two centuries of experience also suggest, unsurprisingly, that our federal courts, in particular the Supreme Court, are more likely to be receptive to lawsuits setting limits on the executive's wartime powers that are brought at the end of a war than to those brought in the war's midst. [127] The end of the Cold War thus seems an opportune time.) The judiciary shouldn't decide what wars we fight, but it can insure that Congress play its constitutionally mandated role in such decisions. It has become imperative that one way or another it do so.

CHAPTER 4

The (Unenforceable) Unconstitutionality
of the "Secret War" in Laos, 1962–1969

> The roar of the bombs and the noise of the planes frightened me
> terribly. Our life . . . was without tomorrows. Each day, across
> the forests and ditches, we sought only to escape from the
> bombs. When looking at the face of my innocent child, I could
> not stop crying for his future . . . . Why do the men in this world
> not love each other . . . [a]nd why do they kill each other this
> way? . . . In any case, in all that happens, it is the innocent people
> who suffer all the terrible consequences so fatal and tragic.
> —Laotian Refugee, 1971[1]

> You can't let your people know what the government is doing
> without letting the wrong people know—those who are in oppo-
> sition to what you're doing.
> —Ronald Reagan, 1983[2]

OFTEN over the past couple of years, as I told one or another friend I was
writing about the war in Indochina, I was greeted with a quizzical look.
"The war in Vietnam," I'd quickly add, and then they'd understand—kind
of. It is not the point of this vignette to suggest that my friends are dull-
witted. It's rather that the general picture most of us had of the American
war in Indochina—certainly it was the picture our government was giving
us—was that we were fighting to defend the Saigon government from a
North Vietnamese invasion (and, initiates understood, indigenous Communist insurgence as well). To the extent the war slopped across the borders,
as we knew it did into Cambodia in 1970 (and suspected it had in minor
ways all along), that was because the North Vietnamese were using the
eastern rim of that country (and probably southeastern Laos as well) as a
transport and staging area for its assault on South Vietnam.

In many ways this picture was closer to the truth than radical critics
would have had us believe at the time. There really was a North Vietnamese infiltration of the South, and there really was a "Ho Chi Minh trail"
stretching down through Laos and Cambodia,[3] just across the western border of South Vietnam. However, the picture we were getting was seriously
incomplete. The United States was engaged in a hot war against "Commu-

nism" throughout all of Indochina, siding with the governments in Saigon, Phnom Penh, and Vientiane against a Communist threat that in each case did involve an element of North Vietnamese aggression but also importantly involved Communist elements (Viet Cong, Khmer Rouge, and Pathet Lao) that were indigenous to the country involved.

In chapter 2 I concluded that the first of these wars—the "war in Vietnam" our government told us about—was constitutional under currently prevailing notions of congressional authorization. (Chapter 3 suggested the need to clarify those notions in ways that will more effectively force Congress to face up to its constitutional obligation to decide on war and peace.) In this chapter and the next I shall suggest that the rest of the American war in Indochina (the part they didn't tell us about) was (essentially for that reason) unconstitutional.[4]

AMERICA'S ROLE IN THE WAR IN LAOS

> They made a wasteland and called it peace.
>
> —Tacitus

> The least goddam thing somebody could do is come back and say "I'm sorry."
>
> —"Pop" Buell[5]

At Geneva on July 23, 1962, fourteen nations, including the United States and North Vietnam, signed agreements guaranteeing the neutrality of Laos. They outlawed "foreign military personnel" in Laos and prohibited the introduction of arms and war materials into that country except for "conventional armaments . . . necessary for the national defense." "Foreign military personnel" was defined to include "members of foreign military missions, foreign military advisers, experts, instructors, consultants, technicians, observers and other foreign military persons . . . and foreign civilians connected with the supply, maintenance, storing and utilization of war materials."[6]

Initial American compliance with the 1962 Geneva agreements was better than that of the North Vietnamese. Although we withdrew all of our 666 military advisers by the October deadline, they pulled out a mere handful, leaving somewhere between 6000 and 10,000 North Vietnamese fighting men in Laos.[7] "But [e]ven as it complied with the letter of the treaty," the United States "violated Geneva's spirit by increasing covert military operations."[8] "Military advisers and CIA personnel moved across the border of Thailand, where they were flown in every day like commuters by Air America,"[9] and it was not long before we were back in Laos in several very big ways, participating in what amounted to two wars.[10] One was over the

Ho Chi Minh trail, a network of roads, waterways, and trails in the eastern part of the Laotian panhandle that the Communists were using as a corridor for the transportation and provisioning of their troops in South Vietnam and Cambodia. This campaign was basically an adjunct of the war in Vietnam and thus an almost exclusively American show: Laotian troops rarely participated. The other was for control of northern and central Laos, and involved a struggle between Laotian government forces supported by their American and Thai allies, and the Pathet Lao and their North Vietnamese allies. American participation in these campaigns took several forms: (1) training anti-Communist troops (sometimes even accompanying them into battle), (2) supplying them with arms, food, and other equipment, (3) transporting them in and out of action, and (4) supporting them by heavy bombing of Communist positions.

General Vang Pao's "Secret Army" (Armée Clandestine) fought (with comparative effectiveness) on the government side of the war in northern Laos.[11] It comprised some 40,000 to 70,000 Hmong ("Meo") tribesmen[12] augmented later by somewhere between 17,000 and 21,000 American-paid Thai "volunteers," most of whom "resigned" from the Thai army to fight in Laos but were guaranteed reinstatement without loss of benefits upon their return.[13] This Secret Army was trained and guided by Central Intelligence Agency employees, a contingent that in turn substantially comprised Army Special Forces troops who had switched their official employment after the 1962 Geneva Agreements.[14] As Under Secretary of State U. Alexis Johnson testified in 1971: "Under the Geneva Agreements we were prohibited from having American military personnel in Laos and that is the brief answer . . . . CIA is really the only other instrumentality we have."[15] Some of these Green-Berets-turned-CIA-operatives reported that they were "fed up with having their hands tied" in Vietnam.[16] These "ex-Green Berets train[ed] government troops, assist[ed] reconnaissance teams, and help[ed] plan terrorist and psychological warfare operations."[17] Sometimes they actually accompanied Vang Pao's troops into battle, though generally not, as American casualties risked publicizing the fact that live Americans had been there.[18]

The United States supplied virtually all the military and other equipment for the Armée Clandestine, often channeling it through the Agency for International Development (AID), which generally served as a cover for CIA operations.[19] Air America (a CIA subsidiary) and Continental Air Services (a private airline working closely with the Agency)[20] moved Vang Pao's troops and supplies, and evacuated his wounded.[21] Most Air America and Continental pilots had (at least officially) resigned from the United States Air Force to fly for these carriers; some "returned" to the Air Force when their Laotian chores were completed.[22] Americans also operated the air bases.[23] The Secret Army was thus "armed, equipped, fed, paid, guided strategically and tactically, and often transported into and out of action by the United States."[24]

> By the mid-1960s the CIA in Laos had grown to immense proportions. No longer did the CIA just organize a small army of [Hmong] tribesmen numbering 11,000, but the CIA found itself commanding an army numbering more than 100,000. The CIA station in Laos had created an organization of huge numbers of [Hmong], Lao, and Thai peasants, U.S. military advisors, mercenaries, diplomats from the U.S. Mission in Vientiane, Army and Air Force attaches, members of the International Voluntary Services, people from the United States Information Service, some Americans in the Agency for International Development, and pilots from the Navy, Air Force and Marines to form a paramilitary group to conduct the ground and air war in Laos.[25]

As if that weren't enough, official United States armed forces units often got involved. In "Operation Prairie Fire," which apparently lasted from 1967 to 1972, Green Beret units periodically and secretly crossed the border to fight in Laos.[26] "Prairie Fire executed over 250 missions in 1967, including patrols penetrating as far as twelve miles into Laos. By 1968, in addition to the Green Berets serving with the 5th Special Forces Group, there were another 598 Americans assigned to Prairie Fire."[27] Reportedly over 1,000 such border crossings occurred during 1969 and 1970.[28]

In the spring of 1964, when the war was going badly for government forces, American fighter-bombers began striking targets in northern Laos.[29] This was not at the beginning a large campaign: There were only twenty such sorties during 1964. In the autumn of the same year, at American request, Laotian planes began to bomb North Vietnamese supply routes along the Ho Chi Minh trail. In 1965, as we sent our first actual combat troops into South Vietnam, American aircraft took over this mission. (Many Americans' first suspicions that we were bombing Laos incorporated an assumption that we were doing so to close off supply routes to South Vietnam. That indeed became much of the point, but the chronology, as well as the relative tonnage involved, demonstrates that a prior goal, which remained important throughout, was support of the Vientiane government. Of course, our support of Vang Pao's Secret Army was directed almost entirely toward that goal as well.)

Throughout the 1960s American bombing of Laos intensified enormously, especially during those purportedly dovish intervals when the bombing of North Vietnam had been halted.[30] "The only difference was that bombs that might have fallen on North Vietnam were dropped instead on similar targets in the jungles of Laos."[31] (Unfortunately it made eco-

nomic sense: "We couldn't just let the planes rust";[32] Laos was a convenient place to use them; and their use there would be secret.) This therefore
became "the heaviest sustained bombing campaign in history"[33]: By late
1969, the United States Air Force was flying at a rate variously estimated
by responsible commentators as somewhere between 300 and 500 sorties a
day over Laos.[34] By the time the bombing stopped in 1973, United States
planes had flown approximately 600,000 sorties there, which computes out
at about "one planeload of bombs every eight minutes around the clock for
nine years."[35] We dropped somewhere between 1.6 and 2 million tons of
bombs on Laos all told,[36] more than we had loosed on all of Europe and the
Pacific theater during World War II.[37] (By way of contrast, during Operation Desert Storm we dropped on Iraq and Kuwait "only" about 5 percent
of the total tonnage dropped during World War II.[38])

Until 1969 the American people, and to a lesser degree the Congress,
were kept in substantial ignorance of these various American involvements
in Laos. In September and October of that year, however, *The New York
Times* began running detailed articles about our role. At first the government resolutely maintained the cover-up. However, when government
troops captured the Plain of Jars in September of that year (temporarily, as
it turned out) the temptation to gloat apparently proved irresistible and
"sources" within our government confirmed that the victorious troops were
actually CIA protégés, and that we had provided "heavy" air and logistical
support.[39] (The next day the State Department, speaking corporately, "refused to confirm or deny" this story.[40]) In October 1969 a subcommittee of
the Senate Foreign Relations Committee chaired by Stuart Symington held
closed hearings on our role in Laos. On April 20, 1970 a heavily censored
transcript of these hearings was released, and on December 21 of the same
year a brief and similarly unenlightening subcommittee report was issued.
However, several of the senators present indicated that what came out in
the hearings substantially confirmed the 1969 *New York Times* stories,
which covered a good deal of what I have reported here.[41]

Secret wars are prima facie unconstitutional, since they haven't been
authorized by Congress, let alone exposed to the scrutiny of the American
public. There are, however, four conceivable defenses of the constitutionality of the American war in Laos, which I will discuss in turn: (1) that it
shouldn't count as a "war" for constitutional purposes because it was
largely fought by the CIA (and Laotians and Thais acting under its tutelage)
as opposed to American armed forces; (2) that in fact it *was* authorized by
Congress at the same time the war in Vietnam was authorized, most pointedly in the Tonkin Gulf Resolution; (3) that there were compelling military
justifications for keeping the war secret from Congress and the American
people, and thus for not seeking authorization; and (4) that the American

war in Laos actually wasn't a secret, in that any alert member of Congress or the public could have learned what was happening by careful attention to the right public reports—and thus, I guess the argument is supposed to run, Congress authorized it by not cutting any of the appropriations they might have surmised were being used to fund it.

DEFENSE 1: BECAUSE IT WASN'T FOUGHT BY OUR "ARMED FORCES," THE CAMPAIGN IN LAOS WASN'T COVERED BY THE CONSTITUTIONAL REQUIREMENT THAT WARS BE AUTHORIZED BY CONGRESS

Obviously no such defense could even be attempted with regard to the most destructive components of our war in Laos[42]—the massive bombing campaigns, which involved United States Air Force and Navy planes—or to the actions of Green Beret and Marine units in Laos. In light of contemporary events, however,[43] it is worth going on to discuss the applicability of the Constitution's War Clause to operations run by the CIA (or some other arm of our "intelligence" apparatus) that employ, as troops, either non-American military personnel or "civilian" CIA employees. Such operations are proving increasingly attractive, and here the argument undoubtedly *would* be made, at least by the CIA General Counsel's office,[44] that the United States is not at war.

The increasing attractiveness of "paramilitary" operations and proxy battles has at least two causes. First, the consultation and reporting requirements of the War Powers Resolution apply only to the commitment of "United States Armed Forces."[45] Second, using foreigners to fight our battles (though probably not American "civilians") is cheaper for the United States, not only monetarily but in terms of American lives as well. As former Under Secretary Johnson testified in 1971:

> The only U.S. Forces involved in Laos are in the air. We have no combat forces stationed there. And I personally feel that although the way the operation has been run is unorthodox, unprecedented, as I said, in many ways I think it is something of which we can be proud as Americans. It has involved virtually no American casualties. What we are getting for our money there, as the Ambassador said, is, I think, to use the old phrase, very cost effective.[46]

As another witness pointed out, "[W]hen they die, you don't have to ship them home, you bury them right there on the spot."[47] This kind of thinking not only appeals to government cost-benefit analysts, but also is likely to reduce domestic opposition to the war in question. Americans will understandably be more concerned about a war in which there is a danger that they or their loved ones will die.

Understandable, yes, but morally indefensible: Hmong and Thai lives count too. In addition, while such situations may not be covered by the War Powers Resolution, they *are* covered by the War Clause of the Constitution. The fact that few American lives were at risk in Laos (at least as compared with the lives of locals) doesn't seem like something that should take this out of the constitutional category of war. In fact, in explaining why they were trying to make wars difficult to get into, the founders mentioned their financial costs as well as their human ones.[48] And even wars that aren't particularly costly to the United States in either of those terms, such as the "walkover wars" of the Reagan-Bush era, carry moral and political costs. Naturally we're all happier when Americans don't die, but at the same time we don't want our country risking the lives of significant numbers of foreigners—either as enemies or as soldiers on our side—without careful and constitutional consideration. Moreover, "[w]hat is initially intended to be a minor effort, perhaps involving only a bloodless show of force, can easily grow into a major war, even a nuclear one."[49] In any event, significant numbers of Americans were put at risk, and killed, in Laos.

Neither can the fact that many of the Americans fighting and managing the war in Laos were not officially members of the United States Armed Forces make a constitutional difference. That would make the War Clause a hollow joke indeed: All the president would have to do is redesignate a couple of Army divisions as "CIA" and use them accordingly[50]—or, perhaps less flagrantly, let the membership of the Armed Forces dwindle while the membership of the CIA, or whatever, is beefed up to the point where it can manage, perhaps even fight, full-scale wars.

In February 1970 Senator Charles Mathias argued that the presence of the Green-Berets-turned-CIA-operatives in Laos constituted a violation of Congress's earlier ban on American ground combat troops in that country.[51] Such a "veil piercing" analysis certainly seems to make a lot of sense in the statutory context for which Mathias proposed it. However, one doesn't have to reach it in the constitutional context, as the commissioning of nonmilitary and even private groups to take military action on behalf of the United States is a situation precisely contemplated by the War Clause. "In the eighteenth century, war had not yet become the exclusive domain of the state; many governments contracted out the business to private citizens or groups, or foreign units and mercenaries . . . ."[52] As we noted in chapter 3, the marque and reprisal provision was designed to insure that authority to license such acts of war or lesser hostilities in behalf of the United States, like the authority to authorize full-fledged wars, would be unambiguously vested in Congress. That such hostilities were undertaken by private parties (let alone agencies of government not officially designated "armed forces") was irrelevant: They still had to be legislatively authorized.[53] (As the quoted passage also suggests, hostilities contracted out to *foreign* mercenaries, like the Thais we hired to fight on our side in Laos, were also covered by the clause.[54]) It is therefore as clear as any conclusion of constitutional law can be that the fact that part of the American war in Laos was fought by a combination of the CIA and its protégés did not eliminate the necessity of congressional authorization.

DEFENSE 2: THE TONKIN GULF RESOLUTION AUTHORIZED THE WAR IN LAOS

Section 2 of the Tonkin Gulf Resolution, enacted in August of 1964, authorized the president to use armed force to assist any SEATO protocol state (which Laos was) "requesting assistance in defense of its freedom" (which Souvanna Phouma did). Section 1 didn't even require a request from the country in question: It simply "supported the determination" of the president to "prevent further aggression." True, there was no legislative history indicating that Laos was to be among the countries to which we would be lending our assistance. However, as noted earlier, declarations of war generally don't specify allies, they specify enemies. And the Resolution's Preamble, which referred to the "campaign of aggression that the Communist regime in North Vietnam has been waging against its neighbors," not only identified the "enemy" but also indicated with some specificity the set of nations to which we might be lending assistance. "Neighbors" is plural, Laos abuts North Vietnam, and at the time of enactment North Vietnam was engaged in aggression against the Vientiane government.

One problem for this defense of the American war in Laos is that both of its aspects were begun substantially in advance of the enactment of the Tonkin Gulf Resolution—our training and support of the Secret Army by years, the bombing campaign by months.[55] Beyond that, however, even the staunchest supporters of presidential power in this area grant—indeed this is a critical premise of their argument that the constitutional requirement of advance authorization can be ignored—that if Congress does not like the way a war is being conducted it can pull the financial plug on it (and by extension that if the public does not approve of the war, it can pressure Congress thus to end it).[56] That constitutional safeguard is eliminated, however, if the way the war is being conducted, let alone the fact that it exists, is being kept secret from Congress and the American people. The validity of this defense of the war in Laos—even *after* August 1964—is therefore entirely dependant upon the validity of the next, that is, upon the existence of a compelling military justification for the secrecy. The fact that a resolution was once passed which facially appears to have authorized a given war cannot by itself constitutionally justify keeping the progress of that war secret, let alone its very existence.[57]

DEFENSE 3: THERE WERE COMPELLING MILITARY REASONS WHY
   CONGRESS AND THE AMERICAN PUBLIC COULD NOT BE
   TOLD ABOUT THE WAR IN LAOS, AND THUS WHY
   AUTHORIZATION COULD NOT BE SOUGHT

We obviously need to begin by questioning whether such a defense should be entertainable even in theory. Plainly military officers can undertake secret campaigns during a war—secret at least in the sense that no advance warning is given—in order to surprise the enemy, rendering him more vulnerable and increasing our chances of military success. It is some distance from that, however, to the conclusion that the president can covertly *start* a war simply because there is a military justification for doing so. (As there might be: Pearl Harbor is an example that readily comes to mind.) The argument that he should not be able to do so is obvious and strong: Such a beginning leaves the body constitutionally vested with authority to get us into wars, namely Congress, entirely out of the loop.[58]

On the other hand, we can construct hypothetical cases in which most of us might instinctively want to say that the president should be able to begin a war clandestinely—the case, for example, of a country that reliable intelligence sources tell us (a) is planning to launch a nuclear attack on the United States in forty-eight hours, and (b) can be stopped by covert military action not involving the use of nuclear weapons. His doing so would also seem to fit within any sensible contemporary rendition of the constitutional principle that he can repel "sudden attacks" without first coming to Congress.[59] In addition, it will often be debatable whether the clandestine operation in question is a "separate war" or merely a separate campaign in a war of whose existence we are all aware.[60] Thus on neither theoretical nor practical grounds does it appear fruitful to stake one's constitutional analysis on whether the covert campaign in issue constitutes the commencement of a new war.

In order to make Laos even debatable, however, one's rendition of the rationale underlying the exceptional power to repel sudden attacks must be extended not only (1) to encompass reactions to situations not actually involving assaults upon United States territory—itself a debatable extension, but one of which I convinced at least myself earlier[61]—but also (2) to deem the president constitutionally "unable to come to Congress" not simply when there is not time to do so, but in certain other situations as well—for example, where secrecy is essential to military effectiveness. That move too is highly debatable, though I suspect many of us would come out the same way on our nuclear attack hypothetical even if the intelligence estimates were that the president had a month to move. (Exposing a military plan that far in advance to the entire Congress would obviously pose a grave risk of compromising its secrecy.[62]) Still another assumption is needed before Laos becomes arguable, however, and that is (3) that the constitutionally acceptable military justifications for presidential secrecy are not limited to a desire to surprise the enemy.[63] It is not easy to come up with another plausible example of such a justification—and I say that having reviewed the various excuses the administration actually came up with—but there may be no reason in principle why that should be the only one. The reason for the cagey language is that once the *enemy* knows of our military campaign—and thus is in a position to tell whomever it wants—a convincing defense of the proposition that Congress shouldn't know about it becomes essentially inconceivable. Nonetheless, for purposes of the ensuing analysis I shall assume, though we have made a number of highly debatable assumptions to get to this point—one or more of which it would not surprise or disappoint me if you had rejected[64]—that any convincing military justification for keeping our role in Laos secret from Congress and the American people would have justified the president in doing so, and proceed to consider the excuses the administration actually threw at us when the United States' role in Laos was finally revealed in 1969 and 1970. We shall see that even with the benefit of all these questionable legal concessions, none of the administration's excuses will work.

The Agreement with Souvanna Phouma

First, "the State Department said the American government had agreed with Souvanna Phouma to keep such activities secret."[65] Some such understanding does indeed appear to have existed, but our first answer should be, "So what?" Agreeing with a foreign leader to circumvent the constitutional requirement of congressional authorization does not justify the president in doing so.[66] The secrecy arrangement had domestic political benefits for the leaders on both sides. Souvanna could at least attempt to maintain his image as a "neutral" rather than a hapless dependant on United States aid, and Johnson (and later Nixon) could avoid domestic protest both within and outside of Congress. Souvanna's attempt at image-maintenance was plainly rather silly. Virtually everyone in Laos knew what we were up to anyway, as did the governments of North Vietnam, China, and the Soviet Union. Only Congress and the American people were effectively kept in ignorance.[67] And even if it had worked, helping a foreign leader appear to his people to be something he isn't hardly constitutes an excuse for violating the United States Constitution. Neither does the goal of avoiding criticism here at home: In fact that's the essence of the constitutional offense.

A variation on this first excuse that was suggested at least once was that if we made the bombing public, "Souvanna Phouma, himself, in order to maintain his 'neutrality,' would ask us to cease the bombing that was being carried on in support of his forces."[68] In order to make it into even the arguably relevant category, this version has to incorporate the unspoken premise that such a request on Souvanna's part would have been damaging to our national security. In the first place it seems unlikely that such a request would have been made. As we noted, the Laotian people and the various Communist governments Souvanna might have wished to impress with his "neutrality" already knew we were bombing, and yet he made no request that we stop. (It seems suspiciously convenient that when the administration starts worrying about Souvanna's embarrassment it defines "making the bombing public" as telling the United States Congress about it.) And indeed when the administration *was* finally forced by media and congressional attention officially to acknowledge that we were bombing Laos, Souvanna didn't ask us to stop doing so, and we didn't.

But suppose he *had* asked us to stop. You'll note that the quoted excuse is ambiguous as to whether we would have done so. Perhaps the idea was that we wouldn't, and that would have further embarrassed Souvanna. But if that was the idea, it is one we dealt with above: Reducing embarrassment to a foreign leader doesn't justify ignoring the Constitution. If on the other hand the implication was supposed to be that we *would* have stopped, it was most misleading—at least insofar as it was supposed to convey the idea that *his request alone* would have induced the administration to do so.

It is conceivable that under such circumstances we would have stopped bombing *northern* Laos: If Souvanna didn't want our help in keeping his government in power, I suppose he might have (though he might not have) been accommodated. However, it is simply not believable (and note that no one actually said) that the administration would voluntarily have stopped bombing the Ho Chi Minh trail, as that effort was felt to be important to protecting our troops and otherwise prevailing in Vietnam. "Souvanna Phouma often stated that his government had no control over the trail region and could not prevent American or North Vietnamese activities there."[69]

All the while we were bombing the trail the administration was preparing defenses in terms of "hot pursuit" under international law and claims that the territory just west of the Vietnamese border was not "really" part of other sovereign nations, since so few people lived there and so many North Vietnamese troops operated there.[70] Had Souvanna complained, I'm sure the administration would have denied the charge (or at least denied intentionality), hauled the international law excuses out as a plea in the alternative, and continued bombing. Souvanna's desires just were not that important to us,[71] and the only reason it was sometimes implied they were was that they dovetailed beautifully with the desire of the Johnson and Nixon administrations to hide the bombing from Congress and the American people.

Am I therefore accusing administration spokespersons of lying when they implied that a request from Souvanna might result in a bombing halt? Note that what I said was that it is not believable that *by itself*—without the intercession of Congress or the American people—such a request could have had that effect. I do not mean to deny the possibility, though in retrospect it too seems a very long shot,[72] that such a protest from Souvanna— which might have called attention to the bombing so dramatically that our legislative representatives would have had trouble continuing to look the other way—would have induced *Congress* to put such pressure on the executive that he would have decided to stop bombing. (More likely, of course, it would have led to some ineffectual grousing, though that too is something the administration had every incentive to avoid.)

So no, members of the administration weren't exactly *lying* when they said, "If Souvanna asks us to stop, we'll have to stop."[73] What such a statement conjures up was a simple administration accession to the request, and that is not believable. But technically it could also mean, and in the heat of conflict even relatively candid officials are liable to assimilate the two,[74] "If Souvanna asks us to stop, we'll have to stop . . . because congressional pressure will make us stop." There is, however, a world of *constitutional* difference between the two versions of the claim, as it can never count as a valid excuse for the president's not telling Congress about a particular warlike activity in which he is engaged that they might instruct him to stop it. Its right to do so is precisely the constitutional point.

The Desire to Preserve the 1962 Geneva Accords

It was next asserted that we did not wish publicly to confess to our violation of the Geneva Accords, because we continued to harbor hopes of putting them back together again.[75] This excuse can be dispatched more quickly. Both United States and North Vietnamese forces were flagrantly violating the Geneva Agreements, and everybody in the area knew it. As Senator Fulbright rhetorically asked at the Symington hearings, "If both sides are not living up to the Geneva Agreements, what is the use of pretending it is of any value?"[76] If we had really wanted to put the Accords back together, we could have cut down on the flagrancy of our violations.

The Wish to Retain Discretion to Withdraw

It was also argued that making our role in Laos public would make it more difficult for us to walk away from that role if and when we decided that would be advisable.[77] This too seems like post-disclosure rationalization. Certainly the secrecy of the operation did not appear to incline us toward withdrawal, and in fact our eventual admission of our role appears to have played a part in moving everyone toward settlement.[78] Beyond these factual problems, however, it is simply inadmissible to permit the president unilaterally to wage war and then to cite as an excuse for not seeking authorization the consideration that he wished also to retain for himself unilateral discretion as to when to make peace.

The Fear of a Propaganda Disadvantage

The fourth explanation was that if we were to admit our violations of the Geneva Agreements, while the North Vietnamese had not admitted *their* violations, we would suffer a "propaganda disadvantage."[79] Actually, we probably wouldn't have, since everyone was aware that the North Vietnamese were also violating the accords. We had made much of that fact and undoubtedly would have continued to do so. Beyond that, a desire to shield our conduct from political scrutiny and criticism is the paradigm example of a defense that shouldn't count.

Concern Over Possible Soviet Reaction

The final explanation was to the effect that an official acknowledgment on our part "might require the Soviet Union to take more positive action in support of our adversaries in Laos than it had theretofore done."[80] The first answer to this is a recurrent one, that everyone but the American public—including the Soviet government—was already aware of what we were doing in Laos. The North Vietnamese made much of our violations of the Geneva Accords,[81] and "Soviet propaganda for several years had excoriated the United States for the bombing" without inducing the feared reaction.[82] The idea must thus have been that if *we* admitted what we were doing, the Soviets would feel obligated to react somehow.[83] Was the fear that they would actually intervene? That seems a little absurd: Our role in Vietnam was certainly admitted, and the Soviets made no move toward intervening there.[84] No, a State Department spokesman admitted, that was not the fear.[85] Perhaps, then, they would provide other sorts of military assistance to the Pathet Lao? Also not likely: There is every indication that Moscow was quite satisfied "watching us dissipate our assets in this Far East tragedy."[86]

By the time the State Department spokespersons had finished their dialogue with the Symington Subcommittee, it seemed that the feared "Soviet threat" was that they would withdraw their official recognition of the Souvanna Phouma government.[87] Even if that had been true it would seem to have come under the "big deal" heading, certainly not enough to justify a failure to comply with the Constitution. Anyway it too was implausible.

The Soviets knew perfectly well that we were bombing Laos and providing on-the-ground assistance to Vang Pao. And indeed, when we finally did confess our role publicly, none of these things actually happened: The Soviets did not intervene, they did not send significant military aid to the Pathet Lao, and they did not even withdraw their recognition of Souvanna's government. As a matter of fact our "going public" in 1970 seems to have been taken quite the other way. As one respected contemporary account put it: "One purpose of Nixon's statement may have been to dramatize U.S. firmness in Laos for the benefit of the Communist powers and particularly the Soviet Union, which U.S. officials still believed might eventually persuade North Vietnam to abandon some of its aims and cooperate with the Vientiane government."[88]

The final reason this fifth excuse cannot count, however, is the most basic of all: It could be adduced in every single case of covert presidential war. The War Clause cannot be such a charade that it can be ignored simply on the basis of a presidential fear that if he made his covert war public more enemies would be arrayed against us (or those who were already our enemies would be even more miffed). Some such allegation of this sort could always be made—indeed it could probably always be made in good faith. An exception that totally swallows the rule it is supposed to qualify is not admissible.

The Perennial Invocability of the Administration's Excuses

Indeed, if you think about it, all five of the administration's excuses share this characteristic.[89] (1) A president embarked on a secret war could always find some ally with whom to agree that he would keep the matter secret from Congress and the public. He could always aver that he was keeping his war secret so as both (2) to increase the chances that a prior peace could be restored and (3) to leave himself more flexibility to withdraw at will. (4) Every war could also be kept secret—indeed, here, the more horrendous the war the stronger the proffered "defense" would become—on the theory that exposing it would subject us to a "propaganda disadvantage." (5) And as we just noted, every war could be hidden in order to minimize the number of parties giving assistance to the enemy. Thus each of the excuses was incredible, and it's doubtful that any of them should have been allowed to count even if it hadn't been.

The Real Reasons

There appear to have been two actual reasons for the secrecy. The first was that bureaucracies generally like to operate without scrutiny whenever they can get away with it, and that the CIA in particular displays this preference with a vengeance. As the Symington Subcommittee's 1971 follow-up report on Laos put it: "CIA is not used to prosecuting a war in public and does not see what purpose would be served by doing so."[90] Indeed, in testimony before the Church Committee in 1975, Secretary Kissinger admitted that the CIA had been used in Laos "*because* it [was] less accountable."[91] The other actual reason for the secrecy about Laos within the United States was to still domestic criticism of what our government was up to there.[92] All the while the administration was working so hard to keep the facts about Laos from Congress and the American people, it was its policy to *publicize* our Laotian efforts to the South Vietnamese, so as to keep up their morale.[93] This obviously undercuts further the administration's various post facto rationalizations for the cover-up and speaks volumes concerning the cover-up's real purpose. That purpose, however, is what made it unconstitutional.

DEFENSE 4: IN FACT THE "SECRET WAR" IN LAOS WAS NO SECRET

The excuses for keeping our war in Laos secret having so swiftly collapsed, the more fashionable defense of its legality has become that it wasn't really a secret at all, that any knowledgeable American, and certainly Congress, was aware of what was going on all along.[94] (The argument presumably would continue that because Congress did not qualify its various appropriations so as to exclude Air Force and CIA operations in Laos, it should constitutionally be deemed to have authorized them.)

Was "Congress" on Notice of the American War in Laos?

Responding to allegations that the administration had hidden much of what was going on in Laos from the Senate Foreign Relations Committee, Secretary of State William Rogers told the Symington Subcommittee, "I had thought Congress was familiar with the developments in Laos . . . . I thought Congress understood it."[95] This attitude soon was affected by the executive branch generally: Professions of surprise on the part of the members of the subcommittee were dismissed by State Department insiders as feigned, a "political gimmick."[96] Just as predictably, Congress responded that it hadn't known. Senate Foreign Relations Chair Fulbright testified, for example, that he "had no idea we had a full-scale war going on" in Laos.[97] Admittedly Fulbright made a minor specialty of being misled,[98] but in this he spoke for many others, including Symington: Congress hadn't known.

Where does the truth lie on this issue? Even after months of studying the record I have to confess I don't really know. Given the executive's incentive to assert that Congress was on board and Congress's interest in professing ignorance, this has proved a maddening inquiry. Certain things are plainly the case, however. One is that the administration *tried* in many ways to keep Congress from getting the facts about Laos. And since we are here judging the constitutionality of the administration's behavior, what they were trying to do is very much to the legal point—unless, I suppose, they totally failed in their attempt, in which case we could count it harmless error. Plainly, however, they did not totally fail.

"None of the appropriate committees of Congress [was] notified about the full extent of U.S. involvement in Laos."[99]

> Congress was ignorant of the situation because no action regarding Laos had been requested openly by the executive and the war had been conducted almost entirely by executive order to bodies such as the CIA, USAID, USIS, and the armed forces, which are responsible only to the President. The United States has no treaties or written agreements with Laos which would have required congressional scrutiny or approval.[100]

Nor was Congress's investigating arm, the General Accounting Office, allowed to refer to the CIA's books for most of the war, let alone to go out in the field to see what was happening.[101] And as often happens, the classification of certain information helped keep Congress in the dark.[102] The Symington Subcommittee report observed:

> [B]y classifying the number of daily missions flown by United States aircraft over northern Laos since 1964—as distinguished from those missions flown over the Ho Chi Minh Trail and thus directly connected to the Vietnam war—the Executive Branch hid from the Congress as well as the people that additional major commitment, in men and dollars, undertaken to support the Royal Government of Laos.[103]

Neither, on those rare occasions when they did testify about Laos, were administration officials always candid.[104] For example, Deputy Assistant Secretary William H. Sullivan, who as Ambassador had essentially run the war in Laos from 1964 to 1969, testified as late as 1969—during *a secret session* of the Senate Foreign Relations Committee, no less—that the United States "[does] not have a military training and advisory organization in Laos" and went on to imply unmistakably that the only bombing in the north was being done by the Laotian Air Force.[105] Confronted with this testimony a year later at the Symington hearings by Senator Fulbright, Mr. Sullivan contended that he did not recall the details of what he had testified to earlier, but suggested that he would have answered truthfully had there been "any *direct* questions asked of me about U.S. air operations."[106]

Couldn't members of Congress go to Laos and see for themselves? Mr. Sullivan testified before the Symington Subcommittee that "every Congressman who has ever come to Laos anytime I was there was fully and completely informed on all our actions . . . ."[107] In fact, congressmen who visited that country were seriously misled by the officials who were there to "brief" them. The CIA went so far as to help Vang Pao maintain two headquarters: the real one at Long Cheng (or Long Tieng), which was "strictly military and strictly clandestine" and another, much smaller, six miles to the north in Sam Thong. "Militarily," *The New York Times* reported in October 1969, Sam Thong "is only a show window, a place for the general to receive visitors who are not supposed to know of the clandestine army and the American support for it."[108] Fred Branfman reports that he

> accompanied two congressmen during their visit to Laos in the summer of 1967. American officials made a consistent attempt to mislead them throughout their stay. Particular emphasis was placed on obscuring American military involvement in the Long Cheng–Sam Thong operation. The attitude of resident officials was illustrated during a visit to Sam Thong. As the congressmen proceeded down a long line of welcoming [Hmongs], who draped them with Hawaiian-style leis, the author joined a group of USAID officials, including the present Deputy Chief of USAID James Chandler and "Pop" Buell [who ran the AID mission at Sam Thong]. During the course of the conversation, Buell asked Chandler, "Do they know anything?" "Don't worry, Pop," Chandler replied, "Hurwitch [then deputy chief of mission] gave them a beautiful snow job, complete with maps. They were very impressed."[109]

Jerome J. Brown was an Air Force Captain assigned to Vientiane, whose covert assignment in 1967–68 was to pick our bombing targets in Laos. (He wore civilian clothes and carried papers identifying him as an AID employee.) In 1972 he told *New York Times* reporter Seymour Hersh, "I couldn't come out of my little cubicle, which was hidden at the back end of the air attache's office. If there was somebody there who wasn't supposed to be there, such as a Congressman, I had to stay back in the corner of my room."[110]

At the same time, however—whatever the members of Congress would have us believe—the cover-up wasn't complete. One can piece together a good deal of circumstantial evidence that certain members were briefed on certain aspects of our Laotian operations at certain times[111]—probably more often on the bombing of the Ho Chi Minh trail than on the CIA's activities or the bombing in the north—though naturally they sought to minimize their knowledge. The following mind-twisting 1971 interchange between Fulbright and Allen Ellender, the former Chair of the CIA subcommittee of the Senate Appropriations Committee pretty well sets the tone:

> MR. FULBRIGHT: It has been stated that the CIA has 36,000 [men in Laos]. It is [now] no secret. Would the Senator say that before the creation of the army in Laos they came before the committee and the committee knew of it and approved of it?

MR. ELLENDER: *Probably so.*

MR. FULBRIGHT: Did the Senator approve it?

MR. ELLENDER: I was not—*I did not know anything about it. . . .* I never asked, to begin with, whether or not there were any funds to carry on the war in this sum the CIA asked for. It never dawned on me to ask about it. I did see it published in the newspapers some time ago.[112]

William Colby, whose reputation for veracity is good for a spymaster (which is short of saying it's stellar[113]) has also consistently insisted that Ellender simply was not telling the truth in claiming ignorance.[114]

Senator Symington also appeared surprised:

That is what they said in the beginning in Laos when I was there . . . that they were intelligence people . . . . [T]he large majority of Congress was deceived by Laos . . . . We now get reports that Americans died in Laos and that we had been lied to, because we were told they died in Vietnam. We are getting pretty sick of being lied to . . . . I learned most of my information about Laos from the newspapers . . . .[115]

As to Symington too, however, the record strongly suggests that he knew a great deal more than he was here implying.[116] The most generous reading of such statements may therefore be that he felt most of Congress and the American people had been deceived: He seems to have skirted saying that he personally had been seriously misled, at least for very long.[117]

Plainly a number of senators and congressmen knew more than they let on in 1969 and thereafter.[118] Like Captain Renault in *Casablanca*, they were "shocked, *shocked* to find that gambling is going on here!" At the very least they had been told enough to induce them, had they been inclined, to investigate further. Admittedly this would have been an aggravating and politically unrewarding inquiry. As Senator Fulbright responded (too gently, in my view) to Mr. Sullivan's "explanation" that he had not been asked "direct questions" about U.S. Air Force bombing:

You see, we do not know enough to ask those direct questions, and this is what I meant about quibbling about whether the U.S. role in Laos is exclusively advisory. When you take a group of Senators who are primarily concerned with their own States, and only incidentally in this foreign affairs area, the responsibility for which we are given by the Senate, we do not know enough to ask you these questions unless you are willing to volunteer the information. There is no way for us to ask you questions about things we don't know you are doing.[119]

This is certainly an understandable reaction—though Fulbright's self-description as "only incidentally concerned" with foreign affairs is arresting—but it does not seem adequate. Congress was aware that it was getting a snow job, and when that happens the appropriate response is to keep shoveling until you hit something.

But Congress didn't get the whole story, because nobody—not the president, and not Congress itself—wanted it to. As the Symington Subcommittee concluded, "The Congress did not inquire into, nor was it kept informed of, United States military activities in and over Laos."[120] Thus its knowledge was spotty at best. Fulbright again: "I knew we were doing a little of this and a little of that in Laos, [but] had no idea it was a major operation of this kind."[121] And what awareness existed was much more likely to concern the bombing of the Ho Chi Minh trail than either of the campaigns in the north.

> The U.S. Congress was not informed about the extent of the bombing, and the appropriate committees of Congress did not press the executive on these matters. The few members of Congress who were selectively informed about the administration's Laotian bombing were led to believe that the bombing was minimal and that it was related "solely to operations around the Ho Chi Minh Trail and the war in Vietnam."[122]

Thus to a significant degree the administration succeeded in maintaining secrecy. Though this was partly due to willful ignorance, a unwillingness to ask what should have been the obvious next question, "[r]evelations about U.S. involvement shocked and surprised many members of Congress in 1969 and 1970."[123] Indeed, a 1970 memorandum from Dr. Kissinger to President Nixon essentially admitted that "the Senators" had not known "what is going on in Laos" prior to the Symington hearings.[124]

Is Notice to the Congressional Leadership, or to Congress More Generally, Constitutionally Sufficient?

If the constitutional test were whether the "congressional leadership" was aware of what was going on in Laos prior to 1969, this would be a tough case (as all such cases would be, given the cross-cutting incentives of the executive to claim the leadership knew, and the leadership to claim they didn't). But although people often talk as if it were, leadership awareness cannot be the test. At the very least the requirement must be that the entire Congress be aware of what is going on (as it plainly was not in this case). For one thing, it is by no means clear exactly who should count as the "leadership": The potential for a president's confiding in his yes-men and a few trustworthy hawks and calling it "notification of the leadership" is manifest. More fundamentally, there is no theory of which I am aware on which the acquiescence of the leadership (even assuming we could agree who they were) can fulfill a constitutional requirement of authorization by "Congress."[125]

I am certainly aware that telling something to the entire Congress might run a serious risk of leaks, and that there are occasions on which a leak could prove so damaging militarily that any reasonable person would wish to avoid it. However, we have been proceeding on the assumption that where premature disclosure would cause palpable military damage, the requirement of advance congressional authorization should be inapplicable (leaving only the requirement that the president come to Congress for approval as soon as his military move has become evident to the enemy). A fortiori, advance notice to "the leadership" or a relevant committee would be adequate in such a situation (a device that has been employed in post-Vietnam intelligence legislation[126]). Laos was not such a situation, however; no real reason existed to keep what we were doing there secret, except to still criticism on the home front.

I personally would go further and argue that where secrecy is not a military necessity, even notice to the entire Congress is insufficient to satisfy the constitutional requirement: *We the people* are part of the process too. This suggestion may sound as American as apple pie, but when I made it in an earlier article[127] it evoked some criticism. Drawing on sources as diverse as *Federalist* 63 and Bruce Ackerman's recent work,[128] the critics argue in essence that so long as our representatives are adequately informed of the facts bearing on their decisions, it is not the business of the Constitution what the people are or are not told. I've thought about it, and I confess I still don't get it.

That our representatives will on occasion quite properly interpose their consciences to deny the majority what it wants[129] is no reason to let them hide from us the facts that indicate that that is what they're doing: Democracy demands at a minimum that we be able to *evaluate* our representatives' intercessions. Granting, further, that there are periodic "constitutional moments," when the people participate more directly in our nation's fundamental decisions than we do at others, similarly seems to me to furnish no excuse for withholding crucial facts from us on others (or what our representatives deem to be others). Isn't it, for one thing, up to *us* to decide whether to "make the moment 'constitutional'"? It may not sound so much like a champagne ad, indeed I confess it's somewhat earthbound, but I see nothing here to justify dispensing with the theory that if Congress doesn't approve of a war it can pull the plug, and if the people don't approve we can pressure Congress to do so. (Please do not forget that I am talking about a situation where there exists no military justification for keeping the facts from us.)

But even if you're not with me in democratic theory, there are practical grounds on which it seems to me you have to be. An essential term of the tacit deal that has existed in recent decades, at least in the area of war and peace (and arguably more broadly[130])—that the president will take the responsibility as long as he can make the decisions, and Congress will live with a lack of power as long as its members don't have to be held accountable—must be that neither Congress's leaders nor its rank-and-file ever have to tell exactly what they knew at the time the decisions were actually being made. What they get in exchange for their agreement not to try to influence policy is the right to come along later and scold, "*Now* look at what you've done!" However, one consequence of the fact that they aren't really expected to find out what's going on (before media and public outrage force them to), and then aren't expected to come clean about how much they knew at the time, is to render any test geared to the knowledge of either Congress or its leadership unadministrable. Laos may seem like a textbook example, but given the various incentives at work here it's actually pretty typical.[131] We'll never be able to get a reliable direct measure of congressional acquiescence in what has become a controversial policy, which suggests our best measure of what they knew must approximate what most reasonably well-informed citizens knew. This provides another reason for concluding that the operative test in such situations has to be what (I at least believe) the theory of our government suggested it should have been all along, whether the American people were on notice of what was going on.

Were the American People on Notice of the American War in Laos?

As it did with Congress, the administration certainly *tried* to keep the American public in the dark about Laos.[132] The most elementary method employed was that of telling us things that just weren't true. "Seeing the Laotian conflict solely in the context of the Cold War, many American officials view[ed] lying not only as a tactical aid but also as a patriotic duty."[133] Thus, for example, "[f]rom May 1964 until President Nixon's March 1970 statement on Laos . . . American officials denied, publicly and privately, that the United States was bombing in Laos."[134] (If the evidence got dangerously incriminating, they would indicate that we were flying nothing more than "armed reconnaissance" flights over northern Laos.[135]) Sometimes the administration let others do its lying for it. As late as 1969, for example, Souvanna Phouma was regularly making dishonest public statements—that there were no foreign troops (specifically no Americans or Thais) fighting on his government's behalf, that American planes were not intentionally bombing northern Laos (though they might occasionally get confused about the location of the Vietnam/Laos border)—and our government did nothing to correct them.[136]

More often, though, administration claims may have been merely misleading. As one respected account put it:

> To say, as U.S. officials have said repeatedly, "There are no American ground combat forces in Laos," is true but misleading. As in every modern army, most

soldiers do not fight the enemy directly. But they draw the plans, operate the radios, fuel the aircraft, direct the bombers, repair the equipment, move the supplies, and give advice (which may be tantamount to orders) to the men who do fight. American planes, with American pilots, drop bombs on roads, bridges, trucks, villages, and Pathet Lao and North Vietnamese troops. U.S. planes and helicopters are shot at and shoot back. On the ground, American officers and civilians (many of whom were formerly in uniform in Vietnam) work with Laotian soldiers in their base camps. The Americans fight when attacked, and several dozen have admittedly been killed. For this work, they have received "hostile fire" pay since January 1966. In the ordinary meaning of the term, they are at war.[137]

This was written in 1972 and we now know that the administration's drumbeat claim that we didn't have ground troops in Laos was not simply misleading but (by even the narrowest definition of ground troop) at least recurrently false.[138] However, the quotation's overall drift must be right: I'm sure the truth was merely skirted rather than actually ravished whenever that choice seemed available.

The preferred option, though, was that of simply hiding the facts.[139] Newspaper reporters, authors, and television teams were generally not permitted to get anywhere near our operations in Laos—theoretically on grounds of "military security," although it seemed clear to most observers that the real reasons were political.[140]

> The infrequent visits of newsmen to sensitive areas have been rather carefully managed. Military personnel and foreign mercenaries are withdrawn; a briefing is given by Laotian generals in which the emphasis is on the North Vietnamese invasion of the given areas; American involvement is denied; North Vietnamese prisoners and Pathet Lao defectors are made available for interviews; and stocks of captured communist weapons are exhibited.[141]

Officers assigned to Laos "weren't allowed to associate at all with journalists under threat of court-martial,"[142] and three reporters with sufficient initiative to walk from the show headquarters at Sam Thong to the real one at Long Cheng were taken into custody and shipped back to Vientiane—in 1970, no less, after our activities had theoretically become more open.[143]

Finally, the stonewalling was monumental, and continued to be so to the bitter end. Even after the *Times* had run its series of articles, and the Symington Subcommittee had held its hearings, President Nixon took the position at news conferences that we had no combat troops in Laos, and that while it was true that we were bombing the Ho Chi Minh trail, "public opinion would not be served" by providing the nation with further details.[144] There was, in addition, a five-month delay in the release of the transcript of the Symington Subcommittee hearings, occasioned by the necessity to negotiate with the executive branch over what could be published.

What emerged was less than helpful. The fact that CIA Director Richard Helms had even been a witness was deleted from the transcript, as, incredibly, were *all mentions of the CIA!*[145] So also were anything resembling helpful information about the Air Force's bombing of northern Laos; references to the amount of tax money used to assist regular and irregular Laotian forces, to finance our bombing campaigns, and to maintain the air bases in Thailand from which our bombers operated; and details about the participation, including our financing, of third country nationals (mainly Thais) in the war in the north.[146] This clumsy attempt to hide the legislatively relevant facts from the American people came in 1970, after most of them had appeared in the establishment press, and thus speaks quite loudly to the administration's willingness to mislead us earlier. Yet supporters of presidential power assured us then, as they assure us now, that if we don't like the way a war is being fought, we need only pressure our representatives in Congress to do something about it: The people hold the ultimate trump.

As I noted above, the fact that the administration was trying so hard to keep us from learning the truth about Laos is entirely to the constitutional point—unless, perhaps, its efforts were so plainly unavailing as to render them in effect harmless error. That they were just that—that despite the administration's efforts to keep it quiet, the Laos story was well known to at least the alert segments of the American public—thus became the last line of constitutional defense of the war. This has not been articulated very often, but it certainly was with enormous self-confidence in a 1970 *Foreign Affairs* article by Robert Shaplen:

> The truth of the matter, which bears directly on the current situation and on the fuss and fury that have attended the secret Laos hearings held by the Symington subcommittee of the Senate Foreign Relations Committee is that nobody was fooled by anything, including that portion of the American public willing to read the newspaper and magazines with a modicum of care. Throughout Asia, let alone in the United States, the bombings of the Ho Chi Minh Trail were a matter of common knowledge, and there were repeated articles in the press about the so-called "secret war" in Laos backed by the CIA and the "hush-hush" airlines, Air America and Continental Airlines.[147]

Or as Henry Kissinger put it in his memoirs (having minimized our involvement in Laos, which made what followed closer to true): "Most of this was occasionally reported in the press . . . ."[148]

Confident claims that "every sophisticated person knew *x* all along" seldom encounter contradiction, not simply because no one wants to admit he isn't hip, but also because of the tricks our minds play about exactly when we actually learned something (as opposed to beginning to wonder whether it might not be true). Well, I'm so hip I call my girlfriend "Man," so I'll risk it. (The fact that I've done a good deal of research on what was in the media helps too.) Dr. Kissinger knew what was going on at the time, perhaps more than anyone else on earth. And to a degree Mr. Shaplen probably did as well: At least some of what the United States was up to was indeed common knowledge in southeast Asia, where he spent the relevant period.[149] But most of us in this country (yes, Mr. Shaplen, even those of us who can read) did not.[150]

"[T]he CIA managed to keep happenings in Laos their own private game. Its coverage by the world's press was sketchy in the extreme, the barest outline, and often misleading."[151] For evident reasons, Laos (unlike Vietnam) received essentially no television coverage. Neither was it really covered in the daily newspapers. ("In the war next door in Vietnam a fluctuating press corps of around five hundred men and women covered the story, while in Laos there were rarely more than half a dozen visiting journalists, and only one permanent American correspondent."[152]) What got out generally were therefore ill-formed assertions of long-term patterns of behavior, better suited to magazine-style summaries than to news reports per se.[153] Thus there was sporadic coverage in the mainstream American newsweeklies, though given the administration's campaign of obfuscation it was understandably underinformed. By the mid-1960s reports began to surface that we were bombing the Ho Chi Minh trail as an adjunct of our efforts in Vietnam, necessarily without anything resembling details concerning volume. Also creeping out were indications that we had supplied the Royal Laotian Air Force with old T-28 fighters and the Hmongs with various supplies (rice and ammunition being most often mentioned). Lacking during this period were descriptions of the CIA's role in the operations of the Secret Army and indications that we were bombing other than on the trail in support of our troops in Vietnam.[154]

Thus as late as 1968, in a story titled "Spillover into Laos," *Time* reported that the "U.S. regularly bombs the Trail to slow the flow. But unlike Hanoi, Washington has been unwilling to violate the ban on foreign troops in Laos . . . ."[155] As we moved into 1969, the reports began to hint that we were bombing the north as well, and that Americans were somehow "involved" in the guerrilla struggle there, though such reports necessarily remained brief and allegational.[156] In September and October of that year *The New York Times'* series appeared—so detailed it remains one of the best sources on the war—and the Symington hearings began.[157]

So far as the foreign press was concerned (particularly the foreign press to which some Americans are accustomed to looking for a "different" perspective[158]), *The Economist's* coverage of Laos was essentially identical to that of the American media.[159] *The Far Eastern Economic Review* was understandably a couple of years ahead[160]—it was even sensible enough to report that despite awareness in Asia, Laos was not getting coverage in the United States[161]—though even it could be seriously ill-informed.[162]

Admittedly a Vietnam junkie could have located such stories—*The Far Eastern Economic Review* is not a terribly obscure publication—and assuming she believed the right ones, thereby placed herself ahead of what American media were reporting on Laos (though still not in a truly knowledgeable position). I'm sure a number did. Indeed, to pursue this line further, as early as 1964 Soviet English-language periodicals were charging (albeit without supporting detail) that American warplanes were engaging in "barbarous bombing raids" on "areas controlled by patriotic forces" in Laos.[163] A number of Americans, albeit a smaller one, must have believed them too. Or maybe we all should simply have noted the occasional references and allegations in American newsmagazines and drawn the inference that the truth must be (as it was) much worse. It's a sad commentary, but I'm sure that today (precisely *because* of episodes like Laos) a good many more of us would do just that—draw the conclusion that Kissinger and Shaplen have suggested we should have drawn then, that our government was lying to us. However, the limited coverage of what was happening in Laos available in this country in the mid-1960s was plainly inadequate to support the inference that is needed if the war's legality is to be sustained, that the American public actually knew and acquiesced in what was going on.

The information available concerning Laos was inadequate for several reasons. (1) What coverage there was was not in the daily media, which is how most of us get our news. Thus neither Congress nor the rest of us could rely on the usual presumption that if it's important *The New York Times* and *The Washington Post* will tell us about it. (2) It was, in addition, quite sporadic, most often foreign, and greatly overwhelmed by Vietnam and then Cambodia.[164] (3) The events in question took place halfway around the world. (4) The reports were, of necessity, most often either explicitly or by clear implication based on rumor or allegation, rather than the direct observation of the person writing the story. (5) The allegations were most often explicitly or by clear implication those of (gasp) Communists. (6) Perhaps most important, the allegations were consistently denied, publicly and privately, by official spokespersons for the United States government. Most of us want very much, and thus tend, to believe our government, especially when it is reassuring us that it hasn't been behaving unlawfully.[165] To the extent that last seems naive to you—and it doesn't to me, even today— remember that this was before Watergate, when we were all more innocent, and it took a genuine radical to believe allegations that our government was lying to us.[166]

Mr. Shaplen thus seems to have been quite wrong in asserting that "nobody was fooled" about Laos. Many of us were—which undoubtedly is one reason our government's activities in that country did not elicit anywhere near the kind of domestic opposition its more public activities in Vietnam and Cambodia did.[167] Dr. Kissinger's memoirs may suggest that it was all "in the press," but this is the same Dr. Kissinger who had written President Nixon a memorandum in 1970 acknowledging that the Senate hadn't really gotten the facts about Laos until the Symington hearings; the same memo implied that the public did not *yet* know "what we are really doing" there.[168]

Earlier I tentatively stipulated the possibility of a harmless error defense here, for that is what it seems is being proffered. Actually I don't buy the stipulation: I do not see how our government can lie to us and then successfully claim as a defense that we were actually on notice as to the truth, because we should have known the government was lying. In any event, the facts defeat the defense. It is, at root, an argument that despite the administration's lies, we the American people were on sufficient notice of the nature of our government's activities in Laos that by not pressuring our representatives to stop them, we tacitly acquiesced. Such an argument is nonsense. The administration sought to hide the war in Laos from both the Congress and the American people, and to a substantial degree it succeeded. Because there was no convincing military justification for doing so, even assuming such a justification should count, that war was unconstitutional.

What is the Remedy for a Secret War?

> The illegal we do immediately, the unconstitutional takes
> a little longer.
>
> —Henry Kissinger[169]

Congress has at least the theoretical power to pull the plug on a war of which it does not approve. In order to figure out whether you approve, however, you need to know what's going on, something the executive was busily engaged in withholding from Congress and the rest of us as well. Well, shouldn't Congress have been more tenacious about *getting* the facts about Laos: Shouldn't it have run those rumors down? Of course in an ideal world the answer to that question would be yes, but even a commentator of my considerable self-righteousness has trouble casting the first stone here, as we know perfectly well that further congressional inquiries would only have received a royal runaround. Well then, again theoretically, Congress could threaten to pull some financial plugs—though knowing which plugs were relevant was itself at the heart of the dilemma—unless it got a complete and convincing account of what was going on in Laos. Here, however, a member of Congress runs into a dilemma. What is she to do when she reads in some semiobscure journal an allegation that the United States is bombing northern Laos and inquires of what she takes to be the relevant executive official, who tells her the report is not true or stonewalls her in a way that suggests that she is not quite getting the whole story?[170] Since political careers are broken by charges that one is insufficiently solicitous of national security, we can be pretty sure that Congress would not have the hardihood—and frankly it's hard to get huffy here—to start pulling plugs under such circumstances.[171]

If substance would only cooperate more completely with esthetics, I would attempt to parlay this condition of substantial legislative impotence into a further argument for my central contention that the *judiciary* should generally abandon its hands-off attitude in this area: Okay, agreed, Congress lacks the tools as well as the will to dig out the facts on wars the executive is intent on hiding, which is why, the argument would run, it is important that courts stand ready to entertain lawsuits to do so. Even passing the courts' likely reluctance to do any such thing, however, this plainly cannot be the answer either. For the very secrecy of the war will guarantee a shortage of plaintiffs who are able and willing to bring a lawsuit. That the lawsuits challenging the war in Indochina were about Vietnam, the public 1970 ground incursion into Cambodia, and the 1973 bombing of that country—and not about Laos and the secret bombing of Cambodia—is hardly a coincidence: Those were the campaigns we knew about, most certainly the only campaigns we knew enough about to assemble a complaint that would have a prayer of making it past a motion to dismiss. And even assuming such a case could somehow be made before a court, developing the actual facts about a war the executive branch is intent on keeping secret would prove frustrating at best. What media exposés there are will be only suggestive and often inaccurate, and those in possession of the facts will almost certainly—at least given present attitudes—give the plaintiff and even a sympathetic judge a runaround that would make what they did to Congress seem like child's play.

Obviously the sort of statutory changes recommended in chapter 3 and the appendix can make a contribution of sorts, by reaffirming the original constitutional principle that decisions about whether we fight wars are to be made by the legislative process. Their direct contribution respecting wars the executive is intent on hiding from Congress and the American people is likely to be slight, however—it's essentially impossible to write a statute that cannot be effectively defied by a president prepared to lie to cover his tracks—unless they are accompanied by a process of socialization, a growing acceptance on all sides of the constitutional norm that wars must be authorized by Congress.

Here the participation of the courts is indispensable. Not only must commentators (and politicians for that matter) refrain from irresponsible generalizations suggesting that it is within the constitutional prerogative of the executive unilaterally and secretly to fight wars lasting the better part of a decade, but the courts—the Supreme Court of the United States in particular—must hold in no uncertain terms that the decision whether to go to war is constitutionally vested in the legislative process. Statutes or no statutes, cases or no cases, the central problem here is the big lie that was born in 1950 and has been nurtured by the executive branch fairly consistently ever since, that decisions whether to go to war, whom to go to war against, and how much to tell the rest of us about what's going on, all rest with the president. It is critical that the moment be seized to lay that lie to rest for good, and on that score the courts have been failing us as fully as the Congress.

Obviously we're not yet to the point where the courts can generally be counted on to reaffirm the arrangement of the Constitution on this subject, however, and we certainly weren't in the 1960s either: Does that mean there was nothing to be done about the executive's unconstitutional war in Laos? I noted above that prior to 1969 there were not sufficient facts about that war in even the realm of respectable rumor to embolden Congress to get tough. But what about *after* the Symington hearings? At that point Congress had learned that for almost a decade the executive branch had fought an unauthorized war and systematically misled Congress and the American people about its progress and even its very existence. Why shouldn't President Nixon have been impeached at that point? There is little legal doubt that such a serious and willful violation of the separation of powers should count as a "high crime or misdemeanor" for purposes of the Constitution's impeachment provision.[172]

But this too is fantasy: There was never any chance of Congress's impeaching President Nixon, or anybody else, over the war in Laos. (Although one of the articles of impeachment on which the House Judiciary Committee ended up voting concerned the secret bombing of Cambodia, none mentioned Laos.) There appear to have been three reasons for this. First, although the executive branch worked hard, and to a large degree successfully, to keep Congress from getting the whole story, Laos was considerably short of an airtight secret. Various members of Congress knew various things about various aspects of it—surely enough to have triggered a further investigation, if they'd been doing their job.

Second, when most members of Congress finally did learn what was going on in Laos, their concern turned almost entirely toward the possibility that Laos would become "another Vietnam"—specifically that the administration was about to send regular American troops there. Thus, "in line with the expressed intention of the President of the United States,"

Congress barred only the "introduction of American ground combat troops into Laos or Thailand."[173] Neither CIA assistance to Vang Pao's Secret Army nor continued bombing of either the Ho Chi Minh trail or northern Laos was prohibited.[174] As the author of the enacted provision, Senator Frank Church, indicated: "We are not undertaking to make any changes in the status quo. The limiting language is precise. And it does not undertake to repeal the past or roll back the present. It looks to the future.[175] Technically, the fact that Congress voted to continue the war in Laos once it was disclosed does not mean that the executive branch had committed no offense in previously hiding its existence. At the same time, though, it powerfully helps to explain why impeachment on this ground was never seriously considered. It takes righteous indignation to argue for impeaching a president. "You committed a very great wrong in not telling us what you were doing, but you have our permission to continue doing it" is an entirely coherent declaration, but not one that readily lends itself to indignant delivery.[176]

Finally, this war (and its cover-up) were in very substantial measure the work not only of President Nixon but also of Presidents Kennedy and Johnson before him.[177] Given a sufficiently horrendous offense, Congress should impeach the person in office, even if his predecessors were also culpable. However, in light of the facts that a substantial number of those in Congress had an inkling (or more) of what was happening in Laos all along, and Congress didn't do anything to end or even scale down the war once it found out about it, the offense here did not, at least not by Congress's lights, fall into that category.

If that is the end of the analysis, however, it is difficult to see—at least until we experience a general rededication to the principles of the Constitution—what will deter presidents from acting much the same way in the future, embarking on "secret wars" free from congressional and public scrutiny and then, if and when the press finally forces Congress to take notice, facing no sanction more severe than the termination or limitation of the war (which we have seen is also unlikely). There are two further things Congress can do, though. First, at the risk of sounding like a wimp, I would suggest that one thing Congress should do in such a situation is pass a resolution of censure. In fact the House of Representatives, having granted President Polk the funds necessary to pursue the Mexican War to a decisive victory, proceeded to vote a resolution—Representatives John Quincy Adams and Abraham Lincoln both concurring—to the effect that Polk had got us into it unconstitutionally.[178] It isn't impeachment, but it's certainly not something any president would welcome either: Members of Congress faced with censure resolutions generally fight like Turkish prisoners of war to avoid them. (The 1973 Senate vote, or at least the "debate," on the confirmation of Dr. Kissinger as Secretary of State would also seem to have been an appropriate place to register disapproval of the secret war in Laos.[179])

The other thing Congress can do is make damn sure that on the rare occasion when the facts converge in such a way as to make impeachment a politically viable option—where the secret of the war is actually kept from Congress, and only one president is involved—it *does* impeach him for fighting an unjustifiably secret and unauthorized war. Deterrence can work even at high levels. Of course the facts will seldom add up that way. If you think they won't ever, though, you should read on.

CHAPTER 5

The (Enforceable) Unconstitutionality
of the Secret Bombing of Cambodia,
1969–1970

> The American people cannot and should not be asked to support
> a policy which involves the overriding issues of war and peace
> unless they know the truth about that policy.
>
> —Richard Nixon, 1969[1]

ON March 18, 1969—some thirteen months before our public ground incursion into Cambodia—United States Air Force planes began bombing Communist sanctuaries in that country. Those responsible for this bombing campaign kept it a very tightly held secret. "A dual reporting system was set up to by-pass the command and control procedures of the Strategic Air Command":[2] All records of the actual Cambodian targets were incinerated, and South Vietnamese targets were recorded and reported in their place. The bombing was thus not simply concealed; the records (classified records at that) were actually falsified.[3] The State Department, Secretary of the Air Force, and the Air Force Chief of Staff were not informed of the campaign—that clause may bear rereading—nor, obviously, were the relevant congressional committees.[4] (Dr. Kissinger went so far as to suggest "that the B-52 bomber crews not be told that their targets were in Cambodia," but was convinced that was impractical.[5]) Although a small handful of co-operative members of Congress—I make it eight[6]—apparently were told, those the administration subsequently identified understandably tended to belittle the extent of their notification,[7] and in any event they did not pass the word along to their colleagues or to the American people.

From March 18, 1969 to May 1, 1970, when the United States publicly initiated ground combat operations in Cambodia, there were 3,875 secret American sorties into Cambodia, dropping 108,823 tons of bombs.[8] Throughout the course of our ground incursion the bombing of Cambodia was quite open, and as the troops were withdrawn at the end of June 1970, President Nixon announced his intention to continue bombing that country. However, the fact that we had been bombing Cambodia from March 1969 through April 1970 remained secret until 1973.[9]

Under other circumstances it might be tempting to begin our analysis of the secret bombing of Cambodia where we ended our analysis of the public land incursion into that country—with the question (which could be answered comfortably in the affirmative) whether the bombing constituted a rational means of supporting our troops in South Vietnam or could otherwise be fit within the authorization of the Tonkin Gulf Resolution. Having devoted so much time to the war in Laos, however, we can readily see that this would be an error. The 1969–70 Cambodian bombing campaign stands on an entirely different constitutional footing from the 1970 land incursion, for the reason that it was kept secret (very effectively, in this case) from Congress and the American public.

When the story of the secret bombing finally did become public, President Nixon explained that those who had not been advised of it (a group that included all of Congress except perhaps eight members, to say nothing of the rest of us) had neither "any right to know or need to know."[10] A better understanding of the Constitution was displayed by Hal Knight, the man whose job it had been in Vietnam to falsify the Cambodian bombing records and who ultimately blew the whistle on the operation: "I am not opposed to the war but I believe that full disclosure is necessary for the people of this country. It is my firm conviction that the American people, through their elected representatives, have the right to know how the war has been conducted."[11]

THE SIHANOUK SCENARIOS

Mr. Knight had it right, but naturally the administration had to throw some sand in our eyes. The basic theme—whose implications were generally left indeterminate—was that although Prince Sihanouk was now saying things very much to the contrary, he had actually welcomed the American bombing of his country. One's natural first reaction, again, is to ask, "So what?" Sihanouk's consent might conceivably have some relevance as a matter of international law, but what could it have to do with the demands of the United States Constitution?

Needless to say, changes were rung on the Sihanouk explanation that purported to make it matter. When the bombing was revealed in 1973, President Nixon stated in a speech to the Veterans of Foreign Wars: "Had we announced the air strikes, the Cambodian Government would have been compelled to protest, the bombing would have had to stop, and American soldiers would have paid the price for the disclosure and this announcement with their lives."[12] Two weeks later Dr. Kissinger said much the same thing during his confirmation hearings for the position of Secretary of State:

[Sihanouk was] in a difficult position. We [had] respect for him. We [did] not want to make his position more difficult. It is clear that it was in his power to stop it if he had protested, and he did not do so. But I can also understand why in his present position, where he is dependent more on his former opponents, he will take a different tack.[13]

Once again it is not clear that such an excuse—"We couldn't tell Congress we were waging this war because if we had, x would have had to protest, at which point we would have stopped"—should be allowed to count. Of course it begs the question whether the war in question is desirable, which is precisely what Congress is supposed to decide. But then so does *any* excuse rooted in "military necessity," and we have assumed at least for the sake of argument that some such excuses for hiding military operations from Congress should be admissible. In addition, it is an excuse that seems always capable of articulation and never subject to verification. We've seen that before though, too. Once again, therefore, let us assume, very much arguendo, that it can be a valid excuse: In this case too it's incredible.

Certain critics notwithstanding, the part of the scenario that holds that Sihanouk at least acquiesced in the bombing appears to be correct[14] (which helps account for how the secret could be kept[15]). However, the risk that he would have protested if it had been revealed to Congress seems less clear.[16] More fundamentally, it seems most unlikely that if he had protested the administration would actually have stopped bombing.[17] More likely, it would have given earlier impetus to the coup that deposed him in March 1970.[18] Again I should stress that my denial is only that the administration would have stopped the bombing of its own accord had Sihanouk protested. It *is* possible (and note that both Nixon's and Kissinger's remarks can be read to say only this) that if Sihanouk had protested, *Congress* would have forced the president to stop bombing Cambodia—or more realistically, that the administration feared that under such circumstances Congress might have become peevish.[19] We covered that train of events above, however: A fear that Congress might overturn (or complain about) executive policy is not a constitutional excuse for not telling it what's going on.

Thus this version of the scenario turned out to have a short half-life. Neither Nixon nor Kissinger mentions it in his memoirs, though the secret bombing of Cambodia is rationalized in each. For Nixon, protest from Cambodia now seems amalgamated with protest from within the United States—as something that would get in the way of his policy and thus something he felt justified in avoiding by secrecy.[20] Kissinger now reports that "a Cambodian or North Vietnamese reaction" was "firmly anticipated":[21]

We would have been willing to acknowledge the bombing and defend it if there had been a diplomatic protest. There was no protest; Cambodia did not object, nor did the North Vietnamese, nor the Soviets or the Chinese. Proceeding secretly became, therefore, a means of maintaining pressure on the enemy without complicating Cambodia's delicate condition, without increasing international tensions in general, and without precipitating the abandonment of all limits.[22]

A determination to "acknowledge and defend" the bombing upon receipt of an anticipated protest does not signal a disposition to stop it, so Kissinger's suggestion is now that a public announcement of the bombing would have constituted "a gratuitous blow to the Cambodian government" that would "complicate its delicate position."[23] The idea now thus seems to be that by announcing we were bombing Cambodia we would have undercut Sihanouk's claim of neutrality, thereby weakening his hold on his office.[24]

This version is, if anything, more unbelievable. The notion that such a train of events would have forced Sihanouk from office seems highly improbable: The effective political opposition to Sihanouk within Cambodia was from the right, or pro-American, side. More fundamentally, there is not the slightest indication, indeed there is every counterindication, that during this period our government would have been the least bit chagrined by the thought of Sihanouk's leaving office. There have been persistent published allegations of various CIA plots to assassinate Sihanouk over the years and of its complicity in the coup that succeeded in March 1970.[25] Whether or not these charges can ever be proved, the evidence that we welcomed the coup, and helped it along at least around the edges, seems irrefutable.[26]

That is more than enough to render incredible both Sihanouk scenarios—that the bombing of Cambodia had to be concealed from Congress and the American people because making it public would have (a) induced Sihanouk to protest, at which point the administration would have voluntarily stopped bombing, or (b) weakened his domestic position, which also would have undercut perceived American security interests. But two further nails can be put in the coffin. The first is that neither version, even if true, could reasonably justify *falsifying* classified records before submission to the relevant congressional committees, as opposed to simply withholding a public announcement[27]—a conclusion Secretary Kissinger may silently concede by accompanying his defenses of the cover-up with a (contested) denial that he and the President knew the extent of it.[28] If the extent of the cover-up does not fit the proffered defenses, however, it fits the goal of avoiding congressional interference like a glove.

Second, and if this doesn't put the old tin lid on it I can't imagine what would, even after Sihanouk was ousted from office and replaced by the palindromic and proudly pro-American Lon Nol—and thus all basis for either version of the "Sihanouk" justification had been removed—the administration continued to keep the bombing campaign secret from Congress and the American people. This began with President Nixon's lie, after sending troops into Cambodia in April 1970, to the effect that the United States had "scrupulously respected" Cambodia's neutrality theretofore and had not previously "moved against" the sanctuaries.[29] It continued when, in 1971 and again in 1973, the Pentagon not only submitted to the Senate Armed Services Committee falsified documents that did not list any B-52 raids on Cambodia at all during the thirteen months when they actually were taking place almost nightly,[30] but flatly assured the Committee there had been "no B-52 bombing in Cambodia of any kind during the entire year of 1969."[31] The truth did not come out until Mr. Knight blew the whistle in mid-1973—if you don't recall being shocked by his revelations it is probably because they were buried by the Watergate hearings, which were going on at the time—and even then the Defense Department continued, for a time, to lie to Congress.[32] The lies soon became untenable, however, and the explanation was devised that the cover-up was designed to keep Sihanouk, in the alternative, (a) from protesting, or (b) in office. At that point, however, the lies had gone on for three years past the point when either version could have claimed remotely colorable validity.

By now the actual reason for the cover-up is obvious. When Major Knight asked his commanding officer why he was being told to falsify the records, he was told that "the purpose is to hide these raids." "Who from?" Knight asked, and the answer was given, "Well, I guess the Foreign Relations Committee."[33] Chair of the Joint Chiefs Earle Wheeler testified that President Nixon had ordered him, no fewer than six times, not to disclose the Cambodian bombing "to any member of Congress."[34]

The admiring biography of Dr. Kissinger by Marvin and Bernard Kalb (written with his cooperation) reported:

> Kissinger had no trouble justifying the deception. He felt that if it became known that the United States was widening the war geographically, extending the bombing into Cambodia, this would prompt a wave of angry denunciations from an increasingly disillusioned Congress and anti-war critics across the country. This kind of nationwide uproar would only complicate the Administration's plans for peace in Vietnam.[35]

And in his memoirs President Nixon admitted that one reason for the secrecy—the other, as noted, was to discourage *international* protest—"was the problem of domestic anti-war protest. My administration was only two months old, and I wanted to provoke as little public outcry as possible at the outset."[36]

WHAT IS THE REMEDY FOR A SECRET WAR IN WHICH CONGRESS ISN'T COMPLICIT?

> Now who among the Soviets voted that they should invade Afghanistan? Maybe one, maybe five men in the Kremlin. Who has the ability to change that and bring them home? Maybe one, maybe five men in the Kremlin. Nobody else. And that is, I think, the height of immorality.
> —Defense Secretary Caspar W. Weinberger, 1984[37]

The secret bombing of Cambodia almost made it into the final version of the Articles of Impeachment. Congressman John Conyers introduced an article charging that President Nixon had violated his constitutional oath of office when:

[O]n and subsequent to March 17, 1969, [he] authorized, ordered, and ratified the concealment from the Congress of the facts and the submission to the Congress of false and misleading statements concerning the existence, scope and nature of American bombing operations in Cambodia in derogation of the power of the Congress to declare war, to make appropriations, and to raise and support armies . . . .[38]

Twelve members of the House Judiciary Committee supported the article when it came to a vote, while twenty-six opposed it.[39]

As I noted earlier, a serious and willful violation of the separation of powers constitutes an impeachable "high crime or misdemeanor." Moreover, to the extent anyone remains in doubt about either version of the Sihanouk explanation,[40] an impeachment inquiry would have been well designed to unravel alleged executive motives and determine which among them constituted only post facto rationalization. Unlike the war in Laos, the secret bombing of Cambodia was an offense consummated by one and only one president. Also unlike Laos, it was a well-kept secret[41]—involving measures as extreme as hoodwinking the Air Force Secretary and Chief of Staff and providing falsified secret documents to the relevant congressional committees for up to four years after the events. The fact that Congress will not be in a moral position to impeach when it has in effect been part of the conspiracy makes it all the more important that it do so in the rare situation where it wasn't.[42]

It is true that other presidents have masked changes in military strategy in order to avoid criticism from Congress and the public. Lyndon Johnson certainly did some things along these lines at earlier stages of the war in Indochina, McKinley led Congress to believe that our actions in the Philippines during the Spanish-American War were purely defensive, and other examples could be cited. Indeed, whenever the president acts in excess of congressionally delegated power, he is technically violating the separation of powers and thus the Constitution. It is, however, the job of Congress in an impeachment proceeding to make just such distinctions of degree. The offense here, even viewed in historical context, was flagrant—the brutal violation of a neutral country (with, we know in retrospect, results of almost unimaginable, and continuing, horror) covered up by a meticulous falsification of records that was reiterated for years beyond the expiration of the only remotely colorable (though ultimately incredible) "innocent" justification for the deception.

I'd have impeached him for it. Surely it would have been a more worthy ground than the combination of a third-rate burglary and a style the stylish couldn't stomach.[43] As Congressman William Hungate put it: "It's kind of hard to live with yourself when you impeach a guy for tapping telephones and not for making war without authorization."[44]

CHAPTER 6

"Covert" War Today

> [A]nother important requirement is an aggressive covert psycho-
> logical, political and paramilitary organization more effective,
> more unique, and if necessary, more ruthless than that employed
> by the enemy . . . . There are no rules in such a game. Hitherto
> acceptable norms of human conduct do not apply. If the U.S. is
> to survive, longstanding American concepts of "fair play" must
> be reconsidered.
> —1954 "Doolittle Report" on Covert Operations[1]

> The greatest strength of the totalitarian state is that it will force
> those who fear it to imitate it.
> —Adolf Hitler[2]

AT THE TIME of the war in Indochina there weren't really any statutes bearing on covert war. Since then (and partly as a result) Congress has enacted
a series of relevant, if limited, "reform" statutes. Whereas "conventional"
wars fought by uniformed armed forces personnel are covered by the War
Powers Resolution and thus theoretically subject to a requirement of advance congressional approval (well, approval within ninety days) "covert"
wars are not. However, covert wars are now statutorily required to be (a)
based on a presidential finding that they are important to the national security, and (b) at least ordinarily reported to the Senate and House Intelligence Committees.[3] The statutes are explicit that these committees have no
power to veto such operations, but they are at least given the opportunity to
try to talk the president out of his more harebrained schemes (and, the idea
must be though it is seldom put this way, if they saw an overwhelming
disaster coming they could go at least semipublic and attempt to generate
from their congressional colleagues a statute of disapproval supported by a
sufficiently overwhelming majority to survive its likely veto). This new
statutory scheme leads all too easily to an erroneous corollary affecting the
contemporary legality of campaigns like those we covered in the two preceding chapters: "With respect to Laos, the currently accepted procedure
authorizing covert wars (which does not involve congressional authorization) seems to contradict Ely's thesis."[4]

The first problem with this corollary—it has another, more basic, which
we will identify presently—is that the most central and destructive aspects

of our war in Laos, the massive bombing campaigns, were conducted by U.S. Air Force (and some U.S. Navy) planes, and thus *would* be fully subject to the War Powers Resolution's requirement of congressional authorization.[5] It's true, however, that the Resolution applies only to actions of "United States Armed Forces," language pretty plainly meant to be read narrowly, as Senator Eagleton's floor amendment to apply it to "any person employed by, or under contract to, or under the direction of any department or agency of the United States Government who is either (a) actively engaged in hostilities in any foreign country; or (b) advising any regular or irregular military forces engaged in hostilities in any foreign country"[6] was defeated fifty-three to thirty-four.[7] Thus war conducted by U.S. agents other than official members of our armed forces was left for regulation by subsequent statutes.[8]

HAVE COVERT WARS BEEN CONGRESSIONALLY AUTHORIZED EN MASSE?

At first blush it would seem—given an appropriately broad reading of the constitutional clause assigning decisions to "declare War, grant Letters of Marque and Reprisal, and make Rules concerning Captures on Land and War" to Congress—that such military actions (even limited ones) require congressional approval. Some commentators argue that covert wars have been granted blanket congressional authorization, while others argue just as confidently that they have not. As usual, given Congress's aversion to clarity in this area, the question yields no easy answer.

The latter commentators seem correct in denying that such authorization can responsibly be found in the National Security Act of 1947, which put in place our contemporary national security apparatus. The most often cited source of such power to be found in that act[9] is the catchall (at any rate catchmuch) section 102(d)(5), which empowered the (newly created) CIA "to perform such other functions and duties related to intelligence affecting the national security as the [also newly created] National Security Council may from time to time direct."[10] And indeed it is difficult to deny that any warlike act (up to, for example, the nuclear destruction of the Soviet Union) could be said to be "related to intelligence" (because, after all, our ability to do it would be in part the result of intelligence, and for that matter doing it would be powerfully preservative of our intelligence apparatus).

From the beginning, however, this has been taken for what it is, an irresponsibly pickwickian reading that far outruns the manifest purpose of the legislation. "[C]overt operations had been in no one's mind when the National Security Act was passed,"[11] or at least if they were in some people's minds (as in retrospect it seems pretty clear they were) the thoughts weren't communicated to Congress.[12] Thus a 1947 memorandum from Lawrence

Houston, the CIA's first general counsel, to Roscoe Hillenkoetter, its first director, concluded:

> Taken out of context and without knowledge of its history, these Sections [102(d)(4) and (5)] could bear almost unlimited interpretation, provided that the services performed could be shown to be of benefit to an intelligence agency or related to national intelligence . . . . Even certain forms of S.O. [special operations] work could be held to benefit intelligence by establishment of W/T [wireless telegraph] teams in accessible areas, and by opening penetration points in confusion following sabotage or riot. In our opinion, however, either activity would be an unwarranted extension of the functions authorized in Sections 102(d)(4) and (5). This is based on our understanding of the intent of Congress at the time these provisions were enacted.[13]

Ironically, a substantially stronger argument can be made that the missing statutory authority has been supplied by several laws Congress passed *post*-Indochina—during (and after) the "oversight revolution" of the 1970s—with the avowed purpose of curbing CIA abuses. The Hughes-Ryan Amendment to the Foreign Assistance Act of 1974 attempted to inject Congress into the process by prohibiting the expenditure of funds

> by or on behalf of the Central Intelligence Agency for operations in foreign countries, other than activities intended solely for obtaining necessary intelligence, unless and until the President finds that each such operation is important to the national security of the United States and reports, in a timely fashion, a description and scope of such operation to the appropriate committees of the Congress . . . .[14]

(In the Intelligence Oversight Act of 1980 and the Intelligence Act of 1991 Congress preserved this general approach, though it sensibly reduced the number of committees to be reported to—which at one point had reached eight—to the two intelligence committees.[15]) The 1976 Report of the Senate Select Committee to Study Governmental Operations with Respect to Intelligence Activities, more commonly referred to (after its chair) as the Church Committee, recommended several statutory changes designed to make congressional oversight more effective, recommendations that generally were not adopted. In doing so, however, the Church Committee expressed the view that Hughes-Ryan had supplied the statutory recognition that had previously been lacking:

> The significance of the events up to 1974 is that until that date Congress could escape a full share of responsibility for the CIA's covert actions. Enactment of the Hughes-Ryan Amendment, however, does represent formal acknowledgement by Congress that the CIA engages in operations in foreign countries for purposes other than obtaining intelligence.[16]

And so on its face it would seem it had: What would be the point in setting up a reporting system for something that isn't legal?[17] The inference would seem to have been reinforced since the issuance of the Church Committee's report, as the reporting requirements were reiterated in the 1980 and 1991 legislation.

However, this line of reasoning runs us smack into an objection that surfaced in the discussion of the Tonkin Gulf Resolution (which objection turned out to be irrelevant there but seems dispositive here). Although the Declaration of War Clause is not a formalistic straightjacket—it does not, for example, require that congressional combat authorizations actually be labeled "declarations of war"—it *does* require such authorizations to proceed at retail rather than wholesale: Not only must Congress make the decision whether we go to war, it must decide whom we go to war against.[18] The standard inference from Hughes-Ryan and its progeny—that Congress meant therein to authorize the president to fight whatever covert wars he thinks advisable—flatly violates this core command. It is thus time to abandon this "Congress authorized it" rationalization of executive authority to wage covert war, and refocus our attention on an alternative that surfaced earlier, that on a proper reading of the Constitution, covert wars or acts of war (or at any rate some of them, for some limited period of time) do not *require* congressional authorization.

MUST COVERT WARS BE CONGRESSIONALLY AUTHORIZED?

In chapter 4 I made a stab at giving contemporary meaning to the framers' reservation of presidential authority, without advance congressional authorization, to "repel sudden attacks." It seems quite clear that the perceived central animating feature of that situation was that the president would be *unable* to come to Congress before acting, that he would thus have to respond militarily and seek authorization simultaneously. More controversially, I went on to suggest—while admitting that one could reasonably go the other way—that the president might permissibly be deemed "unable to secure advance authorization" for reasons other than a lack of time, specifically for reasons of military effectiveness.[19] This turned out not to matter to the cases examined in the previous chapters, as the rationalizations for keeping our war in Laos and bombing of Cambodia secret turned out to be unconvincing covers for the real reason for the secrecy, a desire to preclude popular objection and congressional interference. At this point, however, the skeleton in the closet has come home to roost: The general propriety of congressionally unauthorized covert acts of war cannot be determined without deciding whether "military effectiveness would be seriously undermined" should, like "there just isn't time," count as a constitutionally acceptable excuse for not securing advance congressional authorization.

Plainly the framers did not have this issue specifically in mind one way or the other, but that's no way to construe the Constitution in any event: Instead we should attempt to map the animating purposes of the provisions they adopted onto contemporary conditions. I also am personally of the opinion that covert wars do our nation and the world significantly more harm than good. (Essentially undebated by people who do not work for the president, sometimes even by the president himself, they stand a greater-than-average chance of being ill-advised[20]—and history suggests that more often than not they are.[21] They are not the kind of wars that play to America's strengths,[22] and in addition breed a general attitude of disrespect for law that plays itself out not only on the battlefield but domestically as well.[23] Given America's position in the world, particularly post–Cold War, it is—in addition to its other detriments—simply a non sequitur that because "the other side" plays dirty, we have to too.) However, common as such inferences are, my feelings about the unwisdom of covert wars provide no basis for interpreting the Constitution: Neither the document nor its apparent animating impulses provide clear instruction respecting their constitutional propriety. Of course advance congressional authorization was the contemplated norm, but it is a norm we know the framers did not deem an absolute when time prevented its implementation, and brood as I may I have trouble distinguishing in principle between "can't come to Congress because there isn't time" and "can't come to Congress because it would serve to defeat our military effort." Indeed, on reflection, the former is but a specific instance of the latter: The *reason* there's "no time" to wait for congressional authorization to respond to a Cuban landing on the Florida beaches is that by the time Congress could act Castro could be halfway to Disney World. So I don't particularly like it, but I'm afraid we must answer the question the subhead poses in the negative: At least sometimes, at least for some limited period, the president can constitutionally engage in covert acts of war without advance congressional authorization.

HAVE I JUST GIVEN AWAY THE STORE?

You will not be surprised to learn that the answer to this question is no. For the second error of the "corollary" quoted at the beginning of this chapter— that given the new "reporting to committees only" statutes the war in Laos would today be legal[24]—is that such statutes are manifestly insufficient constitutionally (and thus necessarily inapplicable) when secrecy is not, or has ceased to be, a military necessity: At that point the claim that the president "can't" come to Congress (and thus the situation resembles a response to a "sudden attack" on the United States) goes entirely out the window.[25]

What's more, we saw in chapters 4 and 5 how quickly executive claims that secrecy is a military necessity tend to dissolve into the likely truth that in fact the secrecy is intended to keep *us* in the dark.[26]

One kind of case where the claim that "we didn't take x to Congress because we had to keep it secret" should not be heeded is the case where x isn't in fact a secret. I know it seems odd I should have to spell this out, but any reader of today's newspapers will readily understand why I do so: Whatever "covert" may or may not mean in bureaucratese these days (the best translation seems to be "we're not going to take this to Congress"), it does not necessarily incorporate the notion of even approximate secrecy. "The details of . . . 'overt-covert' operations are trumpeted not only in the press, but also in published government documents."[27] Thus, "the World Court in the *Nicaragua* case could condemn the United States for 'covert' paramilitary support of the contras on the basis of an evidentiary record drawn largely from official statements and U.S. government documents."[28]

A more recent example is provided by the lead story in January 19, 1992's *New York Times*, whose first paragraph reported: "Saudi Arabia is pressing the Bush Administration to organize a large covert action campaign in Iraq aimed at dividing Iraq's army and toppling Saddam Hussein, United States and allied officials say." Say what? "Covert"? Ah, this must have been a leak by someone trying to kill the idea. So those of you hung up on English usage might suppose, and indeed it does appear that some of those supplying details may have had such motives,[29] but no, this story was authorized: "American and allied officials discussed those plans with a reporter because some believe that the disclosure will by itself instill confidence in Iraqi opposition forces . . . ."[30] The *Times*'s description of the contemplated "covert" action included the following passages:

> In addition to the Saudi option of secretly arming guerrilla forces, a senior Bush Administration official said in an interview this week that the Administration has considered coordinating its efforts with Kurdish and Shiite forces inside Iraq to foment a coup for which Iraqi military commanders would seek allied support.

· · · · ·

> Among the covert options that Saudi Arabia is promoting is the formation of arms-supply and guerrilla-warfare networks organized by allied intelligence services that could challenge poorly trained Iraqi Army units garrisoned in most of the rural areas of northern and southern Iraq.

· · · · ·

"There has to be a combination of a major covert operation and a major air operation and then leave the rest to the Iraqi people," said a senior allied official who
has been discussing strategy with Bush Administration aides involved in the
planning.[31]

Okay, you get the point (that whatever else it may mean, "covert" doesn't
mean covert) and you get the further point as well (that the fact that executive officials slap that label on an operation shouldn't move us an inch in
the direction of concluding that congressional authorization is not constitutionally required).

The only legitimate basis for the delegation in the first place was the need for
tactical secrecy in conducting military operations. Thus, it follows that when
secrecy fails or is no longer necessary to the success of an operation, such action
must be presented to the full Congress and may not continue without formal
legislative authorization. When the United States is controlling the war-making
activities of private forces, which are no secret to the enemy, there is no legitimate reason not to get congressional authorization for the executive's action.[32]

Thus the Constitution requires that "covert" wars that aren't in fact secret receive congressional authorization (which entails the proposition that
those begun in secret must be authorized as soon as they cease to be so).
One kind of war that can't remain a secret is one that goes on for more than
a couple of days. Of course secrecy in planning can help a surprise attack
succeed. And indeed we might be able to wage covert war for a day or two
before the enemy realized it was confronted with something beyond a series of random acts of God, sabotage by its own people, or the same ragtag
band of local guerrillas with which it had been engaged for some time—
which ignorance might indeed help us militarily by delaying an increase in
the force of the enemy's response. (You don't call out the tanks if you think
lightning has been causing those fires in your ammunition dump.) But only
for a day or two: After that even the dullest enemy will catch on to the fact
that reinforcements have arrived. As Senator Moynihan remarked in 1984,
"My first comment about so-called secret wars must be that there is no such
thing. The preparations for war can be kept secret, but once a war com-
mences, whatever its avowed nature, it becomes a public event . . . ."[33]

Aha, you may be thinking, you've caught me in a contradiction: Didn't
my discussion of Laos suggest that a substantial American presence can be
kept secret for a long time, even years? Well, no, because we have seen that
our presence in Laos was effectively kept secret from only the American
people (and to a lesser degree the Congress). In fact little or no effort was
made[34]—how could it have been expected to succeed?—to hide our presence from the enemy. The record is therefore clear that not only the Lao-

tians, but the North Vietnamese, Chinese, and Soviets too, were perfectly well aware of what we were doing all along: "Only the American people are in the dark, for the people in Laos know from firsthand experience what the Americans are doing. The North Vietnamese and Pathet Lao broadcast their versions of the truth about U.S. activities, often years before official admissions."[35]

At this point it might be argued that although it is true we couldn't conceal from the enemy for more than a day or two the fact that a war was going on (or that significant new forces had joined an existing one), we might be able to conceal the fact it was *Americans* who had joined in. To this there would seem to be two answers. The first is that in fact we probably couldn't: For one thing, even Americans get captured and killed. The other, more theoretical, is that a desire to hide the fact of an American presence in an overt war is hard to understand as something that should serve to waive the requirement of congressional authorization. Hiding the fact of an impending attack surely can help militarily, and so, I have bent over backward to concede, might concealing the fact that added forces have arrived. Hiding the fact that the added forces are American seems militarily irrelevant, or at least so attenuated that it cannot seriously be suggested as an excuse for not seeking congressional authorization. Naturally one can invent fanciful scenarios: "Those are American planes, all right, but who's flying them? If [and only if] it's Americans, we'd better call up another interceptor wing." I hear the words—as a matter of fact I wrote them—but doubt that anyone would seriously present them as a justification for shelving the demands of the Constitution. (Besides, only one of those planes has to get forced down—as they do at alarmingly high rates in even the most one-sided wars[36]—for the enemy to find out who's flying them.)

Thus during the Cold War the argument was sometimes refined further, to admit that we couldn't long hide our presence from the enemy, but argue that nonetheless we would suffer militarily if we admitted it openly, thus destroying the "facade of deniability" that minimized the chances of direct U.S.-Soviet confrontation.[37] The further I got into the subject the less this struck me as anything much beyond yet another in the long list of excuses the administration devised for not seeking congressional authorization. We have seen how that's about all "deniability" meant in practice—everyone got to know about Laos except Congress and the American people—and might note as well that in neighboring Vietnam, where our role was entirely open, there was never a serious risk of Soviet intervention.[38] At all events the Cold War is over (at least in any sense that is relevant here): Excuses for keeping Congress in the dark rationalized in terms of a danger of bringing the entire "Eastern bloc" down upon us should be interred along with it.[39]

So no, I haven't given away the store: Presidents *can* constitutionally fight unauthorized secret wars, sometimes, but not for more than a couple of days. That returns us to the issue whether the War Powers Resolution should be amended to cover "covert" as well as overt wars. On first reading Senator Eagleton's amendment, simply treating all American agents engaged in or assisting hostilities as if they were American armed forces, may have seemed wooden: Surely *some* difference in treatment must be in order! But once you work it through, it turns out that Eagleton was right again.[40] Whether the secrecy of an operation has been blown or is otherwise no longer necessary is something courts would be fully capable of deciding in many cases—they can read newspapers and public government documents as well as the rest of us—though admittedly there would be others in which we would be uncomfortable with their substituting their judgment for that of even interested experts. That, however, is the reason the statutory test should not be put in such terms[41] but rather should follow Eagleton's approach of simply making the ordinary time limits applicable.

The War Powers Resolution currently gives the president an effective ninety free days to fight even an overt war, though I have suggested that that represents an indefensible estimate of how long it should take to seek congressional authorization, and thus should be reduced to twenty days.[42] Within *either* of those periods the sorts of secrets that can legitimately be counted as militarily relevant—that significant new forces have initiated acts of war or joined a war already in progress—will have long since been blown.

Admittedly that observation doesn't quite get us there, however, as the Resolution requires a report to Congress within forty-eight hours of—under my proposed substitute, simultaneously with—the commencement of such operations. In most cases, though, the arrival of extra forces will be immediately obvious to the enemy. If the executive doesn't believe that, however, it always has the option of reporting to Congress in executive session or otherwise in a fashion that is not entirely public. Of course there's a chance, I'll even grant it's substantial, that despite such precautions the operation will leak before a great deal of additional time has passed, though in that regard two facts should be noted. The first is that although I have not followed the common tactic of denying the possibility of a congressional leak, it is also the case that the danger is routinely overstated by advocates of unfettered executive power. At least some studies—though admittedly it's hard to find one on "either side" that does not begin with an apparent point of view—have suggested that leaks from within the executive branch (where, of course, numerous people are likely to be involved, as are officials of various foreign governments) are more likely and common.[43] The second is that one way to get people to act like adults is to treat them as such. But okay, grant that it will leak: The important point for present purposes is that it is not likely to do so before the enemy on the battlefield has figured out that new forces have joined the fray. I have consequently added what is essentially Eagleton's amendment to the Combat Authorization Act recommended in the appendix. Whether or not the War Powers Resolution is ever amended, the Constitution requires no less.[44]

Toward a War Powers (Combat Authorization) Act That Works

As PROMISED, I hereby tender, with supporting commentary, a revised version of the War Powers Resolution that is calculated to achieve more effectively the goal of forcing the president to seek congressional authorization before (or if necessary simultaneously with) involving the nations's troops in armed combat, and thus forcing Congress to perform its constitutional duty of deciding whether we go to war. The first section of this appendix suggests the elimination from the existing Resolution of a good deal of nonoperational "noise" that serves only to confuse its constitutional status and otherwise to encourage continued presidential noncooperation. The second section suggests specific strategies—centrally involving the insertion of the federal judiciary into the process—for inducing presidential and congressional compliance. The suggested new statute concludes the discussion.

PROVISIONS THAT DON'T DO ANY GOOD AND ONLY GIVE THE PRESIDENT AN EXCUSE TO FLOUT THE RESOLUTION

The Title

Despite the fact that (just like a statute) the War Powers Resolution was passed, by a two-thirds vote of each house, over the President's veto, and thus is understandably often referred to as the War Powers Act, it is officially a "Resolution." I used to suppose that designation was chosen on some theory that "resolutions" are appropriate vehicles for congressional elucidation of the meaning of the Constitution. More recently I have been advised (admittedly by a former Senate staff member) that "Resolution" sounded more weighty and distinguished to the House leadership than "Act." However reasonable that may have seemed at the time—I find it mildly baffling—the effect has been just the opposite, and people who should know better sometimes slip into suggesting that because this is a "mere resolution," it has less stature than a statute[1] (whereas in fact a statute and a joint resolution are of equivalent legal status). Unfortunately, a joint resolution, which this is, sounds suspiciously like a concurrent resolution,[2] which in turn begins to sound a little like a resolution that one house of Congress might pass commending its doorman. It should be called an Act.

I'd go further, however. As we've seen, the War Powers Resolution (or War Powers Act, in almost equally common parlance) has in the two decades since its passage acquired a bad aura—partly because of overdrawn allegations of its unconstitutionality, partly because our presidents, the Congress, and the courts have all essentially ignored it. It therefore seems best, assuming amendment for the better to be possible at all, to try to kill the association by choosing an entirely new title. The "Use of Force Act" isn't bad, but that one has been taken, by a proposal whose heart is in the right place but in my opinion retains many of the defects of the existing Resolution.[3] Thus my choice of the Combat Authorization Act.

Section 8(d)

Section 8(d), which provides that "[n]othing in this joint resolution . . . is intended to alter the constitutional authority of the Congress or the President," was obviously inserted as a hedge, to indicate that should the Resolution's provisions begin to stray across constitutional bounds, they are to be reined in. Having given (understandably) closer attention to the Resolution's constitutionality, however, we are in a position to understand that its only aspects that are even arguably unconstitutional are the concurrent resolution provision, section 5(c)—which is arguable[4]—and Congress's gift to the president of sixty (actually ninety) free days to fight any war he likes. My statute eliminates both of these, and thus any possible need for the 8(d) hedge.[5] But what harm, you may be wondering, could there be in saying that nothing in the Resolution is intended to alter the constitutional authority of either Congress or the president? Under my statute it will become superfluous, but so what? Only this, and it is something: It gives the president a peg on which to hang his defiance. ("The Resolution itself says it isn't supposed to cut into my prerogatives, but if I followed 4(a) and reported this to Congress that would cut into my prerogatives, so by disobeying the Resolution I am actually following the Resolution."[6]) Congress should therefore get rid of it.

Section 2(c)

Section 2(c) provides:

> The constitutional powers of the President as Commander-in-Chief to introduce United States Armed Forces into hostilities, or into situations where imminent involvement in hostilities is clearly indicated by the circumstances, are exercised only pursuant to (1) a declaration of war, (2) specific statutory authorization, or (3) a national emergency created by attack upon the United States, its territories or possessions, or its armed forces.

It ended up in the Resolution as a result of a compromise between the Senate and House forces. The House's approach had been the more "procedural"—not telling the president when he could and could not introduce forces into hostilities but rather instructing him that when he did, he had to report to Congress and withdraw if their use was not then approved. The Senate's more "substantive" approach is captured by the quoted language. Though admittedly the intended function of section 2(c) is less than entirely clear, its most sensible reading in the context of the full Resolution would seem to be that the only occasions on which the president can commit troops in advance of specific congressional authorization—that is, the only occasions on which the report-and-approval mechanism of sections 4(a) and 5(b) will become relevant—are those mentioned in its subsection (3), involving "a national emergency created by attack upon the United States, its territories or possessions, or its armed forces."[7]

Plainly section 2(c) has not been heeded: To name but three, the *Mayaguez* rescue operation, the naval war against Iran, and the invasion of Grenada—none even by a stretch responding to an attack on U.S. territory or troops—were patent noncompliers. No one has paid much attention to such violations, however, for two reasons. First, even such strong supporters of the Senate approach as Senators Javits and Eagleton admitted subsequent to passage that 2(c) had ended up too narrow.[8] Second, section 2(c) appears in a part of the Resolution entitled "Purpose and Policy," where all agree it is operational only to the extent the president chooses voluntarily to comply.[9] It thus begs to be ignored, and functions only to help breed contempt for the entire Resolution.

Repeal is not the only possible reaction, however, and some commentators have suggested that the cure for the Resolution's anemia may lie in taking 2(c) (or some revised version of it) out of the "Purpose and Policy" section and making it legally "binding."[10] I can certainly understand the impulse, but on analysis this turns out to be a nonstarter. In the first place there seems to be a consensus that if 2(c) is to be made "operational," it will have to be broadened. Virtually everyone agrees that it should have included the protection of American citizens as one of the justifications for presidential military action in advance of congressional authorization.[11] That omission could obviously be remedied, but it would not do the trick. For example, Monroe Leigh, the Ford Administration's State Department Legal Adviser, testified in 1975:

> Besides the three situations listed in Subsection 2(c) . . . , it appears that the President has the constitutional authority to use the Armed Forces to rescue American citizens abroad, to rescue foreign nationals where such action directly facilitates the rescue of U.S. citizens abroad, to protect U.S. Embassies and Legations abroad, to suppress civil insurrection, to implement and administer the terms of

an armistice or cease-fire designed to terminate hostilities involving the United States, and to carry out the terms of security commitments contained in treaties. We do not, however, believe that any such list can be a complete one, just as we do not believe that any single definitional statement can clearly encompass every conceivable situation in which the President's Commander in Chief authority could be exercised.[12]

Neither does this enumeration seem recklessly open-ended, as it truly is impossible to predict and specify all the possible situations in which the president will need to act to protect the nation's security before he has time to obtain congressional authorization.[13]

Indeed, if one were to think it desirable to retain a 2(c)-type provision "bounding" the situations in which the president can act in advance of obtaining authorization, she would most sensibly end up reiterating the command of the Constitution properly understood—that the president can use military force in advance of congressional authorization only when the national security is clearly at stake and there has not been time to obtain advance authorization. The Use of Force Act proposed by Senator Biden and others does just that:

In the absence of a declaration of war or statutory authorization for a specific use of force, the President is authorized to use force abroad . . . to respond to a foreign military threat that severely and directly jeopardizes the supreme national interests of the United States under extraordinary emergency conditions that do not permit sufficient time for Congress to consider statutory authorization.[14]

If you think advisable a statutory designation of the occasions on which the president can act in advance of authorization, that's probably about as well as you can do. But what will have been accomplished? Its hortatory value seems nil, given its open-ended character and the fact that it simply repeats the existing command of the Constitution: Reiterating it in statutory form is not likely to increase the chances of the president's voluntarily taking it seriously. Neither does it seem a provision calculated to engender timely congressional enforcement, given the (inevitable) open-endedness of the language, to say nothing of Congress's dismal track record on speaking up at the beginning of wars.[15]

That leaves the courts, but while I obviously favor a general move in the direction of making the Resolution judicially enforceable, this is not the way to go about it. It will (at least sometimes) be difficult enough for courts to decide whether our troops are exposed to an imminent likelihood of hostilities (and if they are to refer the question of authorization to Congress)—though that is a task I have suggested the effectiveness of the Resolution inescapably requires the judiciary to assume. They would rightly refuse, however, to second-guess the president on the issue whether the

military threat he is countering is one "that severely and directly jeopardizes the supreme national interests of the United States." And even if they
did, unwisely, decide to take on such an issue, what would the remedy be?
Rather plainly not an order that the president immediately withdraw the
troops,[16] but instead precisely the same sort of "remand" that would already
be in order under the "procedural" provisions of the Resolution, to the
effect that if Congress doesn't approve their presence within the next, say,
twenty days, a declaratory judgment that the troops are being illegally
maintained in the field, and possibly an injunction, will issue.

A "section 2(c)" of any description therefore seems capable of adding
nothing to the rest of the Resolution in terms of altered presidential behavior, or responsible[17] congressional or judicial enforcement either. Thus although my instincts parallel those who would make 2(c) "operational," I'd
repeal it: As the Congress as a whole sensed at the time, the House of
Representatives' "procedural" approach shows greater promise of making
a difference.

Section 5(c)

All "procedural" approaches are not created equal, however, and not all of
those contained in the existing Resolution are equally susceptible to being
made workable. Section 5(c) provides that within the sixty-day period,
Congress can by concurrent resolution direct the president to remove
troops he has committed to hostilities.[18] A strong argument can be made
that this section was rendered invalid by the Supreme Court's 1983 decision in *INS v. Chadha*.[19] For this reason, it too provides an excuse to
condemn the entire Resolution as "unconstitutional." Since Congress's
proclivities in this area virtually insure that 5(c) would never have been
invoked anyhow, it too should be removed.

My personal opinion is that section 5(c) is not unconstitutional. Even
assuming that *Chadha* makes sense,[20] it seems distinguishable.[21] Section
5(c) does not fit the profile of a standard "legislative veto" wherein Congress has delegated certain powers to the executive branch and then attempted to pull them back by reserving a right to veto executive exercises
of the delegation. Instead, it should be read in the context of sections
4(a)(1) and 5(b), as part of a *package* attempting to approximate in concrete
terms the accommodation reached by the founders, that the president could
act militarily in an emergency but was obligated to cease and desist in the
event Congress did not approve as soon as it had a reasonable opportunity
to do so.

Sixty days is essentially defined by the Resolution (albeit far too gener-
ously in my view) as the *outer limit* of the time Congress can reasonably be
supposed to need to decide. (The additional thirty days for "unavoidable

military necessity" is there to enable our troops to be withdrawn without getting killed.) However, it patently is not the notion of the Resolution that sixty days will always be necessary for such a decision. The scheme contemplates that sometime *within* that sixty days, whenever under the specific circumstances presented Congress can get its act together earlier, it can either authorize continued military activity under 5(b) or terminate it under 5(c). Section 5(c) thus resembles only distantly the sort of legislative veto to which the *Chadha* litigation was addressed.

However, *Chadha* is "a work of mechanical simplicity" that suggests no inclination to distinguish among provisions that bear any resemblance to the one involved in the case,[22] a reading buttressed by the sweeping references of the concurrence and dissent.[23] There is thus a strong likelihood that in the event section 5(c) ever got to court, it would be invalidated. We need not shed many tears over this prospect, however, as experience suggests that Congress would be most unlikely ever to try to invoke it. If it won't acknowledge that hostilities exist in situations like the 1987–88 naval war against Iran and thereby start the clock for its further decision, it certainly isn't going to order the president to remove the troops cold turkey within sixty days of his having committed them.[24]

Such a useless and arguably unconstitutional provision is thus likely only to provide an excuse for denunciation and defiance of the entire Resolution, and it too should be repealed.[25] In one sense this seems a pity, as we can surely understand the motivation that drove 5(c), a desire to avoid giving the president carte blanche to keep troops he has unilaterally committed in the field for the sixty or ninety days the clock is running. (Of course the clock hasn't in fact been running, but that is a problem we will get to presently.) Most of our concern on this score can be allayed by adoption of my proposal to shorten the sixty-day period to twenty days.

Strengthening the Potentially Operational Provisions

The Consultation Requirement

Compliance with section 3—requiring the president to consult "with Congress" before committing troops to hostilities—has been better than compliance with the Resolution's other sections. Admittedly this isn't saying much: It means only that compliance has been sporadic.[26] There is room for improvement.

Though this change should not be necessary, the Resolution should be amended to make clear that consultation requires genuine discussion, a seeking of advice and counsel, rather than—as unfortunately is as close as we have generally come to "consultation"—a mere report of what is about to happen.[27] Another reason section 3 hasn't worked is that a requirement to consult "with Congress" is not very helpful on the subject of who is to be consulted. Logistical and sometime security considerations preclude the idea that consultation can be had with the entire membership of Congress, so everyone has proceeded on the sensible supposition that it is "the relevant leadership" that must be involved. However, that is an unclear concept, and congressional jealousies have made diplomatic selection difficult. Moreover, at least so long as the relevant group has not been officially indicated, those the president decides he should consult may not be available.[28] Such problems of intra-Congress jealousy and unavailability should be allayed by a statutory designation of the leadership group with whom consultation is to be had.[29] Although the proposed amendments of Senators Byrd, Nunn, Mitchell, and Warner can be faulted on a number of counts,[30] the cosponsors of this legislation are certainly experts on who in Congress should be consulted (and who can diplomatically be left off the list). Their recommendations in that regard should thus probably be adopted.[31]

Perceived New Teeth for Section 5(b)

Section 5(b) provides that if the clock runs and Congress has not authorized continued hostilities, "the President shall terminate" the use of United States Armed Forces.[32] Several commentators have suggested that this command be augmented by a provision that once the clock has thus run, funds to support the troops be cut off.[33] While this should be redundant, it probably is a good idea anyhow, as virtually everyone, including apologists for broad presidential power in this area, agrees that Congress has constitutional authority to end a war by terminating its funding.[34] The addition of such a proviso would therefore render presidential obedience more likely. The serious problem, however, has lain not in what happens when the clock runs out, but rather in getting the clock started, a problem discussed in chapter 3 and to which I now return.

The Language of Section 4(a)(1)

Section 4(a) of the Resolution provides:

> In the absence of a declaration of war, in any case in which United States Armed Forces are introduced—
>
> > (1) into hostilities or into situations where imminent involvement in hostilities is clearly indicated by the circumstances;
> >
> > (2) into the territory, airspace or waters of a foreign nation, while equipped for combat, except for deployments which relate solely to supply, replacement, repair, or training of such forces; or
> >
> > (3) in numbers which substantially enlarge United States Armed Forces equipped for combat already located in a foreign nation;

the President shall submit within 48 hours to the Speaker of the House of the Representatives and to the President pro tempore of the Senate a report, in writing, setting forth—

(A) the circumstances necessitating the introduction of United States Armed Forces;

(B) the constitutional and legislative authority under which such introduction took place; and

(C) the estimated scope and duration of the hostilities or involvement.

Section 5(b)'s sixty-day clock is started only by a report under section 4(a)(1): Of sections 4(a)(2) and 4(a)(3) I will have more to say in the next section.

The requirement that imminent involvement in hostilities be "clearly indicated by the circumstances" seems too demanding. Section 4(a)(1) is often paraphrased as if the requirement of a "clear indication" were not present. Some language in the relevant House Report seems to support this loose reading.[35] However, the enacted language, when it is not ambiguous, must prevail, and "clear indication" has a moderately specific and demanding legal meaning.[36] That 4(a)(1) means what it says is also corroborated by the facts: (1) that sections 4(a)(2) and 4(a)(3), which *don't* start the clock, describe situations in which one would ordinarily suppose there is at least some danger of hostilities; and (2) that Congress itself (albeit a later one), in the compromise it eventually reached with President Reagan over Lebanon, found that 4(a)(1) had been satisfied only on the day that four Marines were killed and thirty-eight others wounded.[37] On the other hand, section 8(c) provides:

For purposes of this joint resolution, the term "introduction of United States Armed Forces" includes the assignment of members of such armed forces to command, coordinate, participate in the movement of, or accompany the regular or irregular military forces of any foreign country or government when such military forces are engaged, *or there exists an imminent threat* that such forces will become engaged, in hostilities.[38]

Here the requirement of "clear indication" is omitted. However, it seems irrational to start the clock on a lesser likelihood of hostilities when our troops are accompanying another nation's army than when they are proceeding alone. Apparently Congress was of two minds about whether to require a "clear indication." The language it enacted in section 4(a)(1), however, plainly does so. It should be amended simply to cover all situations in which there is an imminent danger of involvement in hostilities.[39]

That the entire section is keyed to when troops are "introduced" is potentially troublesome, in that on its face the Resolution does not seem to require a report when the troops are already in place and hostilities (or their imminent likelihood) arise later. In Operation Desert Shield/Desert Storm, for example, there were some early (if implausible) indications at least by isolated groups of legislators that the fact we had massed 200,000 troops on the Kuwaiti border presented no imminent danger of hostilities.[40] As talk of moving into Kuwait grew stronger there were indications, up until the very end, that the administration might try to rely on those early indications as establishing that further compliance with section 4(a)(1) was unnecessary. Obviously this was a scenario with many distinguishing twists—at no point did the early indications of apparent satisfaction represent the corporate judgment of Congress; the number of troops was doubled as the talk of invasion escalated—but the point is nonetheless apparent. Section 4(a)(1) should be amended to make clear its applicability when the troops come first and the imminent danger of hostilities later.

Desert Storm demonstrated the need for a related amendment as well. For some time, despite our deployment of 200,000 troops and concomitant number of ships, planes, and tanks on or near the Saudi-Kuwaiti border, the administration took the position that hostilities were not imminent because the Iraqis were likely to be deterred by our presence. (In fact the administration was even then planning to attack *them*,[41] but let's leave that out of the equation for now.) The Resolution should be amended to remind the executive that there is a difference between risks and hopes—to make clear that section 4(a)(1) applies whenever there exists a substantial danger of hostilities, however genuine our wish that the enemy will be intimidated into submission.

Getting the President to Start the Clock

It would be best if the president could be counted on to start the clock himself: He knows the facts best, he knows them soonest, and both congressional debates and lawsuits consume valuable time. However, to the extent the president has deigned to report at all, he has avoided starting the clock by refusing to specify under which subsection of 4(a) he is reporting. For this reason it has been suggested that the Resolution be amended to require him to specify the subsection under which he is filing his report.[42]

This seems unlikely to work. The only effect of such a requirement (assuming it was followed at all) would probably be to insure that the president would file his report under 4(a)(2) or 4(a)(3) and thus avoid starting the clock. (A 4(a)(1) situation is virtually certain also to be a 4(a)(2) or 4(a)(3) situation, so he would not be behaving flat-out dishonestly in such a situation, merely incompletely—"telling the truth but not the whole truth.") Moreover, the filing of such a specific report is likely to have the effect of converting him, in others' eyes, from a defiant noncomplier to a cooperative participant (who has more facts than anybody else and whose judgment is therefore likely to be deferred to).

Indeed, should either Congress or the courts commence undertaking to start the clock when the president has not, he would be clever to respond by habitually reporting and (even without a requirement that he pick a subsection) specifying section 4(a)(2) or 4(a)(3). The fact that this is such an obvious ploy leads me to tender the mildly radical suggestion that sections 4(a)(2) and 4(a)(3) be eliminated from the Resolution: They simply have too much potential as "cop-counts" whereby the president can underreport the situation and thereby avoid starting the clock. (A smart prosecutor puts lesser offenses in the indictment only if she is hoping that the jury will compromise on one of them.) It also appears that on occasion the executive branch, in order to avoid a congressional report entirely—this was back when the possibility of reporting was apparently given consideration—underequipped our troops in deploying them (so as to render them other than "equipped for combat").[43] Congress plainly did not think 4(a)(2) and 4(a)(3) were very critical, as the situations there described require neither consultation with Congress under section 3 nor approval of the operation under section 5(b). Because they provide the president with a clever means of avoiding the application of the Resolution's operationally significant provisions, and an incentive to underequip our troops as well, they should probably be repealed.[44]

What Happens When the President Won't Start the Clock?

Most people in Congress seem to assume that it is up to them to start the clock when the president hasn't.[45] This was not contemplated by the Resolution, but then nothing relevant was. (We have seen that section 5(b) provides that absent congressional authorization, the troops are to be withdrawn sixty days after a 4(a)(1) report is submitted "or is required to be submitted," but little thought and no provision was directed to the question by whom such "requirement" might be determined.) The problem is that it has become clear that we cannot rely on Congress to do so.

For one thing, under *Chadha*, any such congressional action would probably have to be by joint resolution vetoable by the president. Unlike a resolution enacted pursuant to section 5(c), a clock-starting resolution cannot be regarded as a simple indication that Congress has had sufficient time to consider the wisdom of the military venture in question (thereby indicating that the president's constitutional emergency powers have been exhausted). Instead, the clock-starting situation seems somewhat paradigmatic of what the Court appears to have been thinking about in *Chadha*: Congress has delegated to the president authority to decide whether there exist hostilities or the imminent likelihood thereof, he has defaulted in making that decision (or has made it incorrectly), and Congress must therefore withdraw the delegation and make the decision itself.

It also requires no great cynicism to suppose that given the opportunity the president would almost certainly veto such a joint resolution. Consistency will require him to do so, since by hypothesis he has not filed the hostilities report that Congress is now saying is required. Beyond the issue of vetoability is Congress's demonstrated disinclination to start the 4(a)(1) clock anyhow. A few members have apparently doubted that they currently have authority to do so, but most seem to have assumed they do. And still the clock has not been started in situations as protracted and clear as the naval war against Iran.

If, therefore, the constitutional plan—timely congressional consideration of military ventures—is to work, it appears that Congress will have to be *forced* to such consideration. And given the momentum of the situation, we will not be able to achieve this by indicating that the war will continue unless Congress acts to stop it. In such situations, Congress has demonstrated that it will let the war go on (reserving unto itself the right to protest that it is really the president's war and there isn't a great deal it can do about it). The War Powers Resolution was thus wise in its assessment that if consideration is to be assured, the arrangement must be that the war cannot *continue* unless Congress clearly acts to authorize it. The Resolution's optimistic assumption was that the president would effectively force congressional consideration by filing a 4(a)(1) report. He hasn't done so, however, and Congress has demonstrated that in the heat of events it cannot be counted on to force its own accountability either.

It thus seems clear that the courts must be brought into the act. This proposition is so central to my suggested approach that I have discussed it at some length in chapter 3. Any amendment of the Resolution should make clear—though I have argued that the existing Resolution is most responsibly read this way as well—that if the president does not start the clock, one or more members of Congress will have standing to bring suit to do so in federal court, which in such a case should decide the issue whether hostilities (or the imminent likelihood thereof) exist. In chapter 3, I discussed various objections sounding generally in "justiciability"—political question, standing, ripeness[46]—and concluded that none has appropriate general applicability to our situation (though of course each might in a sufficiently eccentric situation). In any event the cases are clear that these barriers can generally be abolished by statute.[47]

Restoring the Presumption of Advance Authorization

I also noted in chapter 3 that the existing Resolution effectively establishes no presumption whatever in favor of advance authorization, instead granting the president the universal option of starting a war, reporting within forty-eight hours, and continuing to fight while Congress takes sixty or ninety days to decide whether the war should be authorized. This scheme is unconstitutional: Advance authorization was to be the norm, not simply an option the president might in his discretion choose. Thus section 4(a) of my proposed statute requires that the placement of troops into hostile situations be authorized in advance, save only where there has not been time to secure such authorization, or requesting it in advance would have destroyed the military effectiveness of our response, in either of which cases the president is permitted to request authorization no later than contemporaneously with the commencement of hostilities.

My statute permits either a member of the armed forces ordered to the theatre of operations, or any member of Congress, to bring suit to enforce section 4(a) in the event the president has not complied with it. What I have in mind here is a suit alleging that hostilities or the imminent likelihood thereof have developed and the president has not requested congressional authorization. Should the court agree with these allegations, Congress will then have twenty days to authorize the president's action or it will have to be terminated. (The fact that the plaintiff has been able to get the case to court and prove his allegations will obviously negate any possible claim that there has not been time to request congressional authorization or that doing so would fatally defeat its secrecy.)

I suppose my statute might also suggest the theoretical possibility of a suit alleging that although it's true that the president sought authorization contemporaneously with his commitment of the troops, he violated section 4(a) by not securing such authorization in advance—a suit, in other words, retroactively challenging the president's judgment that there was not time to secure advance authorization, or that doing so would have defeated the military effectiveness of our response. This seems like a claim a court should *not* entertain—not simply because it might quite sensibly shy away from second-guessing the president on the degree to which advance publicity would have undercut the military effectiveness of our response,[48] but more fundamentally because nothing would turn on it other than a retroactive evaluation of whether the president had misbehaved. By hypothesis a request for congressional authorization will have been filed by the president, and indeed in all likelihood will have been acted upon. The act does not provide for civil liability on the part of the president—now *there*'s a silly (and unconstitutional) idea—and thus all that such a decision could possibly generate is support for an article of impeachment. That should be left to Congress, however:[49] Unaccustomed as I am to uttering such words, I'm not even sure such a lawsuit would present a constitutionally cognizable "case or controversy." Thus that aspect of my statute that shifts the presumption back toward advance authorization (as opposed to authorization within twenty days) is one respecting which we will have to rely not on judicial enforcement, but substantially on voluntary presidential compliance (conceivably prodded by the political process).

Shortening the "Free Period" to Twenty Days

The only legitimate theory that supports giving the president sixty (or ninety) free days is that it approximates the time it will take Congress to gather its thoughts about whether the United States should become involved in the war in question. Either of those, however, represents an indefensibly long estimate of how long it should take Congress to decide whether the president's "emergency" response should be made more permanent.[50] Most of the declarations of war in our history have been considered and voted on almost immediately after the president's request.[51] Yet it was demonstrably the judgment of the framers of the Constitution, as it should be ours, that the only wars in which we ought to be involved are those it is quite apparent are justified.

The fact that declarations of war have generally been immediately forthcoming is a knife that cuts both ways, however, and one might take solace in the existing sixty- or ninety-day period on the theory that although Congress will probably approve anything at first, passions may settle after two or three months.[52] To this there are two answers. The first is practical. Insofar as experience teaches that Congress is likely to support the president at the very outset of a war, it may also teach that it is likely to be a good deal more than a couple of months before Congress sours: It took years in the case of Vietnam. The idea that aborting an ongoing war represents a failure to "support our boys in the field" doesn't really make sense, because an order to withdraw can always be accompanied by provision to protect the troops as the withdrawal is proceeding. But it does appear to convince congressmen, or at least—and for present purposes this amounts to the same thing—it provides a convenient rationalization. There is thus little reason to suppose that Congress is ordinarily going to be more inclined to end a presidential war after two or three months than it would have been at the outset.

More fundamentally, this is an unconstitutional theory on which to construct a free period for presidential war-making. Thus rationalized, the period ceases to be an estimate of how long it will take Congress to consider and resolve the matter and becomes, instead, a delegation of legislative power to the president more open-ended than any declaration of war (because it does not specify in any way—by geographical locale, enemy, or precipitating condition—what war it is the president is entitled to fight for up to ninety days). As such, it constitutes yet another congressional responsibility-avoidance device and offends not only whatever shred of the delegation doctrine survives but, more specifically, the Declaration of War Clause's requirement that wars be authorized on their individual merits and not at wholesale.

It is true that if the enemy knows the deal—that if the war is not approved by Congress within twenty days the troops will have to be withdrawn—it may be encouraged to "hold out" for that period.[53] However, the extent to which the enemy will actually be aware of the niceties of American constitutional and statutory law is one it is easy (and, experience shows, tempting[54]) to exaggerate. Moreover, to the extent the enemy knows that much it is also likely to be aware that when push comes to shove Congress will almost certainly support the president's war. In any event twenty days of "holding out" is plainly preferable, in terms of carnage, to sixty or ninety. And to the extent that opponents of the War Powers Resolution would use the "holding out" phenomenon to argue against *any* deadline, there is a clear sense in which they are right: If we don't let the president fight unauthorized wars for as long as he wants, that does indeed reduce his opportunity to pursue them to total victory. However, this attitude argues not simply against establishing a clock, but against enforcing the Constitution generally:[55] An inevitable by-product of any sort of constitutional requirement of congressional approval is that the enemy may also know that approval is required. The only way around this is to make the president a dictator, but that wasn't, and shouldn't be, the idea.

Obviously I am aware that there could arise a case in which twenty days will not be enough for reasoned consideration (though the longest debate on a declaration of war in our history, that preceding the War of 1812, lasted only seventeen days—and that was when orators strode the halls of Congress). However, it is always within the power of Congress statutorily to authorize the continuation of hostilities for a limited period of time (thus giving itself additional time to consider a more permanent authorization). Let us hope this doesn't become a habit, though even that would be an improvement over the present pattern, as it would suggest that Congress had given the decision *some* consideration.

Section 8(a)

Section 8(a) provides:

> Authority to introduce United States Armed Forces into hostilities or into situations where involvement in hostilities is clearly indicated by the circumstances shall not be inferred—
>
> (1) from any provision of law (whether or not in effect before the date of the enactment of this joint resolution), including any provision contained in any appropriation Act, unless such provision specifically authorizes the introduction of United States Armed Forces into hostilities or into such situations and states that it is intended to constitute specific statutory authorization within the meaning of this joint resolution; or
>
> (2) from any treaty heretofore or hereafter ratified unless such treaty is implemented by legislation specifically authorizing the introduction of United

States Armed Forces into hostilities or into such situations and stating that it is intended to constitute specific statutory authorization within the meaning of this joint resolution.

This section may appear to raise the question how one Congress (in this case the Ninety-third) can bind its successors. It is not difficult to envision some future Congress's enacting, say, an appropriations act, part of whose proceeds they know are to be used to finance some otherwise unauthorized presidential military venture, without indicating therein that it is intended to constitute the authorization the Resolution requires. When opponents protest that one need only look to section 8(a) of the War Powers Resolution to see that this cannot count as authorization, one can certainly anticipate the executive's responding that the appropriations act came later, and an earlier statute does not trump a later one.

It's a fair enough argument, but except under extreme circumstances it shouldn't work. What the War Powers Resolution gave us was a strong rule of construction, telling us how to read the intent of later congresses.[56] The Ninety-third Congress was saying, in effect:

> We know that we have incentives to be ambiguous in this area, and that is very costly in terms of the lives of our young people and the risk to the rest of us. We are therefore hereby providing an unambiguous set of conventions whereby you will be able to tell in the future whether or not we intend the authorization that is constitutionally required. When we do intend such authorization, we will make specific reference to this Resolution. Without such reference, do not construe us as authorizing the war in question.
>
> It is true that the "we" in question will not necessarily be the same people who have enacted this Resolution. However, our successors will certainly be well aware of this Resolution and the conventions it establishes, and thus, until the Resolution is repealed, they also should be presumed not to have intended to authorize a war unless they have included the required reference.
>
> History, and particularly Vietnam, teach that what is needed is a "bright line test" for construing our intention. Others might work as well—such as a requirement of a declaration of war, or a special seal on the document alleged to constitute authorization—but this is the one we are choosing.

If subsequent congresses don't like this, they can repeal the Resolution.[57] Until they do, the conventions it establishes should control.

Section 8(a)(2), providing that no treaty "heretofore or hereafter ratified" can authorize a war unless it is implemented by legislation referencing the War Powers Resolution is at least potentially inconsistent with section 8(d)(1), which provides that "nothing in this joint resolution . . . is intended to alter . . . a provision of existing treaties." In fact it appears that we are not currently party to any treaty that purports to authorize military action without the intervening approval of Congress,[58] but the inconsistency should be resolved nonetheless. The quoted provision of section 8(d)(1) should be eliminated, as it seems pretty clear that it is 8(a)(2) that is in line with the prevailing purpose of the Resolution.

Also mind-twisting is section 8(a)(1)'s patently unintended indication that a law "in effect before the date of the enactment of" the War Powers Resolution can constitute the required authorization, but only if it specifically refers to the War Powers Resolution. Rather than play law teachers' games with this, let us simply recommend that Congress eliminate the reference to preexisting laws. That too is plainly in accord with the Resolution's purpose.

· · · · ·

In chapter 3 I briefly canvassed the question whether there is a chance Congress will enact something like this. I concluded that it doesn't seem very likely in the immediate future. If I thought there were *no* chance, however, I wouldn't have bothered drafting and defending a statute. Stepping up on its own initiative and taking responsibility for whether the president should be permitted to pursue a particular war he has already begun— something Congress has shown itself unable to do of late—and binding itself to make such decisions in advance and outside the context of any particular war are at least potentially different questions. Congress attempted the latter in 1973. It might one day—perhaps in the not too distant future—be persuaded to do so again.

Assuming it did, however, an additional question would then arise: whether its performance under such a new, improved War Powers (or Combat Authorization) Act would be any better than it has been under the War Powers Resolution. That is, when we got down to cases, and a court "remanded" the issue to Congress, would Congress actually be able to follow through and face the issue whether the war in question should be permitted to proceed? Admittedly the matter is not entirely free from doubt. There has to be a point, however, when Congress will want to stop looking ineffectual: Avoiding enforcement of a second, and tightened, version of the War Powers Act would threaten to tarnish its image to what should be an unacceptable degree. Moreover, while Congress has shown a tendency by its indecision to let wars continue, I am unaware of any case of its *ending* one by indecision and, with Secretary Vance, think it most improbable that it would do so.[59] That, of course, is the assumption underlying the existing War Powers Resolution, though it has proved tricky actually setting it up so that the war actually will end unless Congress decides. The suggested new act is designed to make it harder for Congress to wriggle out. One important change is that we would be injecting the judiciary into the process. Rhetoric is the courts' most powerful weapon. It should be within the capacity of most federal judges[60] (certainly within the Supreme Court's capacity) to write an opinion explaining that the Constitution entrusts the choice between war and peace to the legislative process, and that because the conflagration in question meets the statutory criteria, it has become Congress's constitutional duty to decide whether it should proceed—an opinion that Congress simply could not ignore.[61]

My proposed statute follows. The relevant provisions of the existing Resolution appear in the left column, the suggested substitutes in the right.

A Proposed Combat Authorization Act

THE WAR POWERS RESOLUTION	THE COMBAT AUTHORIZATION ACT (*proposed*)
SHORT TITLE	SHORT TITLE
Section 1. This joint resolution may be cited as the "War Powers Resolution."	Section 1. This Act may be cited as the "Combat Authorization Act."
PURPOSE AND POLICY	PURPOSE AND POLICY
Sec. 2.(a) It is the purpose of this joint resolution to fulfill the intent of the framers of the Constitution of the United States and insure that the collective judgment of both the Congress and the President will apply to the introduction of United States Armed Forces into hostilities, or into situations where imminent involvement in hostilities is clearly indicated by the circumstances, and to the continued use of such forces in hostilities or in such situations.	Sec. 2. It is the purpose of this Act to fulfill the purpose of the Constitution of the United States and insure that the collective judgment of both the Congress and the President will apply to the introduction of United States Armed Forces into hostilities, or situations where there is an imminent danger of hostilities, and to the continued presence of United States forces in such situations.
(b) Under article I, section 8, of the Constitution, it is specifically provided that the Congress shall have the power to make all laws necessary and proper for carrying into execution, not only its own powers but also all other powers vested by the Constitution in the Government of the United States, or in any department or officer thereof.	[*eliminated*]
(c) The constitutional powers the President as Commander-in-Chief to introduce United States Armed Forces into hostilities, or into situations where imminent involvement in hostilities is clearly indicated by the circumstances, are exercised only pursuant to (1) a declaration of war, (2) specific statutory authorization, or (3) a national emergency created by attack upon the United States, its territories or possessions, or its armed forces.	[*eliminated*]

CONSULTATION

Sec. 3. The President in every possible instance shall consult with Congress before introducing United States Armed Forces into hostilities or into situations where imminent involvement in hostilities is clearly indicated by the circumstances, and after every such introduction shall consult regularly with the Congress until United States Armed Forces are no longer engaged in hostilities or have been removed from such situations.

CONSULTATION

Sec. 3.(a) Before introducing United States Armed Forces into hostilities or a situation where there is an imminent danger thereof, or retaining them in a location where hostilities or the imminent danger thereof has developed, the President shall in every possible instance consult with the representatives of Congress designated in subsections (b) and (c) of this section, discussing the situation fully and seeking their advice and counsel. So long as such a situation persists he shall consult regularly with said representatives, discussing the situation fully and seeking their advice and counsel.

Secs. 3.(b) and 3.(c) [defining Permanent Consultative Group. Use sections 3.(b) and 3.(c) of "Byrd-Nunn proposal," S.J. RES. 323, 100th Cong., 2d Sess.]

REPORTING

Sec. 4.(a) In the absence of a declaration of war, in any case in which the United States Armed Forces are introduced—

(1) into hostilities or into situations where imminent involvement in hostilities is clearly indicated by the circumstances;

(2) into the territory, airspace or waters of a foreign nation, while equipped for combat, except for deployments which relate solely to supply, replacement, repair, or training of such forces; or

(3) in numbers which substantially enlarge United States Armed Forces equipped for combat already located in a foreign nation;

The President shall submit within 48 hours to the Speaker of the House of Representatives and to the President pro tempore of the Senate a report, in writing, setting forth—

AUTHORIZATION

Sec. 4.(a) Before introducing United States Armed Forces into hostilities or a situation where there is an imminent danger thereof, or retaining them in a location where hostilities or the imminent danger thereof have developed, the President shall have obtained a declaration of war or specific statutory authorization as provided in section 7 of this act. *Provided, however,* that where a clear threat to the national security has developed so rapidly as to preclude Congress's advance consideration of such authorization, or keeping the pendency of the United States's response to such a threat secret prior to its initiation is clearly essential to its military effectiveness, the President may instead, at the latest simultaneously with the introduction of United States Armed Forces, submit to the Speaker of the House of Representatives and to the President pro tempore of the Senate a request for congressional authorization accompanied by a report, in writing, setting forth—

(A) the circumstances necessitating the introduction of United States Armed Forces;

(B) the constitutional and legislative authority under which such introduction took place; and

(C) the estimated scope and duration of the hostilities or involvement.

(1) the circumstances necessitating the introduction of such forces;

(2) the constitutional and legislative authority under which such introduction took place; and

(3) the estimated scope and duration of the hostilities or involvement.

An imminent danger of hostilities exists, inter alia, whenever there exists a substantial possibility that United States Armed Forces will be attacked, irrespective of any hope that the presence of such forces will deter such attack. Any person employed by, or under contract to, or under the direction of any department or agency of the United States government who is either engaged in hostilities in any foreign country or advising any regular or irregular military forces engaged in hostilities in any foreign country shall be deemed to be a member of the Armed Forces of the United States for purposes of this Act.

(b) The President shall provide such other information as the Congress may request in the fulfillment of its constitutional responsibilities with respect to committing the Nation to war and to the use of United States Armed Forces abroad.

(b) [*same as existing 4.(b)*]

(c) Whenever United States Armed Forces are introduced into hostilities or into any situation described in subsection (a) of this section, the President shall so long as such armed forces continue to be engaged in such hostilities or situation, report to Congress periodically on the status of such hostilities or situation as well as on the scope and duration of such hostilities or situation, but in no event shall he report to the Congress less often than once every six months.

[*eliminated as superfluous in light of proposed 3.(b) and 3.(c)*]

CONGRESSIONAL ACTION

CONGRESSIONAL ACTION;
JUDICIAL REVIEW

Sec. 5.(a) Each report submitted pursuant to section 4(a)(1) shall be transmitted to the Speaker of the House of Representatives and to the President pro tempore of the Senate on the same calendar day. Each report so transmitted shall be referred to the Committee on Foreign Affairs of the House of Representatives and to the Committee on Foreign Relations of the Senate for appropriate action. If, when the report is transmitted, the Congress has adjourned sine die or has adjourned for any period in excess of three calendar days, the Speaker of the House of Representatives and the President pro tempore of the Senate, if they deem it advisable (or if petitioned by at least 30 percent of the membership of their respective Houses) shall jointly request the President to convene Congress in order that it may consider the report and take appropriate action pursuant to this section.

Sec. 5.(a) [same as existing section 5.(a), substituting "4(a)" for "4(a)(1)"]

(b) Within sixty calendar days after a report is submitted or is required to be submitted pursuant to section 4(a)(1), whichever is earlier, the President shall terminate any use of United States Armed Forces with respect to which such report was submitted (or required to be submitted), unless the Congress (1) has declared war or has enacted a specific authorization for such use of United States Armed Forces, (2) has extended by law such sixty-day period, or (3) is physically unable to meet as a result of an armed attack upon the United States. Such sixty-day period shall be extended for not more than an additional thirty days if the President determines and certifies to the Congress in writing that unavoidable military necessity respecting the safety of the United States Armed Forces requires the continued use of such armed forces in the course of bringing about a prompt removal of such forces.

(b) Any member of the United States Armed Forces ordered to the relevant theatre of operations, or any Member of Congress, may bring an action in the United States District Court for the District of Columbia to enforce section 4(a) of this Act in the event the President has not complied therewith. Such action shall not be dismissed by the court on the ground that the plaintiff lacks standing, the case presents a political question, the case is unripe, or as an exercise of the court's equitable discretion. In the event the court finds that section 4(a) has not been complied with, it shall enter a declaratory judgment to that effect. A decision either entering or declining to enter such a judgment shall be directly appealable to the United States Supreme Court.

(c) Notwithstanding subsection (b), at any time that United States Armed Forces are engaged in hostilities outside the territory of the United States, its possessions and territories without a declaration of war or specific statutory authorization, such forces shall be removed by the President if the Congress so directs by concurrent resolution.

(c) Within twenty calendar days after a request for authorization is submitted by the President under section 4(a) or a judgment declaring that section 4(a) has not been complied with is entered under section 5(b), whichever is earlier, the President shall terminate any use of United States Armed Forces with respect to which such report was submitted or judgment entered, unless the Congress has declared war or has enacted a specific authorization for such use of United States Armed Forces, or is physically unable to meet as a result of an armed attack upon the United States. Where Congress is able to consider and vote on a declaration of war or specific authorization in fewer than twenty days after said report or judgment, it shall do so.

CONGRESSIONAL PRIORITY
PROCEDURES FOR JOINT
RESOLUTION OR BILL

Sec. 6. [not reprinted]

CONGRESSIONAL PRIORITY
PROCEDURES FOR JOINT
RESOLUTION OR BILL

[*existing provisions to be replicated, as adjusted for twenty-day clock*]

CONGRESSIONAL PRIORITY
PROCEDURES FOR
CONCURRENT RESOLUTION

Sec. 7. [not reprinted]

[*eliminated in light of elimination of existing section 5.(c)*]

INTERPRETATION OF
JOINT RESOLUTION

Sec. 8.(a) Authority to introduce United States Armed Forces into hostilities or into situations wherein involvement in hostilities is clearly indicated by the circumstances shall not be inferred—

(1) from any provision of law (whether or not in effect before the date of the enactment of this joint resolution) including any provision contained in any appropriation Act,

INTERPRETATION OF
THIS ACT

Sec. 7.(a) Authority to introduce United States Armed Forces into hostilities or into situations where there is an imminent danger of hostilities, or to retain them in a situation where hostilities or the imminent danger thereof has developed, shall not be inferred—

(1) from any provision of law, including any provision contained in any appropriation Act, unless such provision specifically authorizes such introduction or retention and states

unless such provision specifically authorizes the introduction of United States Armed Forces into hostilities or into such situations and states that it is intended to constitute specific statutory authorization within the meaning of this joint resolution; or

(2) from any treaty heretofore or hereafter ratified unless such treaty is implemented by legislation specifically authorizing the introduction of United States Armed Forces into hostilities or into such situations and stating that it is intended to constitute specific statutory authorization within the meaning of this joint resolution.

(b) Nothing in this joint resolution shall be construed to require any further specific statutory authorization to permit members of United States Armed Forces to participate jointly with members of the armed forces of one or more foreign countries in the headquarters operations of high-level military commands which were established prior to the date of enactment of this joint resolution and pursuant to the United Nations Charter or any treaty ratified by the United States prior to such date.

(c) For purposes of this joint resolution, the term "introduction of United States Armed Forces" includes the assignment of members of such armed forces to command, coordinate, participate in the movement of, or accompany the regular or irregular military forces of any foreign country or government when such military forces are engaged, or there exists an imminent threat that such forces will become engaged, in hostilities.

(d) Nothing in this joint resolution—

(1) is intended to alter the constitutional authority of the Congress or of the President, or the provisions of existing treaties; or

---

that it is intended to constitute specific statutory authorization within the meaning of this Act; or

(2) from any treaty heretofore or hereafter ratified unless such treaty is implemented by legislation specifically authorizing such introduction or retention, and stating that it is intended to constitute specific statutory authorization within the meaning of this Act.

(b) [same as existing section 8.(b), substituting "Act" for "joint resolution"]

(c) [same as existing section 8.(c), substituting "Act" for "joint resolution"]

[*eliminated*]

(2) shall be construed as granting any authority to the President with respect to the introduction of United States Armed Forces into hostilities or into situations wherein involvement in hostilities is clearly indicated by the circumstances which authority he would not have had in the absence of this joint resolution.

TERMINATION OF FUNDING

Sec. 8. No funds appropriated or otherwise made available under any law may be obligated or expended for any activity which would have the purpose or effect of violating any provision of the Act.

SEPARABILITY CLAUSE

Sec. 9. If any provision of this joint resolution or the application thereof to any person or circumstance is held invalid, the remainder of the joint resolution and the application of such provision to any other person or circumstance shall not be affected thereby.

SEPARABILITY CLAUSE

Sec. 9. [same as existing section 9, substituting "Act" for "joint resolution"]

Notes

PREFACE

1. "The Peace Dividend," N.Y. Rev. Books, June 28, 1990, p. 3.
2. The Cold War also produced disturbing violations of freedom of expression and the privacy of our homes and conversations. Aside from the striking advances that electronic devices have been able to contribute to the cause, however, I'm afraid that all this, while certainly unAmerican (if unAmerican includes unconstitutional) is pretty traditional in this country. Certainly it did not start—as the trends noted in the text essentially did—with the Cold War; throughout our history "subversives" have been searched and silenced.

CHAPTER 1
THE CONSTITUTIONAL FRAMEWORK

1. 2 Debates in the Several State Conventions on the Adoption of the Federal Constitution 528 (J. Elliot ed. 1863).
2. Remarks before the Texas State Republican Convention, Dallas, Texas, June 20, 1992.
3. U.S. Const. art. I, § 8, cl. 11. (In contrast to other provisions, the document doesn't provide that the president is to declare war "with the advice and consent" of Congress (let alone the Senate) or even that Congress is to do so "on the recommendation" of the president.) To Congress also are granted the powers to raise and support armies, to provide and maintain a navy, to make rules for the government and regulation of the armed forces, to provide for calling forth, organizing, and disciplining the militia, to grant letters of marque and reprisal, and to make rules concerning captures. Id. cls. 11–16. "[A]ll these are powers naturally connected with the power of declaring war. All these powers, therefore, are vested in Congress." 1 The Works of James Wilson 433 (R. McCloskey ed. 1967). The clauses providing that habeas corpus is to be suspended only in cases of invasion or rebellion, and that the states are not to make war unless invaded or in imminent danger thereof, are contained in Article I (the legislative article). Article II grants the president but four powers bearing on foreign relations—the power to receive ambassadors (which is his alone), the powers to appoint ambassadors and make treaties (each of which must be exercised jointly, with the advice and consent of the Senate), and the power to act as commander in chief (which depends on Congress's having authorized a war, note 22 infra).
4. The early cases insisted on congressional authorization without pausing to evaluate the size of the conflict. E.g., Bas v. Tingy, 4 U.S. 32, 35–36, 4 Dall. 37, 40 (1800) (Washington, J.) ("every contention by force, between two nations, in external matters, under the authority of their respective governments, is not only war, but public war"); Talbot v. Seeman, 5 U.S. 1, 18, 1 Cranch 1, 27–28 (1801); Little v. Barreme, 6 U.S. 99, 2 Cranch 170 (1804). Clause 11's coupling of the war power

with the power to grant letters of marque and reprisal underscores the founders' intention to require congressional authorization of military actions that fall short of what would conventionally have been counted wars. See pp. 66–67. This makes eminent good sense. "Historically, governments have repeatedly embarked on 'splendid little wars' only to have them turn into long, drawn-out disasters." Allison, "Making War: The President and Congress," 40 Law & Contemp. Prob. 86, 92 (1976). And even wars that stay small carry major moral and political costs.

5. "[T]he ceremony of a formal denunciation of war has of late fallen into disuse. . . ." The Federalist No. 25, at 211 (Hamilton) (B. Wright ed. 1961). See generally J. Maurice, Hostilities Without a Declaration of War (1883). While formal declarations of war experienced something of a renaissance in the late nineteenth century, they are again essentially obsolete, worldwide. The last I have been able to identify was issued during the 1948 Arab-Israeli War (though such a claim is necessarily shaky, given the lack of a bright-line test for determining what ought to be counted as a declaration of war).

In light of the War Clause's manifest purpose of requiring congressional authorization before Americans were sent to die, it would have been farcical to hold that declared wars had to be declared by Congress but the president could on his own involve us in undeclared wars, and the courts did not for a moment consider doing so.

6. Note that the requirement is that wars be authorized by *the legislative process*, which in our system entails (in addition to congressional action) either the approval of the president or passage over his veto by a two-thirds vote of both houses. This refinement is not likely to become directly relevant (suppose they gave a war and the commander in chief didn't come) though it will become tangentially germane to the debate over section 5(c) of the War Powers Resolution of 1973. Note 21 to the appendix.

7. The Butler-Gerry interchange appears at 2 The Records of the Federal Convention of 1787, at 318 (M. Farrand ed. 1911). The relevant Philadelphia debates are usefully summarized in Lofgren, "War-Making Under the Constitution: The Original Understanding," 81 Yale L.J. 672, 675–83 (1972), and Bestor, "Separation of Powers in the Domain of Foreign Affairs: The Intent of the Constitution Historically Examined," 5 Seton Hall L. Rev. 527 (1974).

8. Butler's report of the Philadelphia debate to the South Carolina ratifying convention was a trifle unforthcoming respecting his own earlier role: "Some gentlemen were inclined to give this power to the President; but . . . " 4 Elliot's Debates, supra note 1, at 263.

Of seventy-seven amendments to the Constitution that various states proposed at their ratifying conventions, only one (New York's) dealt with the war power, and that one left it with Congress: In fact it proposed that a two-thirds vote of both houses be required. 1 id. at 330.

9. 1 Farrand, supra note 7, at 316.

10. See also p. 59. Thus, as so often, they pursued a substantive end (the limitation of war to the absolutely necessary) by procedural means (requiring the concurrence of both houses of Congress as well as the president)—a relationship that for reasons themselves elusive has eluded some prominent critics of *Democracy and Distrust*.

11. Letter from James Madison to Thomas Jefferson, Apr. 2, 1798, in 6 The Writings of James Madison 312–13 (G. Hunt ed. 1906). See also, e.g., 2 Farrand, supra note 7, at 319 (George Mason); C. Bowen, Miracle at Philadelphia 60 (1966) (Benjamin Franklin).

12. 2 Farrand, supra note 7, at 319 (Mason).

13. 2 J. Story, Commentaries on the Constitution of the United States § 1166 (1833).

14. See Van Alstyne, "Congress, the President, and the Power to Declare War: A Requiem for Vietnam," 121 U. Pa. L. Rev. 1, 20 (1972).

15. 2 J. Story, supra note 13, § 1166.

16. Though the differences between the House and Senate are no longer so marked as they were at the outset, the effect of congressional debate on public debate is one we all have personally witnessed: The contrast between public discussion prior to Operation Desert Storm and the lack of it preceding the many recent wars that have not been congressionally authorized was stark. Cf. *Pravda*'s commentary on the occasion of the withdrawal of Soviet troops from Afghanistan: "One can say that in the future such vital issues as the use of troops must not be decided in secrecy, without the approval of the country's Parliament." Quoted in N.Y. Times, Feb. 16, 1989, at A4.

17. This was hardly unique to Vietnam (where, we shall see, the authorization was actually moderately clear). For example, California Senator William Knowland, an early enthusiastic booster of the "police action" in Korea, later accused President Truman of involving the United States in "a war which has resulted in 65,000 casualties without a declaration by the Congress." Hearings on the Military Situation in the Far East before the House Comms. on Armed Services and Foreign Relations, 82d Cong., 1st Sess., pt. 2, at 765, 933 (1951).

18. Stockdale, "On Public Virtue," in Thinking About America: The United States in the 1990s, at 479, 480–81 (A. Anderson & D. Bark eds. 1988).

19. See, e.g., Trainor, "Vietnam Experience Has Made the Joint Chiefs Cautious About Using Military Force," N.Y. Times, Aug. 17, 1989, at A13 (remarks of Marine Corps Commandant Alfred M. Gray); C. Arnson, Crossroads: Congress, the Reagan Administration, and Central America 88 (1989) ("After Vietnam, the Pentagon was not about to commit U.S. troops abroad without a solid domestic consensus to back them"); J. Smith, George Bush's War 241 (1992) (remarks of National Security Adviser Brent Scowcroft); N.Y. Times, Nov. 29, 1984, at A5 (speech of Defense Secretary Caspar Weinberger). Cf. Caridi, "The G.O.P. and the Korean War," 37 Pac. Hist. Rev. 423, 440 (1968) ("Eleven generals [pre-Eisenhower, Thomas Dewey] noted, had become American presidents without a major war occurring during the terms of these men . . . ."). Eisenhower himself was unusually deferential to Congress on the question whether to expose troops to hostilities. See, e.g., p. 47; Public Papers of the Presidents of the United States: Dwight D. Eisenhower, 1954, at 306 ("I will say this: there is going to be no involvement of America in war unless it is a result of the constitutional process that is placed upon Congress to declare it. Now, let us have that clear; and that is the answer."). See also id. at 1076–77; J. Smith, supra, at 90; H. Arendt, Crises of the Republic 21 (1972). However, while Eisenhower was chary about committing troops, he was not shy about

using the CIA: The overthrows of Mossedegh and Arbenz both occurred while he was president, suggesting that his concern may have been more with the lives of American soldiers than with constitutional niceties. President Carter, probably our most deferential president since Eisenhower, was a graduate of the Naval Academy.

20. Hearings before the Senate Comm. on Foreign Relations, 97th Cong., 1st Sess. 39 (1981).

21. 2 Farrand, supra note 7, at 318–19. In addition to the Lofgren and Bestor discussions cited in note 7 supra, see W. Reveley, War Powers of the President and Congress: Who Holds the Arrows and Olive Branch? 64, 83–84 (1981). The change from "make" to "declare" was supported by delegates who subsequently refused to sign the Constitution on the ground that it gave too much power to the president. S. Rep. No. 797, 90th Cong., 1st Sess. 8 (1967). The framers generally continued to speak of the power of Congress to "make" war as if no change had been effected. Lofgren, supra note 7, at 684–85. It is also worth noting that articles VI and IX of the Articles of Confederation had used the terms "declare," "determine on," and "engage in" interchangeably when referring to entry into war. See also Adler, "The Constitution and Presidential Warmaking: The Enduring Debate," 103 Pol. Sci. Q. 1, 6 (1988) ("[A]s early as 1552, the verb 'declare' had become synonymous with the verb 'commence'; they both meant the initiation of hostilities.") (footnote omitted).

22. In 1793 James Madison wrote that it is necessary carefully to distinguish the power that a commander in chief has "to *conduct a war*" from the power to decide "whether *a war ought* to be *commenced, continued, or concluded*." 6 Madison's Writings, supra note 11, at 148 (emphasis in original). This accords with Alexander Hamilton's Plan of June 18, 1787, whereby the Senate was to be given "the sole power of declaring war" and the chief executive (styled the Governour) would have "direction of the war" but only "when authorized or begun." 1 Farrand, supra note 7, at 258, 292. Of the plan actually adopted Hamilton—conspicuously the time's leading proponent of executive power—subsequently wrote:

> The President is to be commander-in chief of the army and navy of the United States. [This] would amount to nothing more than the supreme command and direction of the military and naval forces, as first general and admiral of the Confederacy; while that of the British king extends to the *declaring* of war and to the *raising* and *regulating* of fleets and armies,—all which, by the Constitution under consideration, would appertain to the legislature.

The Federalist, supra note 5, No. 69, at 446 (emphasis in original). This position was subsequently endorsed by the Supreme Court, Fleming v. Page, 50 U.S. 634, 646–47, 9 How. 603, 615 (1850), and accords with the colonial usage of the term (denoting the highest military officer in a chain of command). Adler, supra note 21, at 9–13; W. Reveley, supra note 21, at 57; F. Wormuth & E. Firmage, To Chain the Dog of War: The War Power of Congress in History and Law 109–10 (2d ed. 1989). Wholly missing in either the Philadelphia debates or the *Federalist*, A. Sofaer, War, Foreign Affairs, and Constitutional Power: The Origins 36, 48 (1976), or in the ratification debates, W. Reveley, supra, at 103–4, is any broader construction of the term. The Federalists did not construe it broadly in an effort to build the power of the executive, Lofgren, supra note 7, at 686, and neither did the Antifederalists as part of their attack on the inordinate executive power allegedly created by the document they were seeking to defeat. Lofgren, "On War-Making, Original Intent, and Ultra-Whiggery," 21 Val. U. L. Rev. 53, 65 (1986); W. Reveley, supra, at 102–3, 114.

Were there not another constitutional provision so clearly indicating that it is up to the legislature to decide whether we go to war, it might conceivably have been permissible to permit the Commander in Chief Clause to expand over time to encompass that decision. The executive power to "receive Ambassadors," for example, was almost certainly originally intended to be ceremonial only. E.g., The Federalist, supra, No. 69, at 448 (Hamilton) ("more a matter of dignity than of authority"). Yet it has been expanded over time to encompass the substantively more important authority to recognize foreign governments. The overwhelming bulk of foreign affairs powers being assigned by the document to Congress, note 3 supra, this might more reasonably have gone the other way. But it seems a permissible development, as—in both respects unlike our case—(a) the development has been longstanding, unbroken, pursued to the knowledge of and unquestioned by Congress, and judicially recognized, and (b) there is no other constitutional provision indicating that the power in question (here, to recognize governments) is to reside elsewhere. The commander in chief power *has* expanded in some directions plainly not contemplated at the beginning, most notably to encompass authority to decide where to deploy troops in peacetime, which development would seem to accord with these two criteria, at least where such deployment does not create a likelihood of hostilities (in which instance the War Clause would indicate the decision should be Congress's. This last suggests that the House of Representatives was correct in censuring President Polk for unconstitutional behavior in placing our troops so as to induce the attack that began the Mexican War, see p. 96, though it is difficult to imagine such a judgment's becoming judicially cognizable.)

You will be pleased to learn that there is at least one issue I do not propose to try to settle in this book—namely, the point at which congressional limitation of the parameters of a war it has previously authorized becomes a violation of the Commander in Chief Clause. That issue is not implicated by the debate over the Eagleton Amendment ending the bombing of Cambodia, pp. 39–46, as that bombing was at the time all that was left of the American military involvement in Indochina, and all agree that Congress can end a war if it can secure a presidential signature or override his veto. The statute prohibiting American ground troops in Thailand and Laos, see p. 28, is one whose constitutionality I do not discuss. It seems to be assumed that Congress can limit the geographical scope of a war, cf. note 127 to chapter 2, but this statute didn't exactly do that; rather it precluded one kind of military effort in areas it did not otherwise exclude from the theatre of operations. Statutory preclusion of the use of a specific weapon in an otherwise authorized war would seem to present somewhat similar problems. But cf. Little v. Barreme, supra note 4; Act of March 3, 1799, ch. 48, 1 Stat. 749 (defining, inter alia, the rations to which troops were to be entitled—"eighteen ounces of bread or flour, or when neither can be obtained, one quart of rice and an half pound of sifted or bolted Indian meal," etc.).

23. The meaning of this reservation will be explored at pp. 6–7, 76, 108–9.

24. Bork, "Erosion of the President's Power in Foreign Affairs," 68 Wash. U. L.Q. 693, 698 (1990). The suggestion seems out of accord with Judge Bork's usual strongly argued "original intent" approach to constitutional interpretation. Bork,

however, is not alone among "originalists" in his inconsistency on the subject of executive power. See, e.g., Schlesinger, "The Legislative-Executive Balance in International Affairs; The Intentions of the Framers," 12 Wash. Q. 99, 105 (1989) ("Whatever happened to Meese's passion for original intent when his president, without congressional authorization, initiated military action in Grenada, Lebanon, Libya, and the Persian Gulf?").

25. See, e.g., Note, "The Bounds of Legislative Specification: A Suggested Approach to the Bill of Attainder Clause," 72 Yale L.J. 330 (1962); United States v. Brown, 381 U.S. 437 (1965); Note, "Corruption of Blood and Equal Protection: Why the Sins of the Parents Should Not Matter," 44 Stan. L. Rev. 727 (1992); pp. 66–67, 74–75, 106 (Marque and Reprisal Clause).

26. "[P]eople who say the Constitution is not a suicide pact often mean that it is not an inconvenience pact. The Constitution, however, is precisely an inconvenience pact. That is the definition of a constitution." Panel, "The Treaty Power," 43 U. Miami L. Rev. 101, 135 (1988) (remarks of Judge Grover Rees).

27. As an occasional slip makes clear, the real reason such officials find it unthinkable that the approval of another branch might still be constitutionally required—this is hardly unique to this area, we find it throughout the constitutional arguments of those of every political persuasion—is that they're afraid that other branch might "make a mistake" (that is, disagree with them). "The reason for the practice and the rule are rooted in the nature of things. The President is often called upon to prepare or initiate lines of policy for which public and congressional opinion is not yet ready." E. Rostow, President, Prime Minister, or Constitutional Monarch? 26 (1988). (Beware "the nature of things.") See also J. Smith, supra note 19, at 237 (quoting George Bush) ("If I have to go [to war], it's not going to matter to me if there isn't one congressman who supports this, or what happens to public opinion. If it's right, it's gotta be done."). In such sentiments Rostow and Bush are following a familiar Lippmannesque Cold War tradition. See, e.g., R. Barnet, The Rocket's Red Glare: When America Goes to War 15 (1990) ("Dean Acheson once wrote that if you did what the people wanted in foreign policy, 'You'd go wrong every time.'").

28. See, e.g., F. Wormuth & E. Firmage, supra note 22, at 278 (quoting Edwin Corwin); B. Eckhardt & C. Black, The Tides of Power: Conversations on the American Constitution 39–40 (1976). At least in 1993 the world seems divided into potential enemies we so clearly overwhelm that time is not likely to (though admittedly on occasion it might) be of the essence, and those sufficiently strong to require months of mobilization before we could, given what Vietnam is conventionally taken to have taught us about the folly of starting small and ratcheting up, sensibly commence hostilities. See J. Smith, supra note 19, at 85–86.

29. If troops and equipment can be dispatched to the front, a cabinet officer can surely be dispatched to Capitol Hill (even faster, one would suppose).

30. See, e.g., Adler, supra note 21, at 8; F. Wormuth & E. Firmage, supra note 22, at 298–99.

31. A third reading, that the president may without authorization wage "defensive" war (anywhere)—e.g., Emerson, "Making War Without a Declaration," 17 J. Legis. 23, 30 n.51 (1990); Carter, "Going to War Over War Powers," Wash. Post, Nov. 18, 1990, at C4—is unacceptably loose and finds no serious support in the framers' thinking: Today (and to a large extent then as well) "[t]he justification for

nearly every war is self-defense." G. Perret, A Country Made by War: From the Revolution to Vietnam—The Story of America's Rise to Power 150 (1989). Cf. the name change from "War Department" to "Defense Department"; "the best defense is a good offense."

32. See, e.g., Martin v. Mott, 25 U.S. 12, 18, 12 Wheat. 19, 29 (1827) ("In our opinion there is no room for doubt on this point . . . the power to provide for repelling invasions includes the power to provide against the attempt and danger of invasion, as the necessary and proper means to effectuate the object. One of the best means to repel invasions is to provide the requisite forces for action, before the invader himself has reached the soil."). Cf. U.S. Arts. Confederation, art. VI ("No State shall engage in any war without the consent of the United States in Congress assembled, unless such State be actually invaded by enemies, or shall have received certain advice of a resolution being formed by some nation of Indians to invade such State, and the danger is so imminent as not to admit of a delay, till the United States in Congress assembled can be consulted . . . ."). On the one hand this provision seems to assimilate preemptive strikes to defensive actions; on the other, one could stress that the Constitution does not contain comparable language. E.g., Berger, "War-Making by the President," 121 U. Pa. L. Rev. 29, 43–45 (1972).

33. It also seems that committed apologists for executive military power are unusually likely also to be persons who would characterize a wide variety of situations as instances in which no sensible person would suppose we shouldn't respond militarily (and thus in which congressional approval should be treated as a needless formality).

34. I say "properly" rather than "constitutionally" because the metaphysics of this view seem generally to have been that although the executive would technically be acting unconstitutionally in such a situation, he would nonetheless be acting correctly. See J. Locke, Two Treatises of Government §§ 159–60, at 392–93 (P. Laslett ed. 1970); 1 A Compilation of the Messages and Papers of the Presidents 1789–1897, at 428 (J. Richardson ed. 1896) (Jefferson); see generally Lobel, "Emergency Power and the Decline of Liberalism," 98 Yale L.J. 1385, 1392–97 (1989). (Locke's sometime further suggestion that the executive might in an emergency properly act *contrary* to existing legislative direction—again the idea was that he would be acting illegally but should be pardoned for doing so—has not been accepted in this country. 2 Works of James Wilson, supra note 3, at 754–56; Wilmerding, "The President and the Law," 67 Pol. Sci. Q. 321 (1952).)

35. U.S. Const. art. I, § 10, cl. 3 (emphasis added). See also U.S. Arts. Confederation, art. VI, quoted note 32 supra; 6 The Works of Daniel Webster 261 (1851) (right of international self-defense rests on showing of necessity "instant, overwhelming, leaving no means of choice, no moment for deliberation").

36. In contour it resembles the settled and relatively uncontroversial doctrine that the Fourth Amendment requires a search warrant unless emergency conditions have created a situation where there has not been time to procure one (though there is no comparable requirement that a warrant be procured as soon as a warrantless search has been commenced—searches, unlike wars, generally ending within minutes after they are begun).

37. The "no sensible person could disagree" rationale being incapable of principled elucidation, the only plausible alternative would be to read the reservation to require *both* that there be no time to secure advance authorization *and* that the

emergency in question involve an actual attack on United States territory. It seems unlikely, however, that anyone would take the latter requirement entirely seriously (Canada, Mexico, preemptive strikes, etc.), which changes the question from whether to give the reservation a functional interpretation to *which* functional interpretation to adopt.

38. "The invasion of Grenada in October 1983 was neither authorized nor specifically funded by Congress, yet the President was able to employ the standing armed forces nonetheless." F. Wormuth & E. Firmage, supra note 22, at 279. More extended operations will at some point require additional funding, but once an operation has begun, it has become notoriously difficult for Congress to turn off the spigot. Thus although early in our history it might have been responsible to regard the requirement of advance congressional authorization of military action as not that independently important—though even that characterization couldn't make it go away—today it would not be, given the constant availability of forces the president can order into combat without special appropriations (to say nothing of the seriously reduced possibility that Congress might actually vote to end a war the president has started).

Another change, this one recent, that has heightened the importance of the requirement of advance congressional authorization is the abolition of the legislative veto in INS v. Chadha, 462 U.S. 919 (1983). See pp. 119–20.

39. Countries with universal military service, such as Germany, seem to have more widespread public debate on matters military (though admittedly in the case of Germany there are other factors at work).

40. See generally J. Smith, supra note 19.

41. See, e.g., N.Y. Times, Jan. 19, 1992, p. A1 ("White House Weighs Proposals to Topple Hussein Before U.S. Presidential Vote"); Saphire, "Comeback Coming," N.Y. Times, Feb. 27, 1992, p. A19 (predicting election-year military action against Saddam Hussein, Qadaffi, and/or Kim Il Sung). It is to President Bush's credit that he did not succumb. We should not assume, however, that the lesson of what the Falklands did for the Tories has been forever lost.

42. This assumes the war in question is one that should be fought, but that is something else the requirement of advance congressional authorization is designed to help assure. (Authorization provides some assurance of worth; worthy wars should be supported; authorization provides some assurance of support.)

43. Randall McNally, "The Legality of the Decision to Go to War Against Iraq," Mar. 5, 1991, at 20–21.

44. Letter from Abraham Lincoln to William H. Herndon (Feb. 15, 1848), in 2 The Writings of Abraham Lincoln 52 (A. Lapsley ed. 1905).

45. E.g., W. Reveley, supra note 21, at 121–22. Neither is this entirely ancient history: The Desert Storm debate in the Senate was thoughtful, the final vote 52–47. All this does not necessarily mean that Congress has invariably been less "hawkish" than the executive. John Adams courageously resisted congressional calls for an all-out declaration of war against France in 1798; Madison was cajoled into the War of 1812 by a Congress less ambivalent than he; and Cleveland successfully resisted pressures for a war against Spain in 1896, pressures that became so strong that McKinley reluctantly acceded to them two years later.

46. See also A. Schlesinger, Jr., The Imperial Presidency 296–98 (1973). Compare the quarrel between Professors Henkin and Trimble over whether the presi-

dency or Congress is the more "democratic" institution. Trimble, Review of L. Henkin, Constitutionalism, Democracy, and Foreign Affairs (1990), 89 Harv. L. Rev. 1371 (1991). Each is democratic in its own way: That's why the framers required the assent of both before we went to war.

47. Hearings on War Powers, Libya, and State-Sponsored Terrorism before the Subcomm. on Arms Control, International Security and Science of the House Comm. on Foreign Affairs, 99th Cong., 2d Sess. 88 (1986) (quoted by J. Brian Atwood).

48. Powell v. McCormack, 395 U.S. 486, 546–47 (1969).

49. Actually this was basically the question in *Chadha*, supra note 38, and the Court went the other way, overruling what had been a frequent prior practice— sometimes acquiesced in by the executive, sometimes not, but always entirely open, compare p. 10—albeit a practice dating back only to 1932.

50. "The relevance of prior [practice] is largely limited to the insight [it] afford[s] in correctly ascertaining the draftsmen's intent. Obviously, therefore, the precedential value of these cases tends to increase in proportion to their proximity to the Convention in 1787." Powell v. McCormack, 395 U.S. 486, 547 (1969). ("Of these 81 [members of the First Congress], 54 had been members of the Constitutional Convention or of state ratifying conventions; only 7 had opposed ratification." A. Sofaer, supra note 22, at 61. And of course our first president presided at the Philadelphia convention.)

51. Sometimes the argument is made in essence that the Commander in Chief Clause covered the same ground as the War Clause, thereby creating by contradiction the equivalent of an empty vessel whose meaning would have to be supplied by experience. We have seen, however, that no such contradiction was even remotely engineered: The unequivocal meaning of the original document was that Congress was to start wars, the president to fight them. Note 22 supra.

52. For the nonlawyers: "Adverse possession" is the process whereby one person's notorious and exclusive use of another's property over a specified period of years accompanied by a public claim of right can result in his legally acquiring it. In addition to the problems noted in the text, the situations are not analogous, in that the interests of the "property holder" and the "adverse claimant" (here, Congress and the president) are not all that's (or even primarily what's) at stake here.

53. Youngstown Sheet & Tube Co. v. Sawyer, 343 U.S. 579, 610 (1952) (Frankfurter, J., concurring). Frankfurter himself found his test not to have been satisfied in *Youngstown*, and the Court's opinion pointedly rejected even the possibility of such prescriptive acquisition. Id. at 588–89. In addition, *Youngstown* was a naked "legislative power" vs. "executive power" case lacking the intervention of a more precise provision. Compare note 22 supra. All the evidence suggests that none of the nine justices would have accepted the possibility of prescriptive executive acquisition of the war power.

54. "[T]he practice of American Presidents for over a century after independence showed scrupulous respect for the authority of the Congress except in a few instances." S. Rep. No. 797, 90th Cong., 1st Sess. 23 (1967). Such claims of general compliance with a stated norm are difficult to document with anything approaching elegance. Trudging across acres of lawful behavior is unbearably boring for both writer and reader, and placing the arguable counterexamples in perspective often serves only to convey the mistaken impression that the counterexamples represent

the norm. (Cf. J. Ely, Democracy and Distrust: A Theory of Judicial Review 92* (1980): "I realize that by stressing the few occasions on which values *were* singled out for protection, I run the risk of conveying the impression that that is the character of much of the Constitution." This prediction has been amply borne out by much critical reaction.) Two careful and balanced volumes commissioned by the American Bar Association—A. Sofaer, supra note 22, and H. Cox, War, Foreign Affairs, and Constitutional Power: 1829–1901 (1984)—cover the period from the founding through 1901 and strongly support the claim of general compliance throughout that period. Arrays of compliant statements (and behavior) by essentially all our presidents pre-Truman (plus, emphatically, Eisenhower)—to the effect that the decision to authorize acts of war rests unequivocally with Congress—can be found at, e.g., W. Reveley, supra note 21, App. B; A. Thomas & A. Thomas, The War-Making Powers of the President: Constitutional and International Law Aspects, chap. 5 (1982); Adler, supra note 21, at 17–26; Berger, supra note 32, at 61–65; Bickel et al., "Indochina: The Constitutional Crisis," reprinted in 116 Cong. Rec. 15409, 15415–16 (1970) (statement of fourteen prominent law professors and lawyers); Hearings on S. 731, S.J. Res. 18 and S.J. Res. 59 before the Senate Comm. on Foreign Relations, 92d Cong., 1st Sess. 805–8 (appendix to testimony of Leon Friedman).

In search of verisimilitude—cf. Joseph McCarthy's "two hundred and five" Communists working in the State Department—proponents of broad executive power often cite the "exact number" of congressionally unauthorized presidential military incursions in our history. (The number varies from advocate to advocate and, of course, with time.) Thus in 1966, defending the constitutionality of the war in Vietnam, the memorandum of the State Department Legal Adviser's Office stated (without citation or elucidation): "Since the Constitution was adopted there have been at least 125 instances in which the President has ordered the armed forces to take action or maintain positions abroad without obtaining prior Congressional authorization, starting with the 'undeclared war' with France (1798–1800)." Office of the Legal Adviser, U.S. Dep't of State, "The Legality of United States Participation in the Defense of Viet Nam," reprinted in 75 Yale L.J. 1085, 1101 (1966). That's certainly a lot—a Vietnam precedent every sixteen months throughout our history! The memorandum is also dead wrong about the example cited: The undeclared war with France was authorized by Congress clearly, repeatedly, and in advance, as everyone, including President Adams, believed it had to be. It therefore may not surprise that on close analysis these "lists" tend to evaporate. See, particularly, the devastating analysis at F. Wormuth & E. Firmage, supra note 22, at 135–51.

> [T]he majority of the nineteenth century uses of force . . . were minor undertakings, designed to protect American citizens or property, or to revenge a slight to national honor, and most involved no combat, or even its likelihood, with the forces of another state. To use force abroad on a notable scale, the President of necessity would have had to request Congress to augment the standing Army and Navy.

Reveley, "Presidential War-Making: Constitutional Prerogative or Usurpation?," 55 Va. L. Rev. 1243, 1258 (1969) (footnotes omitted). Accord, A. Schlesinger, Jr., supra note 46, at 50–54; Moore, "The National Executive and the Use of the Armed Forces Abroad," in 2 The Vietnam War and International Law 812 (R. Falk ed.

1969); Hearings on S. Res. 151 before the Senate Comm. on Foreign Relations, 90th Cong., 1st Sess. 81 (1967) (testimony of Under Secretary of State Nicholas Katzenbach); Hearings on War Powers Legislation before the Senate Comm. on Foreign Relations, 92d Cong., 1st Sess. 7–8 (1971) (testimony of Professor Henry Steele Commager). Indeed, a large percentage of the episodes on these lists involved action by some military commander that had not been authorized by the president or, often, by any higher authority whatever. Surely the claim cannot be, though logic might suggest such an extension, that "history" has therefore established a constitutional prerogative on the part of *military officers* to initiate hostilities on their own motion.

In addition to their relative inconsequence, these engagements tended to fall into several fairly well understood categories. Professor Corwin summarized them as "fights with pirates, landings of small naval contingents on barbarous or semi-barbarous coasts, the dispatch of small bodies of troops to chase bandits or cattle rustlers across the Mexican border." Corwin, "The President's Power," in The President's Role and Powers 361 (D. Haight & L. Johnson eds. 1965).

> In 1967 the State Department compiled an official list of 137 instances where it asserted the president . . . committed acts of war on his own authority . . . . Careful scrutiny of the examples provided by the government belies this assertion: eight of the acts involved enforcement of the law against piracy for which no congressional authorization is required, sixty-nine were landings to protect American citizens many of which were statutorily authorized, twenty concerned illegal invasions of foreign or disputed territories which were not acts of war since the United States claimed the territory, six were minatory demonstrations without combat, another six involved protracted occupations of various Caribbean states that were authorized by treaty, and at least one was an act of naval self-defense . . . .

Firmage, "Rogue Presidents and the War Power of Congress," 11 Geo. Mason U. L. Rev. 79, 83–84 (1988).

> The vast majority of the incidents involved landings to protect American property or lives abroad. Generally undertaken during periods of disorder or civil unrest when local authorities could no longer provide protection against ordinary outlawry, these landings were, at least superficially, intended to maintain strict neutrality between contesting political factions.

Note, "Congress, the President, and the Power to Commit Forces to Combat," 81 Harv. L. Rev. 1771, 1788 (1968) (footnotes omitted). Further on this "neutrality theory," see A. Schlesinger, Jr., supra, at 50–51; Berger, supra, at 58–59.

Unfortunately if predictably, the exception for "savages" or "barbarous" people—which developed late, as our early actions against various Native American tribes were in general congressionally authorized—degenerated into what in retrospect appears to have been only slightly adorned racism, and was used explicitly or implicitly in the early twentieth century to justify unauthorized incursions against such non-European peoples as the Chinese, and throughout Central America. (Note that we *did* declare war on Spain; the contrast between our treatment of Mexico and Canada is also instructive.) See T. Eagleton, War and Presidential Power: A Chronicle of Congressional Surrender 46–58 (1974); J. Javits, Who Makes War 52, 74, 94, 113–14, 144, 197–98 (1973). Cf. F. Calhoun, Power and Principle: Armed Intervention in Wilsonian Foreign Policy 27–28 (1986), contrasting Secretary of State William Jennings Bryan's pacifism toward Europe, which ultimately led to his resignation, with his pugnaciousness toward our Latin American neighbors. "The secretary feared war with civilized, which he defined as European, powers, but he considered interventions in less developed lands as a duty from which America could not escape." Id. at 130. (Would it be too much of a stretch to suggest that the nations we used to feel merited a declaration of war are the ones we wouldn't dream of going to war against under any conditions now?) Now that we understand (or should) the unacceptability of treating non-Europeans as undeserving of the usual constitutional rules, it is clear that such campaigns should not serve as precedents. Precedent should be found, instead, in the way our forebears felt obliged to treat those they were prepared to recognize as full persons. (Alternative theories sometimes used to justify such interventions were that those we were proceeding against weren't really in a position to fight back, and that the entire Western Hemisphere essentially belonged to us, or at least that the Caribbean was an "American lake." Neither of those seems any more acceptable as a source of precedent applicable to contemporary conditions.)

President Lincoln's actions at the outset of the Civil War are sometimes cited as precedent for presidential military ventures. Although Lincoln did engage in a number of unconstitutional acts during this period, e.g., A. Schlesinger, Jr., supra, at 58, usurpation of the war power was not among them. For me the important fact here is not that Congress retroactively authorized what Lincoln had done, since the reasons why that should count seem murky at best, but cf. note 55 to chapter 4, but rather that for constitutional purposes a domestic rebellion is quite different from a foreign war. In any event, congressional acts of 1795 and 1807 had empowered the president to use the military to suppress insurrection against the government of the United States. The Prize Cases, 67 U.S. (2 Black) 635, 668 (1863).

55. [T]he number of cases in which Presidents have personally made the decisions, unconstitutionally, to engage in . . . acts of war probably lies between one and two dozen. And in all those cases the Presidents have made false claims of authorization, either by statute or by treaty or by international law. They have not relied on their powers as commander in chief or as chief executive.

F. Wormuth & E. Firmage, supra note 22, at 151. See also, e.g., W. Reveley, supra note 21, at 122–23; Sofaer, "The Presidency, War, and Foreign Affairs: Practice Under the Framers," 40 Law & Contemp. Prob. 12, 36–37 (1976). On the beginnings of the Mexican War, see H. Cox, supra note 54, at 141–55 (1984); on the House of Representatives' censure of Polk, see Berger, supra note 32, at 65. "Both Presidents [Wilson and Franklin Roosevelt] were forced [sic] to resort to deception and flagrant disregard of Congress in military deployment decisions because they were unable to rally congressional backing for action essential to national security." Reveley, supra note 54, 1262. On Wilson, see C. Berdahl, War Powers of the Executive in the United States 68–70 (1921). On Roosevelt, see 1 W. Manchester, The Glory and the Dream 268, 282–85 (1974); W. Stevenson, A Man Called Intrepid 155–58, 254 (1976); Bernstein, "The Road to Watergate and Beyond: The Growth and Abuse of Executive Authority Since 1940," 40 Law & Contemp. Prob. 58, 76–77 (1976). Still Roosevelt, like his predecessors, replied to the French in his 1940 "Utmost Sympathy Speech" that his statements carried no promise of military aid. "Only the Congress can make such commitments," he said. E. Corwin, The President: Office and Powers 1787–1957, at 246 (4th rev. ed. 1957). In fact "what seems most striking in this period was not Roosevelt's arbitrariness in pushing the country toward war but rather his caution and restraint." R. Dallek, Franklin D. Roosevelt and American Foreign Policy 531 (1979); see also W. Heinrichs, Threshold of War: Franklin D. Roosevelt and American Entry Into World War II (1988). At no point prior to Congress's declaration of war did he succumb to the more modern tendency to advert to his supposed authority as commander in chief as opposed to powers he had been congressionally granted. A. Schlesinger, Jr., supra note 46, at 113.

Neither, plainly, can either (a) Theodore Roosevelt's "Hey, I was naughty, but I got the job done, didn't I?" boasts, e.g., T. Eagleton, supra note 54, at 48–49, or (b) our Cold War presidents' sometime routine of securing congressional authorization and then announcing they didn't need it, count as precedent for the proposition that they didn't.

56. F. Wormuth & E. Firmage, supra note 22, at 151.

57. Nor was it reassembled throughout the course of the Cold War. It is obviously a central mission of this book to cabin that descensus, to help insure that history will regard it as one of the many constitutional aberrations of the Cold War period. Cf. p. ix.

58. Hearings on Assignment of Ground Forces of the U.S. to Duty in the European Area before the Senate Comms. on Foreign Relations and Armed Services, 82d Cong., 1st Sess. 88–93 (1951) (testimony of Secretary Acheson).

59. Not only was South Korea by no stretch United States territory, it had six months earlier been publicly excluded by Secretary Acheson from our Pacific defense perimeter. 22 State Dep't Bull. No. 556, at 116 (Jan. 23, 1950). Moreover, there seems to have been time to secure authorization prior to the commencement of our military response—for one thing Congress was in session—the failure to do so representing a deliberate assertion of presidential prerogative. See R. Leckie, The Wars of America 850–58 (1968). At all events the claim that we were acting in defense of our national security was valid at most as a justification for seeking authorization simultaneously with such commencement rather than securing it in advance. The Truman Administration did neither.

60. Even assuming that a treaty can constitutionally authorize the commitment of United States troops to combat, see pp. 14–15, the relevant steps contemplated by the U.N. Charter (and the statute laying the basis of American membership, the United Nations Participation Act of 1945, or UNPA, 59 Stat. 619) had not been taken at the time of the commencement of the Korean War, and for that matter have not been taken since. The U.N. Charter contemplated, and Section 6 of the UNPA authorized, the making of "special agreements" committing U.S. (and other nations') troops to the Security Council "on its call for the purpose of maintaining international peace and security," which troops the Council could then employ for such purposes apparently without congressional permission. However, the Charter indicated that ratification of such agreements would be in accordance with the various

member nations' "respective constitutional processes," the UNPA required that they be ratified by Congress, and in fact *no such agreement has ever been concluded* by the United States, or for that matter by any other country—before, during, or after Korea. See, e.g., Glennon, "The Constitution and Chapter VII of the United Nations Charter," 85 Am. J. Int'l L. 74 (1991). (To complicate matters further, though obviously the point is unnecessary at this stage, the completion of such an agreement, committing U.S. troops to combat in totally unspecified future circumstances, would probably be unconstitutional under the Declaration of War Clause. P. 26.)

Franck & Patel, "UN Police Action in Lieu of War: 'The Old Order Changeth'," 85 Am. J. Int'l L. 63 (1991), argues that the absence of the sort of special agreement adverted to in Article 43 of the Charter does not affect the Security Council's authority (without congressional permission) to order American troops into combat under Article 42, simply authorizing the use of force by the U.N. However, this argument is defeated by Section 6 of the UNPA:

> The President is authorized to negotiate a special agreement or agreements with the Security Council *which shall be subject to the approval of the Congress by appropriate Act or joint resolution . . . .* The President shall not be deemed to require the authorization of the Congress to make available to the Security Council on its call *in order to take action under article 42 of said Charter and pursuant to such special agreement or agreements* the armed forces, facilities, or assistance provided for therein: *Provided,* That, except as authorized in section 287d-1 of this title, *nothing herein contained shall be construed as an authorization to the President by the Congress to make available to the Security Council for such purpose armed forces, facilities, or assistance in addition to the forces, facilities, and assistance provided for in such special agreement or agreements.*

22 U.S.C. § 287d (1988) (emphasis added). (Section 287d-1 deals only with noncombatant assistance "not involving the employment of armed forces contemplated by chapter VII" of the Charter; Articles 42 and 43 are both part of Chapter VII.)

It is thus unsurprising that within the Truman Administration the prevailing line was that if the Security Council did not go along, the U.S. would go into Korea alone. E.g., Truman memo to Dean Acheson, July 19, 1950, quoted in D. Acheson, Present at the Creation 415 (1969). (Truman at one point said he "rather wished [the Soviets] would veto," Foreign Relations of the United States, 1950, vol. VII, Korea 181 (1976).) Nor, indeed, did the Security Council authorize the use of force until *after* Truman had publicly announced our air and naval support for South Korea. D. Acheson, supra, at 408. It is thus equally unsurprising that (in contrast to the debates over Korea) hardly anyone in Congress suggested during 1991's Desert Storm debate that the Security Council's resolutions had obviated the need for congressional authorization.

61. Although the Vietnam War lasted almost three times as long—and seared itself much more dramatically into our national consciousness—over two-thirds the number of Americans killed there were killed in Korea (approximately 33,629, as opposed to approximately 46,397 in Vietnam).

62. Note 22 supra.

63. 23 State Dep't Bull. No. 578, at 173 (July 31, 1950). In his memoirs Acheson clung to this outrageous rationale, stating that there has never been a "nonpolitically

inspired doubt" about it. D. Acheson, supra note 60, at 414. It has been suggested that this bold usurpation is one reason the war so quickly lost what support it had. Ambrose, "The Presidency and Foreign Policy," 70 Foreign Affs. 120, 125 (1991–1992). The fact that Truman also, and again without serious congressional consultation, dramatically reversed our overall strategy twice (from halting aggression to "liberating" North Korea, and back again) didn't help either.

64. United States v. Bolton, 192 F.2d 805 (2d Cir. 1951).

65. Unlike most of those raising constitutional objections to Vietnam, and for that matter generally unlike the isolationists of the early twentieth century, most of those opposed to the executive's overreaching in committing troops to Korea supported the war on its merits.

66. Congress, including the Taft Republicans, gave virtually full support to five separate pieces of war-related legislation during the intervention—a bill extending the draft, an emergency aid bill for Asia, a bill lifting the ceiling on the size of the armed forces, a bill to increase taxes by $4.7 billion to help pay for the war, and an act giving the President power over defense production.

Elowitz & Spanier, "Korea and Vietnam: Limited War and the American Political System," 18 Orbis 510, 517 n.11 (1974–1975).

However, Professor Koh's recent testimony that two days before U.S. ground troops went into Korea, the House and Senate had "endorsed" the war by voting a one-year draft extension, Hearings on The Constitutional Roles of Congress and the President in Declaring and Waging War before the Senate Comm. on the Judiciary, 102d Cong., 1st Sess. 137 (1991), is misleadingly incomplete. The bill to extend the draft was pending when the North Koreans attacked. Truman advised selected congressional leaders of his decision to take some military action in response, but only after he had made it, indeed after it had been communicated to the South Koreans. An announcement he read to the leadership spoke only of defending Formosa and the Philippines, and he explicitly advised them that he was *not* planning to send American ground troops to Korea. G. Paige, The Korean Decision 180, 185, 188–91 (1968). Against that background the congressional votes on the draft hardly constituted an endorsement of his commitment of ground forces two days later (a decision of which he also advised the leadership only after it had been taken. Id. at 262).

67. The proposition that an appropriations vote can retroactively authorize combat that has preceded it seems somewhat troubled, see note 55 to chapter 4. On the question whether it should be able to serve as even prospective authorization, see pp. 27-30. On the effect of the War Powers Resolution on this question, see p. 128.

68. See, e.g., Rusk, "The President," 38 Foreign Affs. 353, 357 (1960) ("As Commander-in-Chief the President can deploy the armed forces and order them into active operations"); J. Lehman, Making War: The 200-Year-Old Battle Between the President and Congress over How America Goes to War 40–41 (1992) ("Like Presidents Johnson and Nixon, Bush believed that however vague his authority to actually send forces abroad, once they were there, his powers as commander in chief covered whatever course of action he decided for them, without any need for Congress to approve or disapprove"). The bootstrap here is obvious: The president has

authority to send troops wherever he wishes, and once they're "there," it's up to him to do whatever he wishes with them.

Actually this attitude significantly subsided during the Eisenhower Administration, but has prevailed within the executive branch since 1960—with a brief and limited remission during the Ford-Carter era. (Yes, I do mean to style that combination an era, at least as far as the subject of this book is concerned, though I think in some other ways as well.)

CHAPTER 2
VIETNAM: THE (TROUBLED) CONSTITUTIONALITY OF THE WAR
THEY TOLD US ABOUT

1. Quoted in G. Emerson, Winners & Losers: Battles, Retreats, Gains, Losses and Ruins from the Vietnam War 340 (1976).

2. Interview by Theo Sommer, Die Zeit, July 2, 1976, quoted in W. Shawcross, Sideshow: Kissinger, Nixon and the Destruction of Cambodia 394 (rev. ed. 1981).

3. This book will not discuss whether the war violated international law. It is rather about the question whether it was legal under the American Constitution (which question in turn will require analysis of various U.S. statutes and other actions by Congress, to see whether they had authorized the war as the Constitution requires). Neither will it cover constitutional issues arising out of the war other than those bearing on its legality. I have discussed a number of these other issues before. E.g., Ely, "Legislative and Administrative Motivation in Constitutional Law," 79 Yale L.J. 1205, 1210, 1212–17, 1338–41 (1970) (draft card burning); id. at 1211, 1328–29 (discrimination by draft boards); id. at 1211, 1336–38 (antiwar demonstrations in public schools); id. at 1319–21 (selective conscientious objection); Ely, "Flag Desecration: A Case Study in the Roles of Categorization and Balancing in First Amendment Analysis," 88 Harv. L. Rev. 1482 (1975) (draft card burning and school demonstrations reprised; vulgar antiwar epithets; flag burning and other desecration).

4. See p. 49.

5. The Poetical Works of Robert Southey 658 (A. & W. Galignani pub. 1829).

6. Of course Kennedy had doubts, as did every sane person who ever touched Vietnam, but Oliver Stone seems as right about the fixity of Kennedy's plans to withdraw as he was about the number of gunmen blazing away in Dealey Plaza, and the fact that the things that made the Doors unusually interesting did not include their music. See further note 49 infra.

7. See also R. Secord (with J. Wurts), Honored and Betrayed: Irangate, Covert Affairs, and the Secret War in Laos 29–30 (1992) (secret 1961 U.S. Air Force bombing campaign in Vietnam). A troop strength chart appears in J. Mueller, War, Presidents and Public Opinion 28 (1973). A useful chronology of the war (including troop strength data) appears in S. Karnow, Vietnam: A History 672–88 (1983); other chronologies appear in J. Mueller, supra, at 29–32; A Short History of Vietnam 134–57 (A. Millett ed. 1978); and R. Burns & M. Leitenberg, The Wars in Vietnam, Cambodia and Laos, 1945–1982: A Bibliographic Guide xxix–xxxii (1984). In addition to Karnow, recommended narratives include W. Gibbons, The

U.S. Government and the Vietnam War (1986, 1989) (three volumes published thus far) and Staff of the House Comm. on Foreign Affairs, 97th Cong., 2d Sess., The War Powers Resolution 1–202 (1982) (prepared by John H. Sullivan) [hereinafter Sullivan Study].

8. A. Thomas & A. Thomas, The War-Making Powers of the President 27 (1982). See generally, e.g., R. Burns & M. Leitenberg, supra note 7, at xxiii-xxv.

9. W. Isaacson, Kissinger: A Biography 488 (1992).

10. 6 U.S.T. 81, 83, 209 U.N.T.S. 28, 30.

11. 6 U.S.T. 87, 209 U.N.T.S. at 36.

12. This issue apparently was not considered by the founders. A. Sofaer, War, Foreign Affairs, and Constitutional Power: The Origins 56–57 (1976). In arguing that they thought a treaty *could* authorize hostilities, Dean Rostow points to article XI of the 1778 Treaty of Alliance with France, which guaranteed the "present possessions of the crown of France in America." In so doing, however, he appears to beg the question whether the provision was regarded as self-enforcing. Rostow, " 'Once More Into the Breach': The War Powers Resolution Revisited," 21 Val. U. L. Rev. 1, 24–25 (1986).

13. Wormuth, "The Vietnam War: The President versus the Constitution," in 2 The Vietnam War and International Law 711, 770 (R. Falk ed. 1969); see also, e.g., Van Alstyne, "Congress, the President, and the Power to Declare War: A Requiem for Vietnam," 121 U. Pa. L. Rev. 1, 15, 22 (1972); Reveley, "Presidential War-Making: Constitutional Prerogative or Usurpation?," 55 Va. L. Rev. 1243, 1290 n.155 (1969).

14. U.S. Const. art. II, § 2, cl. 2.

15. See generally Paust, "Self-Executing Treaties," 82 Am. J. Int'l L. 760 (1988).

16. 252 U.S. 416 (1920).

17. Why it was unnecessary to add "and sixteen Senators" this time is left as an exercise for the reader.

18. E.g., M. Glennon, Constitutional Diplomacy 204–5 (1990); Van Alstyne, supra note 13, at 15, 22; Wormuth, supra note 13, at 770.

19. The very clause conferring the war power on Congress also grants it power "to Make rules concerning Captures." U.S. Const. art. I, § 8, cl. 11. That power has long been held to be exercisable by treaty. Note, "Congress, the President, and the Power to Commit Forces to Combat," 81 Harv. L. Rev. 1771, 1799 (1968), and sources cited therein. The power to appropriate money has generally been held not to be thus exercisable. See id. and sources cited therein. However, this result seems defensible in light of the provision in article I, section 9—for which there is no analogue applicable to the war power—that "no Money shall be drawn from the Treasury but in Consequence of Appropriations made by Law." But see Paust, supra note 15, at 780–81 (arguing from the language of other provisions that "made by Law" can be read to include made by treaty). In light of article I, section 7's provision that "all Bills for raising Revenue shall originate in the House of Representatives," the same result would seem appropriate in the case of revenue-raising measures. See, e.g., Edwards v. Carter, 580 F.2d 1055, 1058–59 (D.C. Cir.), cert. denied, 436 U.S. 907 (1978). But see Paust, supra, at 780 ("Just because all 'Bills' for raising revenue shall originate in the House, it does not follow that revenue may be

raised no other way.") (footnotes omitted). This has not been definitively settled. Wormuth, supra note 13, at 772–74.

Having pressed the appropriations and tax examples so hard, Professor Paust seems strangely accepting of the notion that authority to go to war cannot be created by treaty. He notes that the idea of vesting the war power in the president and Senate was considered and rejected, Paust, supra, at 780 n.116, but as we have seen, that one, to the extent it argues at all, turns out to argue the wrong way. He also asserts that the war power is "sui generis" in nature. Id. at 780, 782. Presumably this signals the judgment that war is a more important subject than others covered in Article I, section 8. If I didn't share that judgment of relative importance I would hardly have written this book. It is, however, a highly questionable way to go about interpreting the Constitution. See generally J. Ely, Democracy and Distrust: A Theory of Judicial Review 43–72 (1980).

20. For one thing, authorizing a war in advance by treaty eliminates the "pause" it was one purpose of the Declaration of War Clause to ensure. P. 4. However, that was but one of several rationales, and far from the most frequently or clearly mentioned. More important, the same objection can be made to a conditional declaration of war enacted by both houses of Congress, yet we know that those (a) were historically contemplated, and (b) may often be the most sensible way to proceed. P. 64.

Arguing that the approval of the House of Representatives as well as the Senate should be required for declarations of war, Oliver Ellsworth opined that "It should be more easy to get out of war, than into it." 2 The Records of the Federal Convention of 1787, at 319 (M. Farrand ed. 1911). His reference was to the assumed fact that wars would typically be ended by treaties (which need only the president and Senate): Its implication carried through must therefore be that wars, at least ordinarily, should not be commenceable thus. This was just one statement by one delegate, but it was for the "winning" side—the entire Congress as opposed to the Senate alone was given the power to declare war—and very likely reflected the thinking of most. Ellsworth almost certainly did not have consciously in mind the implications of what he was saying for the question whether wars could be authorized by treaty— there is no evidence that question explicitly occurred to anyone—but his apparent unconscious assumption must be troubling nonetheless.

One tempting escape from the difficulty of distinguishing treaties authorizing wars from other self-executing treaties would be to hold that *no* treaty can be self-executing under our Constitution. Stated that broadly, however, the matter has been settled to the contrary for a very long time; it also seems out of accord with the "intent of the framers," see sources cited in Paust, supra note 15, at 760–64, and more important, next to impossible to reconcile with Article VI's inclusion of treaties along with federal statutes as "the supreme Law of the Land" that is binding on state judges. It may, however, prove possible, though I don't believe anyone claims to have done so in anything approaching detail, to identify categories of "peripheral" matters respecting which self-executing treaties should be constitutionally permissible and "core" matters respecting which they shouldn't (and to demonstrate some degree of correspondence—no one asks for miracles—between those categories and the thinking of the framers). Wedgwood, "The Revolutionary Martyrdom of Jonathan Robbins," 100 Yale L.J. 229 (1990), argues for the historical respectability of such an effort.

21. P. 26.

22. Cf., e.g., Note, supra note 19, at 1783.

23. It is sometimes asserted that the United States is not a party to any treaty pursuant to which "any party [is] required to take any military action." M. Glennon, supra note 18, at 228. This formulation overstates the matter: Such commitments are the very point of mutual defense treaties. More plausible is the claim that we are not a party to any treaty obligating us to take military action except in accord with our own constitutional processes, that is, pursuant to legislative authorization. E.g., L. Henkin, Foreign Affairs and the Constitution 160 (1972). Nor does the former and broader claim follow from the latter and narrower one. A promise to go to war in accordance with our constitutional processes doesn't mean the country isn't obligated: It rather obligates the Congress to take action on behalf of the country, which is surely no less thinkable than obligating the president to do so. The inference that if the nation is obligated by treaty to go to war it must follow as a matter of domestic law that the *president* can do so without congressional authorization, e.g., Glennon, "United States Mutual Security Treaties: The Commitment Myth," 24 Colum. J. Transnat'l L. 509, 511 (1986), is no more valid than an inference from the very same treaty to the conclusion that the Federal Communications Commission could lawfully order the troops into combat. The nation's obligations are to be carried out in accordance with the nation's rules.

The narrower claim, however, that we are not party to any treaty that obligates the United States to go to war without the authorization of Congress—and of course that is all we are concerned with here—appears to be true. See, e.g., North Atlantic Treaty, April 4, 1949, art. 11, 63 Stat. 2241, 2246. The Rio Treaty does not contain this precise language, but it does provide that "no State shall be required to use armed force without its consent." Inter-American Treaty of Reciprocal Assistance, opened for signature Sept. 2, 1947, art. 20, 62 Stat. 1681, 1703. Certainly the implication that the United States can intervene if it consents to do so carries no further implication that, contrary to our usual constitutional processes, the president (or the F.C.C.) can give that consent unilaterally. (One of the principal reasons the Versailles Treaty ending World War I was defeated, of course, was congressional concern with losing the power to decide whether the United States would go to war.)

And even if this narrower claim weren't true, Section 8(a) (2) of the War Powers Resolution of 1973 (which as the juristic equivalent of a statute takes priority over all prior treaty provisions) provides that authorization to introduce American armed forces into hostilities cannot be derived from any treaty, past or future, unless it is implemented by legislation specifically stating that it is to constitute such authorization within the meaning of the Resolution.

24. 78 Stat. 384 (1964) (emphasis deleted and supplied).

25. You will recall that South Vietnam was a SEATO protocol state, and it unquestionably requested our assistance.

26. Fulbright, "The Legislator as Educator," 57 Foreign Affs. 719, 725 (1979) (emphasis deleted). Cf. Hearings on S. Res. 151 before the Senate Comm. on Foreign Relations, 90th Cong., 1st Sess. 84 (1967) [hereinafter National Commitments Hearings] (Sen. Fulbright).

27. 112 Cong. Rec. 4370 (1966).

28. 116 Cong. Rec. 20,750 (1970).

29. A more extensive summary of the legislative history appears in 2 W. Gibbons, supra note 7, at 301–30. The original version, in the Congressional Record, is not that long either.

30. 110 Cong. Rec. 18,132 (1964).

31. Id. at 18,418.

32. Id. at 18,403.

33. Id. at 18,406–7.

34. Id. at 18,409. Concerning the concurrent resolution provision, see also pp. 29–30.

35. Id. at 18,459.

36. Id. at 18,462.

37. Id. at 18,470.

38. Id. at 18,470–71, 18,555.

39. Bickel et al., "Indochina: The Constitutional Crisis," reprinted in 116 Cong. Rec. 15,409, 15,411 (1970) (statement of fourteen prominent law professors and lawyers).

40. Albeit not inevitably. The declaration of the War of 1812 took seventeen days of congressional deliberation.

41. J. Galloway, The Gulf of Tonkin Resolution 80–81 (1970).

42. Sullivan Study, supra note 7, at 36–37; cf. briefly voguish bon mot, Grant Elementary School, San Diego, circa 1949: "I confess—he did it."

43. Quoted in J. Galloway, supra note 41, at 134. See also, e.g., D'Amato, Velvel, Sager, VanDyke, Freeman & Cummings, "Brief for Constitutional Lawyers' Committee on Undeclared War as Amicus Curiae, *Massachusetts v. Laird*," 17 Wayne L. Rev. 67, 150 (1971).

44. See, e.g., J. & S. Stockdale, In Love and War 16–17, 20–23, 34, 92 (1984); 2 W. Gibbons, supra note 7, at 289–97; G. Kahin, Intervention: How America Became Involved in Vietnam 220–23 (1986); S. Karnow, supra note 7, at 366–73.

45. I am, however, advised by a graduate of the Naval Academy who served on a destroyer "doing the same things as the *Maddox* and *Turner Joy*" that "many destroyermen doubt *either* was attacked."

46. L. Gelb & R. Betts, The Irony of Vietnam: The System Worked 100 (1979).

47. See, e.g., 2 W. Gibbons, supra note 7, at 282–88; 3 id. at 9–10; G. Kahin, supra note 44, at 220–21, 224; N. Sheehan, H. Smith, E. Kenworthy & F. Butterfield, The Pentagon Papers as Published by the New York Times 247–48 (1971).

48. 2 W. Gibbons, supra note 7, at 285.

49. Pentagon Papers, supra note 47, at 245; see generally id. at 242–61. Recently declassified documents have given significant additional support to the view of President Johnson as a reluctant participant in Vietnam, who deepened our involvement because he felt President Kennedy had essentially committed us to do so. See, e.g., Economist, May 16, 1992, at 118–19; see generally Foreign Relations of the United States, 1964–1968: vol. I, Vietnam 1964 (1992). Of course the extent of Kennedy's commitment is somewhat unclear, but the trouble with "scenarios" is that they tend to get followed.

50. Pentagon Papers, supra note 47, at 273–75; J. Goulden, Truth is the First Casualty: The Gulf of Tonkin Affair—Illusion and Reality 214–16, 239–42 (1969); 2 W. Gibbons, supra note 7, at 310–14.

51. J. Goulden, supra note 50, at 48; S. Karnow, supra note 7, at 375; D. Halberstam, The Best and the Brightest 417 (1972).

52. 2 W. Gibbons, supra note 7, at 311–16, 320–22.

53. Id. at 307–8. See also, e.g., National Commitments Hearings, supra note 26, at 222–23 (testimony of Sen. Ervin).

54. D. Halberstam, supra note 51, at 414, 417–18.

55. "However [the Tonkin Gulf vote] may now be construed by some Vietnam critics in hindsight, it does nothing to enhance either the role of—or confidence in—the Senate to assert that the Members were 'duped' by bad or insufficient intelligence." Senate Comm. on Foreign Relations, 91st Cong., 2d Sess., Comments on the National Commitments Resolution (1970), in 3 R. Falk, supra note 13, at 588 (1972) (minority views of Sen. McGee). Cf. Symposium, "Foreign Affairs and the Constitution," 43 U. Miami L. Rev. 47, 56–57 (1988) (written comment of William Van Alstyne) (footnote omitted):

[The President] may provide such information to Congress that ought to persuade Congress to adopt his view of the national interest. Indeed, in his capacity to do the latter, there is a definite risk that he may "invent" the information—in other words, he may lie—to get Congress to adopt his proposals. This is a risk the Constitution, by its design, accepts. In the end, however, it will be Congress who will determine whether the President will prevail in securing the necessary authority.

Had Congress been diligent in pressing for the facts, but had the administration continued to lie and the Tonkin Gulf Resolution emerged, I would think the correct legal position would be that the war was unconstitutional, albeit not in any way that would be judicially cognizable; our only recourse would therefore be to impeach the president or take other legislative action. As James Iredell, a delegate to the Philadelphia convention and later a Supreme Court justice, put it:

The President must certainly be punishable for giving false information to the Senate . . . . If it should appear that he has not given them full information . . . and by that means induced them to enter into measures injurious to their country, and which they would not have consented to had the true state of things been disclosed to them—in this case, I ask whether, upon an impeachment for a misdemeanor upon such an account, the Senate would probably favor him.

4 Debates in the Several State Conventions on the Adoption of the Federal Constitution 127 (J. Elliot ed. 1863).

56. E.g., Bickel, "Congress, The President and the Power to Wage War," 48 Chi.-Kent L. Rev. 131, 137 (1971); National Commitments Hearings, supra note 26, at 145 (Sen. Gore).

57. Id. at 138. See also A. Schlesinger, Jr., The Imperial Presidency 179 (1973).

58. 110 Cong. Rec. 18,405 (1964). See also id. at 18,399 (Sen. Fulbright):

The action taken by the United States in retaliation for the North Vietnamese torpedo boat attacks must be understood both in terms of the immediate situation and in terms of the broader pattern of Communist military and subversive activities in southeast Asia over the past 10 years. On both levels the North Vietnamese regime is patently guilty of military aggression . . . .

59. National Commitments Hearings, supra note 26, at 114.

60. Id. at 205; see also id. at 114 (Sen. Hickenlooper), 131 (Sen. Gore).

61. S. Rep. No. 797, 90th Cong., 1st Sess. 21 (1967) (some emphasis supplied). See also J. Fulbright, The Price of Empire 104 (1989) ("The resolution was presented as a way to peace, not war").

62. 2 W. Gibbons, supra note 7, at 322. See also id. at 331 (McGeorge Bundy); 3 id. at 454 (Bill Moyers); J. Fulbright, supra note 61, at 104.

63. Fulbright subsequently reported that in working out his compromise bombing proposal with the White House in 1973, he had been assured by the President (this time Nixon) that there would be no escalation prior to August 15—only to be betrayed once again. See p. 39; T. Eagleton, War and Presidential Power: A Chronicle of Congressional Surrender 184 (1974).

64. 2 W. Gibbons, supra note 7, at 334.

65. We also should recall that Fulbright was the only senator with the good sense and courage to vote not to fund Joseph McCarthy's subcommittee in 1954. W. Manchester, The Glory and the Dream: A Narrative History of America: 1932–1972, at 704 (1973).

66. The delegation doctrine is also often referred to as the nondelegation doctrine. It's like flammable and inflammable.

67. E.g., Mottola v. Nixon, 318 F. Supp. 538, 545 (N.D. Cal. 1970), rev'd, 464 F.2d 178 (9th Cir. 1972); Bickel, supra note 56, at 137–38; Velvel, "The War in Viet Nam: Unconstitutional, Justiciable, and Jurisdictionally Attackable," 16 Kans. L. Rev. 449, 478 (1968).

68. 299 U.S. 304 (1936).

69. A.L.A. Schechter Poultry Corp. v. United States, 295 U.S. 495 (1935), and Panama Refining Co. v. Ryan, 293 U.S. 388 (1935), are the only Supreme Court cases invalidating legislation for excessive delegation.

70. See note 3 to chapter 1; Lofgren, "*United States v. Curtiss-Wright Export Corporation*: An Historical Reassessment," 83 Yale L.J. 1 (1973).

71. Neither was it necessary to the holding: The delegation involved was quite precise.

72. In Zemel v. Rusk, 381 U.S. 1, 17 (1965), the Court argued that "because of the changeable and explosive nature of contemporary international relations, and the fact that the Executive is immediately privy to information which cannot be swiftly presented to, evaluated by, and acted upon by the legislature, Congress—in giving the Executive authority over matters of foreign affairs—must of necessity paint with a brush broader than that it customarily wields in domestic areas." However, the delegation doctrine, "even at its high point, never . . . insisted on more detail than was feasible . . . . Policy direction is all that was ever required . . . ." J. Ely, supra note 19, at 133. The Court's argument thus suggests, at most, that an intelligent case-by-case application of the delegation doctrine would less often end up invalidating statutes bearing on international relations, not that it is inapplicable, or even that it ought to be generally declared more weakly applicable, to all statutes in that category. (Having criticized *Zemel*'s language on this point, it seems only fair to concede that I bear significant responsibility for it.)

73. This point is well argued in M. Glennon, supra note 18, at 198.

74. 381 U.S. at 17.

75. "This does not mean that simply because a statute deals with foreign relations, it can grant the Executive totally unrestricted freedom of choice." Id. The Court thus referred to historical practice, to give more precise content to the statute involved than was reflected on its face, before upholding it. Id. at 17–18.

76. Glennon, supra note 23, at 519–20.

77. J. Ely, supra note 19, at 132. See generally id. at 131–34, 177, and sources cited therein; Ely, "Another Such Victory: Constitutional Theory and Practice in a World Where Courts Are No Different from Legislatures," 77 Va. L. Rev. 833, 857–58 (1991), and sources cited therein.

78. The argument that the doctrine applies uniquely to the War Clause because the debates are explicit that the decision to go to war is to be legislative—see Edwards v. Carter, 580 F.2d 1055, 1058 n.7 (D.C. Cir.), cert. denied, 436 U.S. 907 (1978); Lobel, "Covert War and Congressional Authority: Hidden War and Forgotten Power," 134 U. Pa. L. Rev. 1035, 1098–1101 (1986)—appears to commit the same error we saw respecting the question whether wars can be authorized by treaty: *Every* decision covered by Article I, section 8 was intended ordinarily to be legislative, and the fact that the framers agonized over whether to make something an exception argues, if at all, the wrong way. See p. 15.

79. See J. Ely, supra note 19, at 131–34, and sources cited therein; Schoenbrod, "The Delegation Doctrine: Could the Court Give It Substance?" 83 Mich. L. Rev. 1223 (1985).

80. P. 5.

81. Sidak, "To Declare War," 41 Duke L.J. 27 (1991).

82. Although the argument is constitutional in form, Sidak at times indicates that he may have proved only that a declaration of war is the "preferred" means of authorization as opposed to a mandatory one. Id. at 121. At other times he indicates the contrary. See, e.g., id. at 33. The article's intentions are generally somewhat unclear. Its tone is often sharp toward others who also take seriously the constitutional requirement that wars be deliberately authorized by Congress (Koh, Van Alstyne, Ely) and conciliatory toward those who do not (Crovitz). This suggests the reader might do well to keep his eye on several apparent cross-cutting subtexts— that hostilities short of full-fledged war, not requiring a literal declaration of war, may not require congressional authorization of any sort, id. at 120 (a proposition clearly at war with the document's language and purpose, see pp. 66–67); that wars begun "defensively" (a category he apparently feels includes all wars we have fought since 1846) also may not require congressional authorization, id. at 77–78 (but see note 31 to chapter 1); and that declared wars may not be terminable even by congressional refusal of further funding, id. at 105 (also contrary to intentions of founders and of everyone else since of whom I'm aware, save, perhaps, Sidak, p. 75). However all that may be, the article contains some important insights and single-handedly makes Sidak an important player in this area. It would be a pity if the radicalism of its (apparent) thesis kept those interested in the subject from including it on their reading lists.

83. See note 5 to chapter 1.

84. See Sidak, supra note 81, at 33, 68, 70. The argument is thus one that draws on a Dworkinian distinction between the founders' specific conceptions (here, that authorizations not necessarily be labeled declarations of war) and their more general

constitutional concepts (here, that the legislature take responsibility for deciding on war and peace). The oft-made observation that declarations of wars are "outmoded" is entirely beside the point of such an argument, as indeed it seems beside the point of any sensible constitutional argument one can imagine.

85. Eagleton, "The Form and Function of the Declaration of War," 32 Am. J. Int'l L. 19, 22–25 (1938). See also Draper, "Did Noriega Declare War?" N.Y. Rev. Books, Mar. 29, 1990, at 30, criticizing President Bush's assertion that General Noriega had declared war on us prior to our invasion, on the ground that Noriega had actually said *we* in effect had already declared war on Panama. The problem with Draper's rejoinder is that declarations of war, like scrapping schoolyard boys, have historically recited that the other side "started it": The case of Panama is thus not clear on this score either way. (The lack of a "form book" for declarations of war is one reason we have rightly never accepted the periodically floated suggestion that such a declaration by the other side dispenses with the need for a declaration or other congressional authorization on ours. For example, despite a declaration of war against us by the Bey of Tripoli in 1802, Congress passed a statute authorizing the president to seize Tripolitan ships; the House censured President Polk for "unconstitutionally" starting the Mexican war despite the fact that Mexico had declared war on us prior to its "invited" attack on our forces in disputed territory; and as is well known Hitler's Germany declared war on us before we did on it.)

86. E.g., Note, supra note 19, at 1792–93.

87. E.g., R. Turner, The War Powers Resolution: Its Implementation in Theory and Practice 2–3 (1983). Sidak flags this problem, supra note 81, at 49, but does not appear to assay an answer.

88. Limited declarations of war are entirely precedented historically. (Also, one of the "lessons of Vietnam," which we seemed to have assimilated at least as of Desert Storm, is that we shouldn't get in at all unless we mean to win.)

Under existing law declarations of war have statutorily imposed domestic consequences too, though those could be altered, albeit probably not without some period of dislocation. (In addition, those very domestic consequences might provide an additional reason for Congress to take the decision to go to war seriously—a thesis Sidak is developing in a paper in process.)

As far as bringing in other enemies is concerned, in all the wars I've read about (which by now is enough to last several lifetimes) decisions whether to enter have turned on perceived concrete national interests, not on the titles on papers combatants have filed respecting one another. (The differing decisions of China and the U.S.S.R. concerning entry into the Korean war provide instructive examples.) Mutual defense treaties—certainly NATO and the Warsaw Pact, for example—have also to my knowledge invariably been geared to actual threats, not to whether someone has "declared" war, and in fact countries have quite often militarily ignored declarations of war against them. F. Grob, The Relativity of War and Peace 293 (1949). See, e.g., id. at 290 (Bulgaria, Hungary, and Romania's declarations of war against us ignored for six months, at which time as "a gesture of friendship and support for Soviet Russia" we reciprocated); LaFeber, "The Constitution and American Foreign Policy: An Interpretation," 74 J. Am. Hist. 695, 704 (1987) (China declared war after we intervened in the Boxer Rebellion, without noticeable escalation of goals or action on our part); M. Pusey, The Way We Go to War 55 (1969) ("the Jefferson administration did not care to match Tripoli's declaration of war").

Of course it would be entirely understandable if a court proved insufficiently confident of these assurances to require that combat authorizations be labeled declarations of war: Indeed I suspect that would be my reaction were I a judge, even if I didn't regard such a requirement as insufficiently defensible on other grounds.

89. Cf., e.g., Miranda v. Arizona, 384 U.S. 436 (1966).

90. See note 22 to chapter 1.

91. Arguably there should be a rare exception for the situation where the enemy cannot be designated because it is neither a state nor another entity susceptible to unambiguous description, as where Congress wishes to authorize intervention to protect a friendly head of state from an amorphous collection of insurgents (or to deliver food to starving people). To the extent this translates only into the all-too-frequent desire to keep our options open so that we can switch sides from day to day, it strikes me as just the sort of situation we should steer clear of. Where it isn't that, however, the purposes of the Declaration of War Clause could probably be satisfied tolerably well by an exact congressional description of the situation and our goals. The critical point is that Congress be precise about what it is authorizing, that it violates not only the phraseology but also the purpose of the requirement of a "declaration of war" to permit it to delegate to the president authority to select a suitable enemy and make war on him. The clever among you will have realized my suggestion that there is something special about the language of the provisions bearing on the authorization of combat—*declaration* of war, *letter* of marque and reprisal—that requires unusual specificity to be equivalent in operation to an application of the delegation doctrine to this situation even if it is "inoperative" elsewhere. Since such specificity is unlikely ever to be achieved otherwise—the very existence of Israel as a possible transgressor of any such attempted formula appears almost single-handedly sufficient at least at present to guarantee that—an identification of the enemy seems under ordinary circumstances a minimal requirement. (Obviously nothing I have said outlaws the historical "conditional declaration of war" whereby war was declared against a named country in the event it committed a designated act. See p. 64.)

92. Pp. 65, 108, 127.

93. National Commitments Hearings, supra note 26, at 82.

94. See, e.g., H.R. Rep. No. 267, 90th Cong., 1st Sess. 38, 41 (1967).

95. See, e.g., Brooks v. Dewar, 313 U.S. 354 (1941); Fleming v. Mohawk Wrecking & Lumber Co., 331 U.S. 111, 116 (1947); Ex Parte Endo, 323 U.S. 283, 303 n.24 (1944); Greene v. McElroy, 360 U.S. 474, 506 (1959).

96. 79 Stat. 109 (1965).

97. 111 Cong. Rec. 9282 (1965). See generally id. at 9282–84.

98. Id. at 9497. See generally id. at 9498–9500 (Sens. Javits, Aiken, Church, and Stennis); 3 W. Gibbons, supra note 7, at 244, 246 (1989).

99. Berk v. Laird, 317 F. Supp. 715, 724 (E.D.N.Y. 1970), aff'd sub nom. Orlando v. Laird, 443 F.2d 1039 (2d Cir.), cert. denied, 404 U.S. 869 (1971); see also 3 W. Gibbons, supra note 7, at 247–48 ("[Senator Morse] . . . railed against the 'reservationists,' as he called other Senators who said that their vote for the bill should not be considered an endorsement of Vietnam policy. 'Whom do they think they are kidding,' said Morse"). Cf. L. Richards, The Life and Times of Congressman John Quincy Adams 193 (1986) ("This logic bothered Adams. He found it

'most remarkable' that an overwhelming majority of both houses could sustain the [Mexican] war while 'professing to disapprove its existence and pronouncing it unnecessary and unjust' ").

100. 111 Cong. Rec. 9540–41 (1965); id. at 9772.

101. 79 Stat. 863, 872 (1965).

102. Public Papers of the Presidents of the United States: Lyndon B. Johnson, 1966, at 8.

103. 112 Cong. Rec. 4411, 4474–75 (1966).

104. Id. at 4406.

105. Id. at 4404; E. Windchy, Tonkin Gulf 43–44 (1971). See generally, e.g., Hearings on S. 2793 Before the Senate Comm. on Foreign Relations, 89th Cong., 2d Sess. (1966).

106. S. Karnow, supra note 7, at 106 ("Cambodia" corrected to "Thailand"). Sometimes courts went a little overboard in their proofs of congressional ratification. One cited as proof that "Congress has participated actively with respect to the military effort in Vietnam" the fact that the Senate had recently voted to *repeal* the Tonkin Gulf Resolution. Davi v. Laird, 318 F. Supp. 478, 481 (W.D. Va. 1970). Another pointed to the fact that Congress had voted to punish "persons who tore up their draft cards out of protest at the Vietnam war." United States v. Sisson, 294 F. Supp. 511, 514 (D. Mass. 1968). This is eerily amusing, as it had been central to the government's defense of the constitutionality of the draft card destruction law that it had not been aimed at antiwar protesters. See United States v. O'Brien, 391 U.S. 367 (1968).

107. 112 Cong. Rec. 4382 (1966).

108. Hearings on S. 2793 before the Senate Comm. on Foreign Relations, 89th Cong., 2d Sess. 593, 598 (1966).

109. 112 Cong. Rec. 4409 (1966). See also, e.g., McGovern, Introduction to L. Friedman & B. Neuborne, Unquestioning Obedience to the President: The ACLU Case Against the Legality of the War in Vietnam 12–14 (1972); Velvel, supra note 67, at 465–66 (citing several legislators for much the same proposition); Mitchell v. Laird, 488 F.2d 611, 615 (D.C. Cir. 1973). This is a time-honored congressional rationalization, see T. Eagleton, supra note 63, at 41 (citing use during Mexican War), and persists to this day. See, e.g., Hearing on The Constitutional Roles of Congress and the President in Declaring and Waging War before the Senate Comm. on the Judiciary, 102d Cong., 1st Sess. 64 (1991) (Sen. Simon) ("If . . . we were to take offensive action [in Kuwait] . . . . I think I would vote for funding the troops that are there, even though I would vote against authorizing the offensive action at this point.").

110. See A. Thomas & A. Thomas, supra note 8, at 123–24.

111. At this point the congressional countermove would be to attach the prohibition to a measure raising the debt ceiling or appropriating funds for one of the president's favorite causes—though there is the danger that the political heat will be felt by Congress as well. At all events it never came to this until very late in the war. See pp. 39–41.

112. The war "cost $25 billion in 1966, and added six points to the cost-of-living index in 1966 alone." 3 W. Gibbons, supra note 7, at x.

113. See, e.g., National Commitments Hearings, supra note 26, at 219 (uncon-

troverted testimony of Sen. Ervin) ("Congress could repeal the resolution. The President cannot veto that repeal because the resolution itself gives the Congress the power itself to nullify it."). INS v. Chadha, 462 U.S. 919 (1983), apparently invalidating such concurrent resolution provisions, was years in the future.

114. See note 130 infra.

115. J. McCrae, "In Flanders Fields," in One Hundred and One Famous Poems 11 (R. Cook pub. 1926).

116. 2 W. Gibbons, supra note 7, at 319.

117. D. Halberstam, supra note 51, at 146.

118. H. Kissinger, White House Years 496 (1979).

119. But cf. W. Isaacson, supra note 9, at 268:

> If Nixon had chosen to, the invasion could have been cast in a more muted light: instead of being launched with a fiery presidential address, it could have been announced by General Abrams's press office in Saigon as an expansion of the policy of cross-border operations designed to clear out sanctuaries that were threatening American troops. It would still have provoked protest, but not the explosion that Nixon detonated with his April 30 speech.

120. E.g., Rogers, "The Constitutionality of the Cambodian Incursion," 65 Am. J. Int'l L. 26, 31–32 (1971); McKay, "The Constitutional Issues—Opposition Position," 45 N.Y.U. L. Rev. 640, 645 (1970).

121. E.g., W. Shawcross, supra note 2, at 398. There is evidence, however, that this statement was U.S.-engineered. S. Karnow, supra note 7, at 606. Also, on April 3 Lon Nol had issued the following as part of the official transcript—the question in fact was not asked—of one of his press conferences: "[Question:] [W]ill American troops be called in? [Answer:] I am thinking of the possible intervention of all friendly countries, for example, Indonesia or others." W. Shawcross, supra, at 131.

122. Thus he met with General Haig as with an ally, expressing regret only that he had not received advance notice of the incursion and that the Americans seemed to be pushing the Communists farther into the Cambodian interior. W. Shawcross, supra note 2, at 163, 175. (Sadly, he seemed to miss the point that much of the purpose of the incursion was to support our defense of South Vietnam, and thus precisely to push the Communists away from its borders.)

> When the U.S. invasion began, North Vietnamese forces had spread over one-quarter of Cambodia's countryside; when it was over, they had dispersed to over half the country. Hanoi's troops had also begun . . . . building up the local Khmer Rouge. A ragtag group of five thousand hapless rebels at the time of the invasion, . . . [by 1975] they were a murderous force of seventy thousand intent on brutalizing their own people in order to create the purest nightmare of a communist society.

W. Isaacson, supra note 9, at 272–73.

123. Certainly he was not in on planning the incursion and apparently did not even know about it in advance. W. Shawcross, supra note 2, at 143, 163. Initially upon taking office he had reasserted Cambodia's "strict neutrality." S. Karnow, supra note 7, at 606. Once set upon by a combination of North Vietnamese, Viet

Cong, and Khmer Rouge, however, he seemed to move away from this policy, issuing the April 3 and April 14 statements.

Came the American incursion, however, he asserted that it violated Cambodian neutrality. W. Shawcross, supra note 2, at 149. Concurrently, though, he told the Chinese he could no longer tolerate the Communist sanctuaries, id. at 126, and soon he was meeting with Haig.

124. Id. at 163; D. Kirk, Wider War: The Struggle for Cambodia, Thailand, and Laos 122 (1971).

125. P. 101.

126. P. 21.

127. Critics argued that the administration's logic meant the president was empowered to bomb supply lines or depots in China if they were being employed in the assault on South Vietnam. E.g., Rogers, supra note 120, at 34–35. Representing the administration's position, Robert Bork distinguished bombing China on the ground that "it would involve a decision to initiate a major war" and thus would require additional congressional approval. Bork, "Commentary," 65 Am. J. Int'l L. 79, 80 (1971). Unaccustomed as I am to finding greater executive power than Judge Bork, I find the principle underlying this distinction elusive. Of course China would have been a more formidable enemy than any we were then fighting. But while that certainly bears on the prudence of such a raid, I'm not sure how an "originalist" like Bork, or for that matter anyone, can turn it into a constitutional principle. See also p. 17 (Senator Fulbright agreeing with Senator Brewster that the Tonkin Gulf Resolution would permit the landing of "large American armies" in China).

At all events this is not that case. As the map reproduced at the beginning of this book will remind, Laos and Cambodia are nested within the curve of Vietnam—the proverbial crow flying from Hanoi to Saigon would spend more time over Laos and Cambodia than over the sum of both Vietnams—a geographical relation that accounts for the virtual inevitability of the Ho Chi Minh trail and North Vietnamese staging areas within each of those countries.

128. E.g., Van Alstyne, supra note 13, at 20–21, 27–28; F. Wormuth & E. Firmage, To Chain the Dog of War: The War Power of Congress in History and Law 231 (2d ed. 1989). Even some of the war's supporters argued that repeal would withdraw the authority under which it was being fought. 116 Cong. Rec. 20,750 (1970) (Sens. Ervin & Stennis).

129. Now Senator Fulbright's team overshifts—far to the left—when playing against right-handed hitters. So, the skipper in the Administration dugout signaled for Senator Dole to hit to the opposite field. With a motion to repeal the Tonkin Gulf Resolution, Dole came through with a stinging drive over first base that rolled all the way to the bamboo fence—completely taking the scrambling fielders by surprise. They are now gathered around the pitcher's mound frantically planning how to play the next batter . . . .

Radio editorial (KEX, Portland, Or., week of June 22, 1970), reprinted in 116 Cong. Rec. 22,567 (1970). For a report from the administration's perspective, see J. Lehman, Making War: The 200-Year-Old Battle Between the President and Congress over How America Goes to War 89 (1992).

130. Sensing what the administration was up to, Senator Fulbright ended up as one of the ten to vote *against* Dole's repeal motion.

Read in conjunction with the Byrd amendment [conceding sweeping powers to the President] repeal of the Tonkin resolution in the form sponsored by Sen. Dole may be read as acquiescence in the Executive's contention that the Tonkin resolution was of no consequence in any case because the President . . . has full authority to make war without the authorization of Congress.

26 Cong. Q. Almanac 952 (1970) (Sen. Fulbright). Fulbright's own motion, to invoke the Resolution's concurrent resolution provision—a move he argued would not corroborate the administration's view of executive power—was defeated in the House. E. Windchy, supra note 105, at 337.

131. Id. at 336. Thus the closest thing we have so far to a definitive history of the Vietnam war, Stanley Karnow's 688-page book, does not so much as mention the repeal of the Tonkin Gulf Resolution. (For one thing, the repeal provision ended up as one of thirteen sections in a bill dealing with various subjects as distant as coastal fishing rights. 84 Stat. 2053, 2055 (1971).)

132. See Sullivan Study, supra note 7, at 33, 39.

133. 116 Cong. Rec. 30,683 (1970).

134. 117 Cong. Rec. 20,216, 20,589 (1971).

135. Van Alstyne, supra note 13, at 21.

136. E.g., 85 Stat. 716, 734 (1971). My suspicion is that those readers who find themselves resisting my argument concerning the effect of the repeal do so because they resist the conclusion that even conspicuous appropriations and draft extensions can constitute authorization. This we have seen to be a widely held attitude, and indeed the War Powers Resolution essentially enacted it into law. P. 128. Thus today, a replication of the facts surrounding the repeal of the Tonkin Gulf Resolution *would* put a legal end to the war in question, since there would be nothing left that could count as lawful authorization. Prior to 1973, however, the law appears to have been that earmarked appropriations *could* authorize wars. P. 27. (It does seem likely that after the repeal of the Tonkin Gulf Resolution there survived no operative statute specifically designating North Vietnam as the enemy. Cf. pp. 32–34. As of 1971, however, there could have been no doubt about either who the enemy was or the fact that Congress had approved its selection; this particular "nondelegation" aspect of the Declaration of War Clause thus seems to have been adequately served.)

137. Sullivan Study, supra note 7, at 39.

138. At least that's what they told us at the time.

139. 361 F. Supp. 553, 566 (E.D.N.Y.), rev'd, 484 F.2d 1307 (2d Cir. 1973), cert. denied, 416 U.S. 936 (1974).

140. 414 U.S. 1304 (Marshall); 414 U.S. 1316 (Douglas); 414 U.S. 1321 (Marshall).

141. Had the War Powers Resolution been in effect at the time, the repeal of the Tonkin Gulf Resolution would have legally ended the entire war. Note 136 supra. Absent such a repeal, however, nothing in the War Powers Resolution would have affected the 1973 bombing of Cambodia in particular.

142. R. Turner, supra note 87, at 9.

143. Hearings on S. 1248 and H.R. 5610 before the Senate Comm. on Foreign

Relations, 93d Cong., 1st Sess. 453 (1973) (statement of Secretary of State William P. Rogers).

144. E.g., McDougal & Lans, "Treaties and Congressional-Executive or Presidential Agreements: Interchangeable Instruments of National Policy," 54 Yale L.J. 181 (1945).

145. E.g., L. Henkin, supra note 23, at 177–79.

146. E.g., id. at 177; L. Tribe, American Constitutional Law § 4–5, at 229 (2d ed. 1988).

147. Of course it is unlikely that those who feel the president can do whatever he wants anyway would regard an executive agreement as getting in the way.

148. Glennon, supra note 23, at 513 n.23 (1986) (letter from Ass't Sec. of State Robert J. McCloskey to Sen. Clark).

149. See pp. 14–15.

150. There could be no constitutional objection to the inclusion of "extraneous" terms in an armistice agreement, so long as they were approved by a two-thirds vote of the Senate (and were of some international significance). The suggestion is rather that extraneous terms (unlike the terms defining the cease-fire itself) could not be enforced until they had been thus approved.

151. The administration *had* secretly bombed Cambodia from March 1969 until our ground incursion in April 1970. See chapter 5. Dissenting in *Holtzman*, Judge Oakes claimed that this invalidated Congress's July 1973 grant of permission to continue bombing until August 15 of that year. 484 F.2d at 1316–17. While one can certainly understand Judge Oakes' sense of outrage—the 1969–1970 bombings had been revealed only weeks before *Holtzman*—the legal connection between the two events seems attenuated.

152. Public Papers of the Presidents of the United States: Richard Nixon, 1970, at 538.

153. The administration was never so bold as to count the Marine guards at our embassy in Saigon for these purposes, and to the extent they were knowingly leaving POWs behind—at this writing that point is in high-level dispute—they weren't saying so.

154. 84 Stat. 905, 910 (1970).

155. In fact the second clause did not appear in the 1970 version, but was added to subsequent reenactments, see note 156 infra—in response to the sort of concerns expressed at pp. 38–39. That the full Proviso was thus created in two parts corroborates the account this discussion will suggest, that although it was not intended in its original form to apply to American troops, it was often subsequently assumed to do so. (The need for the second clause becomes attenuated if the first is understood not to apply to American troops.) It does not appear, however, that this subsequent assumption at any point became so clearly and widely held as to imply that one or more of the Proviso's reenactments altered its original meaning in this regard. See note 158 infra.

156. See statutes cited 361 F. Supp. at 554–58.

157. Compare, e.g., p. 38 (Cooper-Church Amendment).

158. E.g., Sullivan Study, supra note 7, at 107 ("Since October 1970 Congress had included in every military appropriations bill a proviso expressly forbidding bombing in Cambodia except for U.S. troop protection"); W. Shawcross, supra note

2, at 277 ("The justification for bombing Cambodia had been to protect Americans in Vietnam. Since October 1970 the Congress had included in every military appropriation bill a proviso expressly forbidding bombing in Cambodia except for that purpose"). I do not wish to overstate here: That the Fulbright Proviso limited American bombing of Cambodia was at no point a dictum on the lips of every American or even every commentator, for at no point was the question widely noticed. (I need hardly point out that the bombing has almost always been debated in other than legal terms.) Neither at any point did a consensus develop *within Congress* that the Proviso had had that effect. (If one had, we would be required to consider the argument—strained under even "pure" conditions—that even though the Proviso as originally enacted had not had that effect, subsequent reenactments of it did.) As the quoted passages indicate, however, on those occasions when a commentator has ventured a legal opinion of the situation, the assumption has tended to be that the Fulbright Proviso limited American bombing of Cambodia. Judge Oakes' dissent in the Second Circuit did make the point I shall end up suggesting, that in fact this was not the meaning of the Proviso, 484 F.2d at 1316, but as the sources quoted indicate, his point seems to have been ignored since.

159. The standard argument to that effect was that the Paris Accords had so altered the situation as to render the Fulbright Proviso obsolete. See *Holtzman*, 484 F.2d at 1313; W. Shawcross, supra note 2, at 277. However, that is at war with the principle suggested earlier that an armistice agreement not approved by the Senate cannot give the president combat authority he did not have before, to say nothing of the boilerplate rule that an executive agreement cannot displace a statute.

160. 84 Stat. 1942, 1943 (1971).

161. 86 Stat. 20, 29 (1972).

162. Id. at 30 (§ 655(d)).

163. Id. (§ 656).

164. S. Rep. No. 431, 92d Cong., 1st Sess. 15 (1971).

165. Id. (emphasis supplied).

166. 86 Stat. 734, 737–38 (1972).

167. 86 Stat. 1184, 1202–3 (1972).

168. 119 Cong. Rec. 17,124 (1973).

169. Id. at 21,778.

170. T. Eagleton, supra note 63, at 174–75.

171. 119 Cong. Rec. 22,305 (1973).

172. Id. at 22,306–7.

173. Id. at 22,307.

174. T. Eagleton, supra note 63, at 176.

175. 119 Cong. Rec. 22,325, 22,636 (1973).

176. 361 F. Supp. at 565.

177. Id.

178. Even though he was the one threatening the veto, President Nixon was quite adroit in putting the blame for the emperilment of benefit programs on Congress. T. Eagleton, supra note 63, at 173–74.

179. 361 F. Supp. at 561.

180. 484 F.2d at 1310 n.1 (affidavit of Secretary of State William P. Rogers, para. 8).

181. I suppose the (strained) idea would be that if the lower extensions of the Ho Chi Minh trail (in Cambodia) were subjected to U.S. Air Force interdiction, its headwaters in Laos would atrophy as well.

182. The entire inquiry is further confounded by the consideration that President Nixon's insistence on continuing to bomb Cambodia seems to have been importantly a product of the fact that it had become one of the few remaining "macho" symbols of his embattled presidency. G. Herring, America's Longest War: The United States and Vietnam, 1950–1975, at 254–55 (1979). We shall see that the choice of targets establishes quite conclusively that the putative military point of most of the bombing must have been to inflict such punishment on the Khmer Rouge that they would be induced to negotiate. However, a regime of bombing with a publicly announced termination date is simply not a rational way to force an enemy to the negotiating table. Of course it was the necessity to compromise with Congress that forced the termination date. But the fact that once that point was yielded Nixon insisted nonetheless on (extremely heavy) bombing right up until the end suggests how attenuated the connection between his motives and military reality must have become.

183. Don't be so sure. I never thought I'd be doing it either.

184. Staff of the Subcomm. on U.S. Security Agreements and Commitments Abroad of the Senate Comm. on Foreign Relations, 93d Cong., 1st Sess., U.S. Air Operations in Cambodia: April 1973, at 8 (1973).

185. 119 Cong. Rec. 12,339 (1973). Understandably in light of the political situation, Senator Fulbright was never forceful about this point. On the other hand he never corroborated the misreading of the Proviso either.

186. 361 F. Supp. at 565.

187. Oliver Ellsworth's dictum that "[i]t should be more easy to get out of war, than into it," 2 Farrand, supra note 20, at 319, was uttered in support of the requirement that both houses (as well as the president) concur before we can get into a war, whereas the president and Senate can end one by treaty. A determination to make x easier than y does not imply than any device to make x still easier must be adopted. And in fact it *is* easier, at least in legal terms, for wars to be ended than started, or at least it would be if our leaders took seriously the requirement of advance congressional authorization to get into one. Not only can they be ended by treaties, but the president alone, by cease-fire or armistice agreement, can effectively do so. Moreover, at least under certain conditions (which we are about to discuss), Congress alone, for that matter one house of Congress, can end a war by withholding further funding, assuming it has the courage to do so.

188. The framers explicitly contemplated that wars could be thus ended. E.g., A. Sofaer, supra note 12, at 57; Fisher, "How Tightly Can Congress Draw the Purse Strings?" 83 Am. J. Int'l L. 758, 762 (1989).

189. President Nixon was very resourceful in locating monies to continue the war—"from contingency funds, from carryover funds, from reprogrammed funds, and from a 'Feed and Forage' act that had not been used since the Civil War." Nathan, "Revising the War Powers Act," 17 Armed Forces & Soc. 513, 516 (1991) (footnote omitted).

190. See, e.g., W. Baumol, J. Panzar & R. Willig, Contestable Markets and the Theory of Industry Structure 6–7 (1982). The connection to our subject was suggested by Sidak, supra note 81, at 95.

191. At least so far as we know. The United States did supply approximately $15 million per year in aid to the coalition of rebels fighting the government the North Vietnamese installed in Cambodia in the late 1970s. N.Y. Times, September 13, 1990, at 3.

CHAPTER 3
INDUCING CONGRESS TO FACE UP TO ITS
CONSTITUTIONAL RESPONSIBILITIES

1. Public Papers of the Presidents of the United States: Dwight D. Eisenhower, 1956, at 380.

2. Stockdale, "On Public Virtue," in Thinking About America: The United States in the 1990s, at 480 (A. Anderson & D. Bark eds. 1988).

3. But see chapters 4 and 5.

4. But cf. note 136 to chapter 2.

5. Most especially, in this age of "volunteer" armies, young people whose disadvantage quota has already been filled.

6. The operative sections of the Resolution are reprinted at the end of the appendix.

7. 99 Stat. 1037 (codified as amended at 2 U.S.C. §§ 901–922 (1988)).

8. I believe the phrase is Professor Casper's. Casper, "Constitutional Constraints on the Conduct of Foreign and Defense Policy: A Nonjudicial Model," 43 U. Chi. L. Rev. 463 (1976). The structure of the Congressional Budget and Impoundment Control Act of 1974, 88 Stat. 297 (codified in scattered sections of 1, 2 & 31 U.S.C.) is quite similar to that of the War Powers Resolution.

9. A. Schlesinger, Jr., The Cycles of American History 291 (1986).

10. In all the reports that have been issued to Congress, the executive has followed nearly the identical script. The contention has been that the report was "consistent with" the requirements of the War Powers Act rather than "pursuant to" the act. In each report, the president has explicitly cited his "authority" attendant to his "constitutional obligation" as commander-in-chief.

Nathan, "Revising the War Powers Act," 17 Armed Forces & Soc. 513, 524 (1991) (footnotes omitted). Thus such "presidential letters have become the executive's signal that it is the president's prerogative to determine the level of cooperation with the Congress in sending U.S. forces into combat." Id. at 514.

On Indochina and Iran, see, e.g., Staff of House Comm. on Foreign Affairs, 97th Cong., 2d Sess., The War Powers Resolution 180–99, 238–46 (1982). Further on the Iran rescue attempt, see S. Dycus, A. Berney, W. Banks & P. Raven-Hansen, National Security Law 260–68 (1990); J. Lehman, Making War: The 200-Year-Old Battle Between the President and Congress over How America Goes to War 100–101 (1992) (succinct demolition of administration's claim of compliance). On Lebanon: see id. at 135–36; Ides, "Congress, Constitutional Responsibility and the War Power," 17 Loy. L.A. L. Rev. 599, 642–52 (1984). On Grenada: Rubner, "The Reagan Administration, the 1973 War Powers Resolution, and the Invasion of Grenada," 100 Pol. Sci. Q. 627 (1986); S. Dycus et al., supra, at 271–72. On the Gulf of Sidra: id. at 255–57. On Tripoli: Hearings on War Powers, Libya, and State-Sponsored Terrorism before the Subcomm. on Arms Control, International Security and Science of the House Comm. on Foreign Affairs, 99th Cong., 2d Sess. (1986); S. Dycus et al., supra, at 274–76. The "tanker war" against Iran dragged on for months, and tragically unfolded so as to highlight the administration's defiance of the Resolution with unusual clarity:

> The situation in the Persian Gulf was one in which "imminent involvement in hostilities" was "clearly indicated by the circumstances." . . . In March [1987] the United States agreed to protect eleven Kuwaiti oil tankers by placing them under U.S. flags and providing U.S. warships to escort them. In May . . . a U.S. frigate, the *Stark* . . . was attacked by an Iraqi fighter aircraft. Thirty-seven American sailors were killed, another twenty-one wounded. In July . . . one of the tankers (*Bridgeton*) struck a mine that had been placed by Iranian Revolutionary Guards. In September U.S. helicopters attacked and disabled an Iranian ship that had been observed planting additional mines. In October armed U.S. helicopters attacked a group of Iranian patrol boats that had fired upon a U.S. observation helicopter, sinking one of them.

B. Blechman, The Politics of National Security: Congress and U.S. Defense Policy 4 (1990).

> By mid-1988 we had some 31 ships patrolling the Gulf. On April 14 a mine blast off Qatar seriously damaged the U.S. frigate *Samuel B. Roberts*, injuring 10 crewmen. U.S. officials blamed Iran for laying new mines, and four days later, on April 18, our forces struck back, destroying the Sassan and Sirri oil platforms with gunfire and explosive charges. Two Iranian Phantom jets approached the ships near Sirri, but fled when the U.S. cruiser *Wainwright* fired anti-aircraft missiles at them. The 173-foot Iranian missile boat *Joshan* fired a missile at the *Wainwright*, but missed. The *Joshan* was then destroyed by missiles from the *Wainwright* and the U.S. frigate *Simpson*, and by bombs dropped by U.S. jets based on the carrier *Enterprise*. Meanwhile, armed Iranian speedboats attacked oil platforms belonging to the United Arab Emirates and a U.S.-flagged supply boat. President Reagan authorized an attack by U.S. planes, which sank one speedboat and damaged two others. Later in the day the Iranian frigates *Sahand* and *Sabalan* fired at U.S. aircraft and warships. The *Sahand* was sunk by missiles from the U.S. destroyer *Joseph Strauss* and by aerial bombs. The *Sabalan* was also crippled by a U.S. bomb.
>
> On July 3 [1988] a regularly scheduled civilian Iranian airliner was mistaken for a warplane and shot down by a missile from the U.S. cruiser *Vincennes*, killing 290 people. Asked to distinguish an episode in 1983 when a Soviet jet downed a Korean airliner, killing 269, the Chairman of our Joint Chiefs of Staff responded:
>
> > [T]he fundamental differences are, of course, that [the earlier incident did not occur in] a war zone, there was not combat in progress, there was not combat there normally . . . .

Defending our action before the United Nations Security Council on July 15, Vice President Bush faulted Iranian officials for allowing the airliner to fly "over a warship engaged in active battle," and a subsequent Defense Department investigation attributed the mistake to the stress of combat. (At the time it fired the fatal missile the *Vincennes* was engaged in battle with Iranian attack boats.) Mr. Bush stood firm: "The Iranians shouldn't be sending an airliner over a combat zone . . . . A captain is under fire in combat."

Despite all this the Administration persisted in its refusal to file a 4(a)(1) report with Congress acknowledging an imminent danger of hostilities. (Its position seemed to be that we were at war but there was no danger of hostilities.)

Ely, "Suppose Congress Wanted a War Powers Act That Worked," 88 Colum. L. Rev. 1379, 1381–83 (1988) (footnotes omitted).

See also R. Bonner, Weakness and Deceit: U.S. Policy and El Salvador 274–75 (1984):

[T]he specific reason that the administration decided not to designate El Salvador as a hostile fire zone was that to have done so would have triggered the provisions of the War Powers Act . . . . Even if a country is not so designated, a soldier is entitled to the extra $65 if he is in fact fired upon. The GAO auditors found that the U.S. military personnel in El Salvador, from early 1981 until mid-1982, were receiving hostile fire pay for 97 percent of the person-months involved . . . . [Yet e]ach of State's monthly reports [to Congress] contained a statement to the effect that there had been no attacks on U.S. soldiers.

President Ford's report on the *Mayaguez* incident is the only one to have included a reference to section 4(a)(1), though even he indicated merely that he was "taking note" of the Resolution. (Also, the operation took less than forty-eight hours and thus was over before the report was filed.)

11. B. Blechman, supra note 10, at 166.

12. He also announced that he did not regard himself as bound by the eighteen-month limit.

13. It gets worse. The president's request was for authority to keep the troops in Lebanon for six months to a year, but Congress gave him eighteen months, thereby pushing the expiration date beyond the November 1984 election.

14. E.g., Ely, supra note 10, at 1383 (naval war against Iran).

15. E.g., M. Glennon, Constitutional Diplomacy 104 n.184 (1990) (Grenada).

16. Hearings on War Powers After 200 Years before the Spec. Subcomm. on War Powers of the Senate Comm. on Foreign Relations, 100th Cong., 2d Sess. 366 (1988). See also, e.g., C. Arnson, Crossroads: Congress, the Reagan Administration, and Central America 157 (1989) (Sen. Biden, characteristically disarming, on the mining of Nicaraguan harbors: "We have lost the resolve to make the system work . . . it would be nice to have an infusion of backbone, myself included"); B. Blechman, supra note 10, at 6–7.

17. Authorization for Use of Military Force Against Iraq, 105 Stat. 3, § 2(c)(1) (1991) ("Consistent with section 8(a)(1) of the War Powers Resolution, the Congress declares that this section is intended to constitute specific statutory authorization within the meaning of section 5(b) of the War Powers Resolution"); but cf. J. Lehman, supra note 10, at 2, inexplicably declaring the War Powers Resolution to have been "irrelevant" because Congress and the President ended up agreeing!

18. Though President Bush did better than his predecessor in this regard, it surely seems overenthusiastic to conclude that he was "careful to involve Congress in the debate over the use of force," Ambrose, "The Presidency and Foreign Policy,"

70 For. Affs. 120, 127 (1991–1992). The invasion of Panama, it should also be recalled, was Bush's. (During the 1992 election campaign Governor Clinton gave no indication of any greater respect for the War Powers Resolution, or for congressional prerogatives in this area more generally, than President Bush, or President Reagan either for that matter.)

19. See Hearing on The Constitutional Roles of Congress and the President in Declaring and Waging War before the Senate Comm. on the Judiciary, 102d Cong., 1st Sess. 120 (1991) (testimony of William Van Alstyne):

> If Congress, in this instance, with half a million armed forces massed for an offensive in the Middle East cannot now reclaim its own constitutional integrity, then this, gentlemen, I put to you is the constitutional moment; it is not Korea, it is not the Civil War, it is not some 19th-century precedent. It is this one which will serve as a monument to the future. The Congress collaborated in the collapse of the separation of powers under the Constitution of the United States.

Despite Van Alstyne's characteristic eloquence, it still took a request from the President to get Congress to move.

20. A randomly selected example is Ely, "Perspective on the Persian Gulf: 'War by Default' Isn't the Law," L.A. Times, Dec. 23, 1990, at 7.

21. See Lewis, "Law Professors Demand War-Making Limits," N.Y. Times, Nov. 27, 1990, at A17 (describing amicus curiae brief filed by eleven law professors in *Dellums v. Bush*).

22. 752 F. Supp. 1141 (D.D.C. 1990).

23. See pp. 58–60.

24. Made despite the fact that the Bush Administration had already begun planning the offensive campaign that eventuated. N.Y. Times, Mar. 3, 1991, at A1. Even *Wall Street Journal* law columnist Gordon Crovitz admits that Bush was in violation of the Resolution at this point. Wall St. J., Mar. 6, 1991, at A9. Accord, J. Lehman, supra note 10, at 45.

25. Drew, "Letter from Washington," New Yorker, Dec. 3, 1990, at 90.

26. See statements cited in Sidak, "To Declare War," 41 Duke L.J. 27, 43 n.75 (1991).

27. Thus our allies were advised of the huge November buildup before Congress was, and the administration, shockingly, tried to mislead Congress into scheduling its debate on American policy in the Gulf for a date a week after the one it had privately set for the invasion. J. Smith, George Bush's War 201–2, 240, 255 (1992).

28. At a joint Georgetown/Center for National Security Studies conference on September 19, 1992, Nicholas Rostow, General Counsel of the National Security Council, indicated that there was a "100% certainty" that Bush would have invaded even had Congress voted the Desert Storm Resolution down. Let us pray this was hyperbole.

29. (By our ambassador to England, John Hay.) The war in Europe that became World War I erupted less than two decades later, and yet almost until its end the American people wanted no part of it.

30. Iraq also has an economic output about the size of South Carolina's, a fact one should not overstress, North Vietnam's being much smaller.

31. Neither do the various U.N. resolutions referenced in the Desert Storm Resolution. Not that it was necessary, but the same day it approved the Desert Storm

Resolution, the House enacted by an overwhelming margin another declaring that any offensive action against Iraq proper would have to be explicitly approved by Congress before initiation.

32. E.g., Bickel, "Congress, the President and the Power to Wage War," 48 Chi-Kent L. Rev. 131 (1971); Ides, supra note 10, at 654. Black, "Reflections on Teaching and Working in Constitutional Law," 66 Or. L. Rev. 1 (1987), takes the congressional self-help line to the extent of recommending that until the president starts complying with the Constitution in starting wars, Congress make a pact to override all his vetoes (on every subject). Somewhat dissonantly, Trimble, "The President's Foreign Affairs Power," 83 Am. J. Int'l L. 750, 753 (1989), takes the "Congress must save itself" line despite having diagnosed the situation in a way that (correctly) suggests the extreme unlikelihood of any such self-salvation:

> Politically, there is often no advantage in having to take a position, through a recorded vote, on pressing foreign policy questions with no immediate implication for local constituencies and with uncertain long-term consequences. To the contrary, it may be preferable to accept presidential leadership and preserve the ability to criticize decisions that turn out wrong.

33. But then, no procedure was. See note 86 infra. Additionally, under INS v. Chadha, 462 U.S. 919 (1983), it seems pretty clear that any such congressional clock-starting resolution would have to be vetoable. It is, if anything, even clearer that it would be vetoed. See pp. 124–25.

34. Separation of powers issues are not the sort voters get exercised about.

35. See note 54 to chapter 1.

36. Okay, Polk before the Mexican War, but his provocation was so flagrant it can responsibly be labeled unconstitutional, as indeed it was by the House of Representatives. P. 96.

37. P. 10. The move also fit the era's "liberal" bias in favor of executive decision-making.

38. Quoted in Rostow, " 'Once More Unto the Breach': The War Powers Resolution Revisited," 21 Val. U. L. Rev. 1, 15 (1986).

39. Ely, "Another Such Victory: Constitutional Theory and Practice in a World Where Courts Are No Different from Legislatures," 77 Va. L. Rev. 833, 855–63 (1991).

40. Id. at 842–54.

41. See generally J. Ely, Democracy and Distrust: A Theory of Judicial Review (1980).

42. Even thoughtful commentators sometimes conflate the two questions: "[E]ven if they seemed so disposed, the courts should not force Congress to act, contrary to the political interests of its members. Foreign policy decisions are normally political and ad hoc, not principled. They should be made by politically accountable officials, not detached, unelected judges." Trimble, supra note 32, at 754.

43. What was revolutionary about *Marbury v. Madison* was its holding that the courts could declare an act of Congress unconstitutional. That they should declare illegal an action taken by an executive official that required but had not received legislative authorization was not in doubt.

At least not until recently. Dean Choper, following Professor Wechsler, has recently argued that "separation of powers" quarrels between Congress and the president—which appear to include claims that the executive is acting beyond his authority—should not be judicially resolved because the "put upon" branch can protect itself politically. J. Choper, Judicial Review and the National Political Process 295– 96 (1980). There is some surface sense in the suggestion: Absent a pretty specific constitutional direction to the contrary, courts should not intervene to take care of those who can take care of themselves. The argument doesn't work in this context, however, as the prerogatives of Congress aren't what's really at stake here. P. 47. At all events the Supreme Court has at no point adopted Choper's suggestion: It has lately been deciding such issues at a fast and furious pace. E.g., Bowsher v. Synar, 478 U.S. 714 (1986); *Chadha*, supra note 33. As the Supreme Court put it as recently as 1990:

> In many cases involving claimed separation-of-powers violations, the branch whose power has allegedly been appropriated has both the incentive to protect its prerogatives and institutional mechanisms to help it do so. Nevertheless, the Court adjudicates those separation-of-powers claims . . . . [T]he fact that one institution of Government has mechanisms available to guard against incursions into its power by other governmental institutions does not require that the Judiciary remove itself from the controversy by labeling the issue a political question.

United States v. Munoz-Flores, 495 U.S. 385, 393 (1990). (For a list stretching back further, see D'Amato, Velvel, Sager, VanDyke, Freeman & Cummings, "Brief for Constitutional Lawyers' Committee on Undeclared War as Amicus Curiae, *Massachusetts v. Laird*," 17 Wayne L. Rev. 67, 115 n.105 (1971).)

44. See Baker v. Carr, 369 U.S. 186, 211–13 (1962); Henkin, "Viet-Nam in the Courts of the United States: 'Political Questions'," 63 Am. J. Int'l L. 284, 286 (1969) ("In regard to foreign affairs, I believe, the Supreme Court has never found a true 'political question' "); Scharpf, "Judicial Review and the Political Question: A Functional Analysis," 75 Yale L.J. 517, 583 (1966) ("the political question doctrine has found only very limited application in the war and security cases"). But cf. Goldwater v. Carter, 444 U.S. 996 (1979) (plurality opinion).

45. U.S. Const. art. III, § 2, cl. 1; art. VI, cl. 2.

46. A small sampling of modern cases (in the nineteenth century the hesitation was not even expressed by commentators) would include Ludecke v. Watkins, 335 U.S. 160 (1948) (power to expel aliens in wartime); Youngstown Sheet & Tube Co. v. Sawyer, 343 U.S. 579 (1952) (seizure of steel mills to assure war supplies); Reid v. Covert, 345 U.S. 1 (1957) (court martial jurisdiction over civilians); Greene v. McElroy, 360 U.S. 474 (1959) (executive employee loyalty and security program); United States v. Robel, 389 U.S. 258 (1967) (employment of Communist Party members in national defense jobs); New York Times Co. v. United States, 403 U.S. 713 (1971) (Pentagon Papers case); United States v. United States District Court, 407 U.S. 297 (1972) (national security wiretaps); Haig v. Agee, 453 U.S. 280 (1981) (power to revoke passports); Dames & Moore v. Regan, 453 U.S. 654 (1981) (agreement with Iran concerning release of hostages); Webster v. Doe, 486 U.S. 592 (1988) (dismissal of CIA employee, despite executive claim that national security information would be compromised by trial).

47. D'Amato et al., supra note 43, at 115–16 n.105.

48. See cases cited in note 4 to chapter 1; E. Keynes, Undeclared War: Twilight Zone of Constitutional Power 94–101 (1982); H. Koh, The National Security Constitution: Sharing Power After the Iran-Contra Affair 81–83 (1990).

49. 5 U.S. 87, 105, 1 Cranch 137, 167 (1803).

50. 6 U.S. 99, 2 Cranch 170 (1804).

51. *Little* also puts into proper perspective (as a statement only about the power to negotiate) Congressman Marshall's oft-quoted and almost-as-oft-abused reference to the president as the "sole organ of the nation in its external relations, and its sole representative with foreign nations." 10 Annals of Cong. 613 (1800).

52. *Chadha*, 462 U.S. at 942–43.

53. Occasionally courts ingenuously admit as much. E.g., Velvel v. Johnson, 287 F. Supp. 846, 850 (D. Kan. 1968), aff'd sub nom. Velvel v. Nixon, 415 F.2d 236 (10th Cir. 1969), cert. denied, 396 U.S. 1042 (1970) ("Though it is not always a simple matter to define the meaning of the term 'political question,' it is generally used to encompass all questions outside the scope of judicial power").

54. The idea that courts should avoid orders evincing "lack of the respect due coordinate branches of government," *Baker*, 369 U.S. at 217, had the potential for swallowing judicial review entirely, as did its companion notion that "multifarious pronouncements by various departments on one question" were to be avoided. Id. See, e.g., Sanchez-Espinoza v. Reagan, 568 F. Supp. 596, 600 (D.D.C. 1983), aff'd on other grounds, 770 F.2d 202 (D.C. Cir. 1985) (noting that certain members of Congress had disputed the President's claim on the issue at bar and reasoning, therefore, that a decision either way would mean that "one or both of the coordinate branches would be justifiably offended"); Lowry v. Reagan, 676 F. Supp. 333, 340 (D.D.C. 1987) (noting that since the members of Congress were divided on the issue in dispute, a judicial decision either way "necessarily would contradict legislative pronouncements on one side or the other of this issue," thus generating multifarious pronouncements). The point, of course, is that judicial decision is often needed to decide which branch legitimately speaks for the government (and thus precisely to *insure* that we will speak with one voice). By answering such arguments with the observation that "it is the responsibility of this Court to act as the ultimate constitutional arbiter," Powell v. McCormack, 395 U.S. 486, 549 (1969), the Court attempted to lay them to rest. See also *Chadha*, 462 U.S. at 942; L. Henkin, Constitutionalism, Democracy, and Foreign Affairs 89 (1990) (noting that most excuses invoked under the "political question" rubric were "contradicted by the institution of judicial review itself"). Hopefully the lower courts will get the idea soon.

55. *Baker*, 369 U.S. at 217.

56. See J. Ely, supra note 41, at 124–25.

57. But cf., e.g., United Steelworkers v. United States, 361 U.S. 39 (1959); United States v. First City Nat'l Bank, 386 U.S. 361 (1967).

58. On the difficulties of a court's determining whether we are either at war or engaged in hostilities, see pp. 60–61, 66–67.

59. "In fact, the Court has noted that it is an 'inadmissable suggestion' that action might be taken in disregard of a judicial determination." Powell v. McCormack, 395 U.S. 486, 549 n.86 (1969) (citing McPherson v. Blacker, 146 U.S. 1, 24 (1892)). This is more than the familiar parental "because I say so": It is one of the several happy miracles of our history that over 200 years all our institutions have assimi-

lated the message that the republic is more likely to survive if they recognize this kind of authority in the Court (though in turn the Court must be careful not to abuse it).

60. E.g., Massachusetts v. Laird, 451 F.2d 26 (1st Cir. 1971); Berk v. Laird, 429 F.2d 302 (2d Cir. 1970), cert. denied, 404 U.S. 869.

61. One of the "lessons of Vietnam" is that we shouldn't start small and ratchet up.

62. E.g., Dellums v. Bush, 752 F. Supp. 1141 (D.D.C. 1990) (Desert Storm; dismissed on ripeness grounds); Lowry v. Reagan, 676 F. Supp. 333 (D.D.C. 1987) (naval war against Iran; dismissed on political question grounds); Conyers v. Reagan, 765 F.2d 1124 (D.C. Cir. 1985) (Grenada; dismissed on mootness grounds); Crockett v. Reagan, 558 F. Supp. 893 (D.D.C. 1982), aff'd per curiam, 720 F.2d 1355 (D.C. Cir. 1983), cert. denied, 467 U.S. 1251 (1984) (El Salvador; dismissed on political question grounds); Mitchell v. Laird, 488 F.2d 611 (D.C. Cir. 1973) (closing phases of Indochina; dismissed as political question); Holtzman v. Schlesinger, described at p. 34 (1973 bombing of Cambodia).

63. From the beginning the Supreme Court has stood ready to entertain "separation of powers" controversies at the behest of private litigants whose interests will be affected by the outcome, even in cases where everyone understood that the private litigants were mere place holders in an underlying struggle between Congress and the president. See, e.g., Myers v. United States, 272 U.S. 52 (1926); F. Frankfurter & J. Landis, The Business of the Supreme Court 315 (1928); Jaffe, "The Citizen as Litigant in Public Actions: The Non-Hohfeldian or Ideological Plaintiff," 116 U. Pa. L. Rev. 1033, 1041 (1968). Against that background the historical reluctance to let representatives of the contending branches represent their own interests in court has never made sense, e.g., Monaghan, "Constitutional Adjudication: The Who and When," 82 Yale L.J. 1362, 1367–68 (1973), and the trend is distinctly in the other direction. P. Bator, D. Meltzer, P. Mishkin & D. Shapiro, Hart & Wechsler's The Federal Courts and the Federal System 80 (3d ed. 1988). The solid line of cases into which ours fits comfortably, permitting members of Congress to sue when an illegal act by the president has precluded a specific vote on their part, is in line with this trend.

Congressional standing in our case also seems sustainable under the theory of Barrows v. Jackson, 346 U.S. 249, 255–58 (1952), in that those most directly affected by the government's act are not, for the reasons noted at pp. 56–57, in a position effectively to litigate in defense of their own rights.

64. See Harrington v. Bush, 553 F.2d 190 (D.C. Cir. 1977). Cf. Ely, supra note 10, at 1413 n.98, suggesting that Lowry v. Reagan, supra note 62, may have been mishandled by styling the complaint thus rather than admitting the point was to start the sixty-day clock. (Of course the court would probably have found some way to dump it no matter what the complaint said.)

65. Note, "The Justiciability of Congressional-Plaintiff Suits," 82 Colum. L. Rev. 526, 542–44 (1982).

66. Goldwater v. Carter, 617 F.2d 697, 702 (D.C. Cir.) (en banc), vacated on other grounds, 444 U.S. 996 (1979). See also Note, supra note 65, at 548; cases cited in Ely, supra note 10, at 1413 n.100.

67. Judge Greene's holding has roots in Justice Powell's earlier suggestion that the courts ought to stay out of such disputes up until the point where the president

and Congress reach an impasse. Goldwater v. Carter, 444 U.S. 996, 997–1002 (1979) (Powell, J., concurring in judgment). That, however, is precisely the point at which Congress *can* be expected to take care of itself. (If the president defies a judgment of impeachment, the Court's intervention is unlikely to make much difference.) It is when Congress is ducking an issue it is constitutionally obligated to decide that judicial prodding may be needed.

68. 752 F. Supp. 1141 (D.D.C. 1990).

69. Stuart M. Gerson, the Assistant Attorney General who argued the case for the administration, exulted that the decision had "left the President's prerogatives for him to act unchanged and unaffected." N.Y. Times, Dec. 14, 1990, at A9. This was a frightening view of the demands of the Constitution for a high Justice Department official to take. The court finds that (although ripeness problems preclude judicial injunction) President Bush's (then) unilateral march toward war to be unconstitutional, and the administration claims . . . vindication!

70. *Dellums*, 752 F. Supp. at 1151.

71. Although there seems to be no good reason they shouldn't be, see note 63 supra, states are rarely plaintiffs in cases challenging congressional action as exceeding federal power, the federal government just as rarely a plaintiff in suits to enforce the dormant commerce clause. Most separation of powers cases are, similarly, brought by someone other the institution or official whose decision authority was usurped. See, e.g., Youngstown Sheet & Tube Co. v. Sawyer, 343 U.S. 579 (1952).

72. Okay, on some occasions only 50 percent, but we can ignore that refinement without losing the point.

73. E.g., 752 F. Supp. at 1151 n.28, 1152.

74. On the connection between Greene's ripeness holding and his implicit construction of the War Clause as requiring congressional approval on only those occasions when Congress wishes to take a stand one way or the other, see note 80 infra.

75. See note 188 to chapter 2.

76. See, e.g., M. Fiorina, Congress: Keystone of the Executive Establishment (2d ed. 1989); Ely, supra note 39, at 855–63, and sources cited therein.

77. N.Y. Times, Dec. 16, 1990, § 4, at 14.

78. 2 The Records of the Federal Convention 319 (M. Farrand ed. 1911). Cf. J. Story, Commentaries on the Constitution of the United States § 1166 (1833) ("It should therefore be difficult in a republic to declare war; but not to make peace").

79. And, presumably, the D.C. Circuit's "equitable discretion" doctrine. See note 82 infra.

80. Greene's language at several points underscored the connection between his "ripeness" holding and his failure to understand that the point of the War Clause cannot be served by leaving it up to Congress whether or not it wishes to take a stand. "[H]ere the [military] forces involved are of such magnitude and significance as to present no serious claim that a war would not ensue if they became engaged in combat, and it is therefore clear that congressional approval is required *if Congress desires to become involved.*" 752 F. Supp. at 1145 (emphasis supplied).

What if the Court issued the injunction requested by the plaintiffs, but it subsequently turned out . . . that the majority of the members of [the legislative]

Branch, for whatever reason, are content to leave this diplomatically and politically delicate decision to the President?

It would hardly do to have the Court, in effect, force a choice upon the Congress . . . .

Id. at 1150–51 (footnote omitted and emphasis supplied). However, since 1950 Congress has made it unfortunately clear that it is unprepared to perform its constitutionally assigned function of deciding on war and peace unless *someone* "forces" it to.

81. Judge Greene's test comes close to making cases like this practically nonjusticiable, in that "if a majority of Congress could demand an injunction from the Court, it could obviously take the more expeditious route of simply denying the president the money to act." J. Lehman, supra note 10, at 48.

82. In recent years the Court of Appeals for the District of Columbia Circuit has given sporadic signs of attempting to displace issues of congressional standing by a doctrine of "equitable discretion" that bars the courthouse doors to congressional plaintiffs in situations where the relief sought could be achieved by a majority vote of the plaintiffs' colleagues. Riegle v. Federal Open Mkt. Comm., 656 F.2d 873 (D.C. Cir.), cert. denied, 454 U.S. 1082 (1981), was the fountainhead "equitable discretion" case. See also Melcher v. Federal Open Mkt. Comm., 836 F.2d 561 (D.C. Cir. 1987), cert. denied, 486 U.S. 1042 (1988); McGowan, "Congressmen in Court: The New Plaintiffs," 15 Ga. L. Rev. 241 (1981). But cf. Humphrey v. Baker, 848 F.2d 211, 214 (D.C. Cir. 1988), cert. denied sub nom. Humphrey v. Brady, 488 U.S. 966 (1988):

We are fully mindful, however, that this circuit's recently minted doctrine of equitable discretion has not even been addressed, much less endorsed, by the Supreme Court. Moreover, several members of this court have previously expressed concern over whether equitable discretion represents "a viable doctrine upon which to determine the fate of constitutional litigation." Those concerns, which all members of this panel share, continue to trouble us. As a panel, however, we are of course bound faithfully to follow and apply the law of our circuit.

In further support of my suggestion of sporadicity, it can be noted that Barnes v. Kline, 759 F.2d 21 (D.C. Cir. 1985), vacated as moot sub nom. Burke v. Barnes, 479 U.S. 361 (1987), which allowed members of Congress to challenge an attempted intersession pocket veto, could have been mooted by Congress's passing the statute in question again more than ten days before the end of the second session.

The doctrine appears to straddle two rationales. Each is questionable to begin with, and in any event neither has plausible application to a suit to invoke section 4(a)(1) or otherwise to insist on a congressional vote of authorization before a war is begun. The first rationale is that by coming to court instead of taking their case to Congress the plaintiffs have chosen the wrong forum, attempting to circumvent the prescribed procedure. E.g., McGowan, supra, at 251. This rationale doesn't make a lot of sense generally: What the plaintiffs are seeking in court is not an opportunity to repeat the political arguments that failed in Congress but rather a decision on a question of law. (If they're not, they should be thrown out on *that* ground.) Nor does the rationale fit our case. If the plaintiffs are correct, the president is already under a statutory (and constitutional) duty, which he has shirked. The idea that they are somehow cheating if they do not secure the passage (over his veto) of an additional statute requiring him to comply with already existing law is elusive at best. (Indeed, it is not even clear that Congress has authority under the Resolution to start the clock or order the president to do so.)

We had therefore better try the other rationale. It is one sounding in ripeness, to the effect that if Congress would only change the law the way the plaintiffs want it to, the legal issue would vanish and the court would not have to expend its capital deciding the case. E.g., McGowan, supra, at 260. The initial problem with this rationale is that every issue courts decide would go away if only the legislature would change the law. The imagined distinguishing factor here, I suppose, is that the plaintiffs are *members* of the legislature and thus in a position to bring the change about. There are two answers to this. The first is that courts do not generally require self-help before hearing legal challenges, and it is not clear why this situation should be different. The second is that it is unrealistic to suppose that in many cases where a group of congressional plaintiffs have troubled to bring a lawsuit, they are well situated to effect the requested change legislatively. Surely this second, "ripeness" rationale is inapplicable to our case. Not only is Congress's proclivity to hide on issues of war and peace legendary, but beyond that, in order to get past *Chadha*, any resolution triggering 4(a)(1) (or otherwise instructing him to do his legal duty) would have to be vetoable by the president. See p. 124. And vetoed it certainly would be. And if by some miracle Congress were to pass it over the president's veto, what reason is there to suppose he would follow it more faithfully than he follows the War Powers Resolution or the Constitution (both of which, after all, have already given him the same direction)? This is simply not an issue with any realistic chance of being resolved legislatively if only the courts will refrain from hearing it.

Indeed, this seems the least plausible context imaginable for a court to turn aside a congressional plaintiff with an admonition to "go persuade your colleagues." Undergirding the War Powers Resolution was a recognition that most members of Congress, left to their own initiative, would dodge decisions of war and peace. The idea, therefore, was that the clock would be started by events and persons external to Congress, which then would essentially be forced to decide the issue. In fact the president has not performed his duty of starting the clock, and consequently—we are supposing—one or more members of Congress have had to come to court in an attempt to do so. In such circumstances it is no answer for the court to respond: "You shouldn't be here. You should go convince your colleagues to be self-starters." The entire basis of the Resolution was a realization that they wouldn't.

It should be noted finally, in particular connection with our discussion of the ways in which the War Powers Resolution might profitably be amended, that the cases are explicit that this equitable discretion doctrine can readily be overridden by statute. Synar v. United States, 626 F. Supp. 1374, 1382 (D.D.C. 1986), aff'd sub nom. Bowsher v. Synar, 478 U.S. 714 (1986); Moore v. United States House of Representatives, 733 F.2d 946, 954 (D.C. Cir. 1984), cert. denied, 469 U.S. 1106 (1985).

83. For example, Ange v. Bush, 752 F. Supp. 509 (D.D.C. 1990), also challenging the initiation of Desert Storm without congressional authorization, decided the

same day as *Dellums* (and dismissed on political question grounds,) was brought by a National Guard Sergeant called up to active duty.

84. Brief for Appellants at 30, Crockett v. Reagan, supra note 62, quoted in Note, "The Future of the War Powers Resolution," 36 Stan. L. Rev. 1407, 1437 n.163 (1984). See also id. at 1438 ("The phrase is not absolutely determinative, but it seems no more vague than innumerable other ambiguous statutes that courts regularly interpret . . . ."). The non sequitur that because one of the parties is prepared in his own interest to articulate a ludicrous construction of a statute, the statute must be unusually ambiguous—have these people never witnessed a lawsuit?—finds surprising favor with those of various political stripes. See, e.g., Biden & Ritch, "The War Power at a Constitutional Impasse: A 'Joint Decision' Solution," 77 Geo. L.J. 367, 401 (1988) (the fact that the Reagan Administration denied that "hostilities" occurred during the naval war against Iran demonstrates the ambiguity of the term). They denied it all right, but the denial was absurd. See note 10 supra. See also, e.g., L. Crovitz, A Presidential Strategy for Repealing the War Powers Resolution 6 (Heritage Soc. Backgrounder 1989) ("The term 'hostilities' is not defined by either the Constitution or the War Powers Resolution . . . . But does 'hostilities' include sending a strike force to spend a few days liberating a Caribbean island?"). It doesn't say what we win if we get this one right. The canons of construction at work on this "hypothetical" are further suggested id. at 9 ("The confusions of other sections also are present here . . . . Arguably, for example, sending a small force to liberate Grenada did not 'enlarge' forces there, because no forces were there before").

85. See cases cited Ely, supra note 10, at 1409 n.88. Courts also seem to experience little difficulty in holding the United States not to have been "at peace" for purposes of dismissing indictments under the Neutrality Act. (See note 8 to chapter 6.) See, e.g., United States v. Terrell, 731 F. Supp. 473 (S.D. Fla. 1989), dismissing indictment against five persons allegedly involved in the "Contra" war on the ground that despite the administration's various denials, the U.S. was not at peace with Nicaragua in 1984–85. A dictum indicates that we were similarly at war with Iran in the Persian Gulf in the 1980s. Id. at 475; but see the various administration denials cited in note 10 supra.

The spectre might be raised that on occasion it will be impossible for a court to tell whether we are engaged in hostilities without delving into military secrets. Two answers suggest themselves. The first would be that while it is entirely proper to keep our military plans secret once a war has been authorized, the evidence bearing on whether we are in fact at war cannot be classified, or the constitutional requirement of congressional authorization would be completely devoured. A second and independent answer would be that the burden of proving that we are engaged in hostilities is on the plaintiffs: If they can make their case, the supporting facts can't be much of a secret. As far as the government's case is concerned, "if U.S. military operations were actually no more extensive than had been publicly acknowledged, what was the danger in demonstrating that fact at trial?" Note, supra note 84, at 1437 n.164.

In fact, on rare occasion, the situation can be a little more complicated than these two answers acknowledge. It would work like this: Part of the plaintiffs' case for the proposition that the United States is engaged in hostilities would consist of the presence during, say, a foreign civil war of a significant number of U.S. military "advisers." The government would then answer that those advisers have not been engaged in hostilities (and indeed, nice trick, are not even exposed to the imminent danger thereof) because in fact they are doing something else. And just what is that something else? That we cannot tell you, the government answers, because to do so we would have to reveal military secrets. (The classified alibi—I know it sounds like the fantasy of a logician turned public defender, but this argument actually was made in the El Salvador litigation.) If this does come up, and if it's plausible, there are ways of dealing with it: They are not entirely satisfactory from anyone's perspective, but they are certainly preferable to declaring the entire inquiry a political question. The first is to instruct counsel not to reveal the contents of the government's files to anyone. Should that prove unacceptable, as on occasion it might, the judge or a special master could review the evidence *in camera* and file a report shielding the classified material. (This technique has been used to explore allegations of illegal FBI informant infiltration. See Socialist Workers Party v. Attorney Gen. of the United States, 642 F. Supp. 1357, 1378 (S.D.N.Y. 1986). The recent North, Poindexter, and Noriega cases all also demonstrated that trials involving much classified information can be handled by able federal judges without generating harmful leaks.) In any event, the time to recognize and cope with an evidentiary privilege is when it is claimed and justified regarding a specific piece of information, not in order to remove an entire legal inquiry from the courts. Ramirez de Arellano v. Weinberger, 745 F.2d 1500, 1513 (D.C. Cir. 1984) (en banc), complaint dismissed in light of intervening statute granting relief, 788 F.2d 762 (1986). Most claims that U.S. forces are engaged in hostilities will not involve a plausible claim that military secrets are at risk. In the Iranian naval war case, for example—Lowry v. Reagan, supra note 62—the congressional plaintiffs moved for summary judgment, since all their proof was based on government statements. (On the off chance you're wondering why I haven't mentioned the Classified Information Procedures Act, it applies only in criminal cases.)

86. In a suit under the War Powers Resolution, a court will confront an important choice of procedure and remedy. Should it:

(1) limit its inquiry to whether we are *currently* in a situation of hostilities or imminent likelihood thereof, and if it decides we are, order the president to file a 4(a)(1) report and thereby start the clock forthwith;

(2) similarly decide only whether we are currently in a state of imminent hostilities, and if we are, start the clock itself;

(3) determine (retroactively) the day on which we arrived at a situation of imminent hostilities, declare the clock to have started on that day, calculate whether sixty days have passed since that day, and if they have, order the President to withdraw the troops; or

(4) adopt some variant of one of these?

This gets kind of tricky—for example, the proposed "Use of Force Act," note 111 infra, simply proffers a court an unguided choice of remedies (1), (2), and (3)—but the best answer seems to be that whereas under a more sensibly reconstituted War Powers Resolution (one with a functionally defensible "free period," such as twenty days) something amounting to alternative (2) would be the most straightforward and sensible approach, under the existing Resolution, with its sixty/ninety-day clock, an altered version of alternative (3) is the one a court should adopt.

The first alternative, ordering the president to file a report and start the clock, seems to be the usual suggestion. For example, the congressional plaintiffs in the Iranian naval war lawsuit, *Lowry v. Reagan*, supra note 62, sought an order requiring the president to file a 4(a)(1) report "within forty-eight hours" of the Court's judgment. This alternative can, however, be rapidly dispatched: Such a judicial order would invite presidential disobedience and, given the alternative of the court's starting the clock itself, it would do so unnecessarily. It thus seems a needlessly risky status degradation ceremony, a little like ordering the president to apologize.

The second alternative—having the court determine whether we are currently in a situation of imminent hostilities and if we are, simply starting the clock itself—is very attractive on the surface. It not only (unlike an unamended version of the third alternative) serves the Resolution's purpose of giving Congress a period to consider the wisdom of the war in question, but also (unlike the first alternative) minimizes the chances of presidential disobedience, in that at the end of the period of congressional consideration, either the war will have been authorized or the courts will have acquired a powerful ally in the unlikely event the president persists in pursuing his war. Although I don't phrase it in terms of judicial clock-starting, this is functionally the procedure the statute I propose in the appendix incorporates. See also Ely, supra note 10, at 1416–17.

My statute, however, shortens the "free period" from sixty to twenty days. Without that change, there is too great a possibility that in operation the second approach, of simply having the court start the clock, would badly disserve the Resolution's central purpose, by insuring maximum delay (often, in these days of quickie wars, probable elimination) of congressional consideration. The rational strategy of a president intent on "preserving executive power" would be not to dream of complying by filing a 4(a)(1) report at the time he committed the troops but rather to pursue his war full blast, defending against the lawsuit only when and if it came. Even if the case were decided before the war was over, *and* even if he lost, he would automatically get another sixty days (which he could readily extend to ninety) to pursue it—and probably a good deal longer, if he appealed and obtained a stay in the meantime. (This would be his rational strategy under alternative (1) as well, and thus counts as another, though superfluous, argument against that alternative. Of course an appeal with a stay will be a possibility under any procedure, including that incorporated in my statute, but that's something we can't—and shouldn't be able to—do anything about, which is one reason my proposed statute makes orders granting or denying a judgment that the criteria of section 4(a) have been met directly appealable to the Supreme Court. Obviously that may not speed things up sufficiently: Due process always carries costs. The values underlying the War Clause will never be fully served until the president is conditioned to comply with the Constitution without a court order forcing him to. See note 61 to the appendix.)

The third alternative—determining when the standard set forth in section 4(a)(1) was met and retroactively starting the clock from that moment, ordering the troops out if sixty days have since elapsed—has an obvious large advantage: It withdraws the troops immediately from what is, by hypothesis, an illegal war, rather than leaving them exposed for another ninety days or longer. It also seems the alternative that best fits the existing statutory command that the troops be withdrawn "[w]ithin sixty calendar days after a report is submitted *or is required to be submitted* pursuant to section 4(a)(1)." (Actually alternative (1) also can be made to fit the Resolution's language fairly comfortably—by regarding the moment of the court's order to the president as the time at which the report was "required to be submitted"— though (1) is inadvisable on other grounds. Making alternative (2)—otherwise a good deal more sensible than alternative (1)—fit the statutory language is a taller order. The court "required" *itself* to start the clock? However, the language was not carefully chosen—Congress never actually focused on what would happen if the president didn't comply—and under such circumstances reference to the Resolution's larger purposes would seem in order.)

Before we leap to the conclusion that the existing Resolution should be construed as adopting alternative (3), however—and I agree that that is basically where we should end up—there are four counterarguments with which we must contend. First, the question whether we are in a situation presenting the imminent likelihood of hostilities can be difficult enough to answer in the present tense. It will often complicate matters to turn it into a historical inquiry, wherein the exact moment when hostilities became imminent must be determined retroactively. Second, such a retroactive judgment more directly questions the president's good faith than one to the effect that we have now arrived at a situation of imminent danger of hostilities, and thus is more likely to risk resistance on his part. (A judgment to the effect that the president has been in violation of the law for some months is quite an indictment, whereas a holding that we are *now* in a 4(a)(1) situation is susceptible to the construction that the president himself might have been on the verge of reaching the same conclusion.)

Third, because (at least unamended) it contemplates an order to the president to remove the troops forthwith (without an intervening period of congressional consideration), this alternative, like the first, quite directly risks presidential disobedience. It is true that unlike the first, it does not do so needlessly, since it would mean (assuming the president complied) that the troops would be withdrawn sooner. However, while presidents do not ordinarily disobey the Court, one reason they don't is that the Court has been careful to shape its orders so as to minimize the possibility. Fourth, although it's true that this third alternative comfortably fits the Resolution's language, as stated it seems not to fit its *purpose* at all. The Resolution's point was not to eliminate war altogether, or to close down those wars respecting which a procedural error had been made at the outset, but rather to assure that we would become permanently entangled only in those wars that Congress had been induced to think about and had clearly authorized. Unamended, this third alternative entirely eliminates the period of congressional consideration and thus hardly fits the purpose of the Resolution.

The problem is that the first alternative has been shown to be unwise under any circumstances, the second equally so under the existing Resolution, with its sixty/ninety-day free period. We thus seem to have painted ourselves into a fine kettle of fish. There is, however, a way out even under the existing Resolution, which consists in altering the third alternative so as to resemble less closely the construct of an academic, and more closely what a real court would be likely to do if confronted with a request that it enjoin a complex governmental program—namely to frame, publish, and justify a judgment to the effect that the war is being fought illegally, but stay its effective date for twenty days in order to give Congress an opportunity to convene and decide whether to authorize the continued maintenance of the troops in the field. (The alert reader will have picked up on the fact that I have just altered the third alternative so as to make it identical in operation—where sixty days have in fact run since hostilities became imminent—to what the second alternative would provide were the free period shortened to twenty days: Either way Congress gets twenty days to approve the war, or the court will issue a final declaration that it's illegal.)

This remedial refinement, granting Congress a reasonable period of consideration and thus maximizing the chances of its support in the unlikely event the president remains recalcitrant, eliminates forthwith the third and fourth objections we noted to the third alternative. The first objection will persist, however, in that this alternative will indeed require a historical as opposed to a present-tense inquiry. This, however, seems like something we'll just have to live with, as just this sort of retrospective inquiry appears to be what the Resolution's language (and the goal of getting the troops out within the foreseeable future) require. For those who remain troubled by this complication, a couple of things can be added. The first is that in the usual case it *won't* be necessary to determine "the exact moment" at which hostilities became imminent: The way lawsuits develop, we are likely to be a good deal more than sixty days beyond any of the plausible dates before the court reaches the point of having to choose among them. And when the question whether the point of imminent hostilities was reached more than sixty days ago *is* close, there is no reason the courts shouldn't (as they do in other contexts) accord the president's judgment some deference: I know it sounds silly to spell it out, but if the court can't say with some degree of confidence that hostilities became imminent before a certain date, it shouldn't.

The second objection to this alternative also persists, sort of: A finding that the president has been in violation of the law for some time is more of an indictment than a "simple" finding that he is now in violation of the law. Ordinarily, however, we operate on the assumption that bigger indictments are precisely what bigger transgressions deserve. To the extent the fear is that a "bigger indictment" will increase the chances of presidential defiance, our modification—granting Congress a period to decide whether or not to authorize the war—should insure the courts congressional support in the event the president persists in his unconstitutional behavior.

87. And, initially (though subject to judicial review), the executive, though in the case under discussion the executive has refused to perform it.

88. Under *Chadha*, supra note 33.

89. E.g., *Lowry, Conyers,* and *Crockett,* all supra note 62. That the two Desert Storm opinions—*Ange*, supra note 83, and *Dellums*, discussed at pp. 57–60—were so radically different in tone was probably mainly a function of the judges' identities, though conceivably it also resulted in part from the fact that only the former added a challenge under the Resolution to the constitutional challenge. If that is so, it is supremely ironic, in that much of the perceived accomplishment of the Resolution was to eradicate the various "justiciability" excuses courts seized upon to dis-

miss lawsuits challenging the Vietnam war. Ratner & Cole, "The Force of Law: Judicial Enforcement of the War Powers Resolution," 17 Loy. L.A. L. Rev. 715, 754 (1984). (*Ange* also suffered from the inclusion of a staggeringly weak due process challenge to the procedure by which the plaintiff's claim of nondeployability on the basis of an ulcer was disallowed: In fact he was examined by several doctors and permitted to submit whatever civilian medical records he wished.)

90. Roberts, "War Resolution is Cited, Skirted—But Never Used," S.F. Banner Daily J., Nov. 30, 1987, at 1.

91. 134 Cong. Rec. S7175 (daily ed. June 6, 1988).

92. Notably Eugene Rostow. See Rostow, supra note 38; Rostow, "Great Cases Make Bad Law: The War Powers Act," 50 Tex. L. Rev. 833 (1972). Professor Rostow was the dean when I was in law school—on some level probably one of the reasons I made the otherwise inexplicable choice to become a dean myself—and is otherwise one of my heroes, not least because of his timely and courageous attack on the Japanese internment program. He was subsequently Under Secretary of State in the Johnson Administration and thus understandably (and correctly, see chapter 2) affronted by undiscriminating charges that the Vietnam war was "unconstitutional." I think he's run rather too far with this reaction, though obviously he would disagree.

93. Pp. 64–65.

94. 462 U.S. 919 (1983). I argue in the appendix that 5(c) is distinguishable, but I doubt the Court would buy the argument. Pp. 119–20.

95. The War Powers Resolution has a separability clause, reprinted at p. 138.

96. E.g., Tuley, "The War Powers Resolution: A Questionable Solution," 1985 A.F. L. Rev. 244, 272. Despite the separability clause and the practical unimportance of 5(c) under any circumstances—because Congress would never summon up the quick resolve to invoke it, p. 120—this "inference" has generated unaccountably intemperate rhetoric from ordinarily temperate commentators. E.g., Statement of J. N. Moore at the Hearing of the Federation of American Scientists, Jan. 7, 1991:

> It is virtually the equivalent of a massive resistance by the Congress of the United States to the Rule of Law that [the Resolution] remains on the books having been struck down, in key part, by the Supreme Court of the United States with respect to the key operative provisions of the Act . . . .

But see, e.g., Hearings on U.S. Supreme Court Decision Concerning Legislative Veto before the House Committee on Foreign Affairs, 98th Cong., 1st Sess., at 52 (1983) (testimony of Deputy Attorney General Edward Schmults) ("[T]he Supreme Court's decision does not affect any of the procedural mechanisms contained in the War Powers Resolution other than the procedure specified in section 5(c) . . . . ").

97. E.g., Crovitz, "Micromanaging Foreign Policy," 100 Pub. Int. 102 (1990).

98. See note 19 to chapter 1. The Eisenhower presidency spanned most of the period between the wars in Korea and Vietnam, and thus most military actions during that period were congressionally authorized—albeit, as in Vietnam, not in the most constitutionally responsible way, cf. p. 26, but rather by open-ended resolutions requested by the President essentially delegating him authority to do what-

ever he wanted in a given area of the world. See generally J. Sundquist, The Decline and Resurgence of Congress 114–18 (1981) (discussing Formosa, Middle East, Cuba, and Berlin resolutions).

99. *Chadha*, discussed at pp. 119–20, invalidated more than two hundred federal statutes dating back to the 1930s, many of them signed by the president. See also p. 10 (Justice Frankfurter on the sort of long-standing and consistent practice needed to shape constitutional development); note 50 to chapter 1 (Court on slight relevance of nonjudicial practice not occurring close in time to founding).

100. U.S. Const. art. I, § 8, cl. 18 (emphasis added). See also Hearings on War Powers Legislation before the Senate Comm. on Foreign Relations, 92d Cong., 1st Sess. 551 (1971) (statement of Professor Alexander M. Bickel) ("Whatever is needed to flesh out the slender recital of Executive functions must be done by Congress under the 'necessary-and-proper' clause. Congress alone can make the laws which will carry into execution the powers of the Government as a whole, and of its officers, including the President."). Enthusiasts of Justice Jackson's concurrence in Youngstown Sheet & Tube v. Sawyer, 343 U.S. 579, 634 (1952), should have little trouble regarding the Resolution as a congressional exercise in mapping the "twilight zone," and therefore plainly constitutional and controlling under the logic of that opinion. (Others of us—including, incidentally, Justice Jackson himself, id. at 642—see the power to authorize acts of war as assigned to the legislative process by the Constitution and thus not in need of rescue from any twilight zone.)

101. See Hearings on War Powers Resolution before the Senate Comm. on Foreign Relations, 95th Cong., 1st Sess. 90 (1977) (testimony of Professor Abraham Sofaer) ("Looking at the War Powers Resolution in historical perspective, I cannot escape the conclusion that it is entirely consistent with established patterns of constitutional conduct"); Cox, "*Raison d'État* and World Survival: Who Constitutionally Makes Nuclear War?" 57 Geo. Wash. L. Rev. 1614, 1617 (1989) ("Critics ignore the fact that the Resolution is essentially a restatement of historical principle").

102. Thus Professor Laurence Tribe, whose treatise gave effusive support to the Resolution's constitutionality (aside from section 5(c)), L. Tribe, American Constitutional Law, § 4–7, at 236 (2d ed. 1988), has more recently characterized it as "largely a dead letter," an assessment that has had the unfortunate effect of leading popular writers inaccurately to infer that "a consensus" has developed "within the legal community that the War Powers Resolution was a hortatory admonition to the president, but nothing more." J. Smith, supra note 27, at 107–8.

103. Compare, e.g., Lakeland, "The War Powers Resolution: Necessary and Legal Remedy to Prevent Future Vietnams," in Congress, the President, and Foreign Policy 153 (J. Moore & R. Turner eds. 1984), and Glennon, "The War Powers Resolution: Sad Record, Dismal Promise," 17 Loy. L.A. L. Rev. 657 (1984), with Berdes & Huber, "Making the War Powers Resolution Work: The View From the Trench (A Response to Professor Glennon)," 17 Loy. L.A. L. Rev. 671 (1984).

104. Letter from Professor Abram Chayes to author, June 7, 1989.

105. See sources cited Ely, supra note 10, at 1412 n.95, 1413–14 n.102; 1416 n.110.

106. See pp. 6–7.

107. During the Cold War we thought we knew who the enemy would be, and where trouble was likely to break out, and thus at least tried to have the troops and equipment appropriately ready. For the foreseeable future it's probably going increasingly to resemble a fun house—some fun, eh?—with bogeymen popping up where we least expect them.

108. Desert Storm also was a situation where there existed what seemed at the time a plausible hope that we could intimidate the enemy into backing down. All the administration's advance public discussion of exactly when we should move into Kuwait eliminated the possibility of any plausible claim that the President was engaged in the contemporary functional equivalent of "repelling a sudden attack" and thus couldn't go to Congress in advance for the constitutionally required authorization. (The exceptional case, where compelling military reasons require that the planning be done (and it in fact *can* be done) secretly, is discussed in chapter 6.)

109. But cf. note 20 to chapter 2.

110. See, e.g., Bandow, "Declare War, Conditionally: We've Done It Four Times in the Past," N.Y. Times, Jan. 3, 1991, at A15; Scigliano, "The War Powers Resolution and the War Powers," in The Presidency in the Constitutional Order 125 (J. Bessette & J. Tulis eds. 1981).

111. Thus the "Use of Force Act" being pushed by Senator Biden, Professor Glennon, and Mr. Ritch extends the free period to 120 days, M. Glennon, supra note 15, at 334, on the theory that this "would provide more flexibility to both the President and Congress." Biden & Ritch, supra note 84, at 404. Indeed it would, and that would compound the unconstitutionality of the existing provision.

112. Ely, supra note 10.

113. Notably the "Use of Force Act," respecting which I make some criticisms in note 111 supra and the appendix, but which is nonetheless a kindred effort.

114. The most prominent recent proposal to change the War Powers Resolution has been that of the powerful combination of Senators Byrd, Nunn, Warner, and Mitchell—Congressman Hamilton has introduced the measure on the House side—to repeal its central provisions. (The Byrd proposal is S.J. Res. 323, the Hamilton version H.R.J. Res. 601—both 100th Cong., 2d Sess. (1988).) Their proposed amendment specifies both a small group (the Speaker of the House, the President pro tempore of the Senate, and the majority and minority leaders of both houses) and a larger "permanent consultative group" (those six plus twelve other congressional VIPs) with whom presidential "consultation" under section 3 is to take place. That is surely a step in the right direction, as presidents since 1973 have complained that they were never sure exactly with whom they were supposed to consult. However, the Byrd-Nunn amendments do not attempt to put teeth into the concept of "consultation," thus leaving open the possibility that it will continue to take the same form it has in the past, that of merely informing the congressional leadership of decisions already reached and respecting which implementation has often already begun.

More important, this limited advance is to be achieved at the cost of the Resolution's central mechanism, the sixty-day clock, which would be excised. No longer would there be a date beyond which troops, if not congressionally authorized, would have to be removed from the battlefield. The sixty-day clock should be removed, the amendments' sponsors explain, because it has proved "unworkable." And so it has—but why? Very simply, because the president has refused to obey the law, and Congress has not had the fortitude to call him on it. The spirit animating the amendments thus seems to be that expressed, pessimistically, by Senator Simon: "maybe realistically we ought to get rid of it because it is meaningless if we do not use it in [an Iranian naval war] kind of a situation." 134 Cong. Rec. S7172 (daily ed. June 6, 1988). *Congressional Quarterly* captured the situation well by reporting that "a major thrust" of the Byrd-Nunn proposal would "be to make the War Powers Resolution less restrictive of prospective military commitments, in hopes that future presidents will acknowledge its validity." Cong. Q., Apr. 23, 1988, at 1051. Repeal *is* one way to decrease noncompliance.

In place of the sixty-day clock (and the concurrent resolution provision) the Byrd-Nunn amendments provide that Congress can pass a joint resolution requiring the president to disengage our troops from hostilities and cutting off funds for their continued support. That, however, is no substitute at all. A joint resolution or statute ending a war by cutting off its funding (each, of course, would almost certainly have to be passed, by a two-thirds vote, over the president's veto) is a possibility that has universally been conceded to be constitutional throughout our history. Mentioning it in the (new, "improved") War Powers Resolution does not add to its stature, or the likelihood of its invocation.

The amendments do give such a joint resolution procedural priority in Congress (though only if it has been approved by a majority of the eighteen-member "permanent consultative group"). Obviously that is not a bad thing, but it is hardly a substitute for the doomed provisions of the existing War Powers Resolution (whose proceedings, incidentally, also receive procedural priority—whether or not they have the approval of the leadership). Congress has not had the mettle to confront the president when he has violated section 4(a)(1) by refusing to file a "hostilities" report. All the procedural priority in the world is not going to get it to take the affirmative step of passing over the president's veto what amounts to a statute instructing him to terminate a war that, under the proposed amendments, he will have entered into with total legality. The Constitution contemplates that before American troops are exposed to the risk of death, the military engagement in question must be affirmatively approved by Congress. Giving that body the "right" to end a presidential war by passing a joint resolution over his veto hardly fulfills the constitutional plan.

Shall we therefore regard the Byrd-Nunn amendments as simply a bad trade—of the existing Resolution's requirement of congressional approval for the trappings of "consultation" that are to be accorded the leadership under the new scheme? Well, no, since it wouldn't really be a trade at all. Congress's performance in this area over the past forty-three years demonstrates that it may prove only too happy to settle back into the pattern of letting the president get out front and then, when the war begins not to play so well, making various feints in the direction of ending it, complaining that it is being stymied by the possibility of a veto and that there isn't much it can do about a fait accompli. Indeed, as Senator Biden and Mr. Ritch have pointed out, enactment of Byrd-Nunn would in one sense return us to a situation *worse* than the status quo ante, in that it would give that status quo ante something it lacked before the enactment of the War Powers Resolution: a moderately clear statutory imprimatur. Biden & Ritch, supra note 84, at 393–94.

115. Technically, jurisdiction would be under 28 U.S.C. § 1331 (1988), which grants federal district courts jurisdiction of all civil actions arising under the Constitution.

116. See also p. 67. Also, the Bush Administration had made some outrageously sweeping claims of unilateral constitutional authority, on which the complainants understandably wished to focus (and which it was important to have authoritatively rejected).

117. The Resolution provides a surrogate, in that most badmouthing of its various provisions actually amounts to badmouthing of the original constitutional understanding.

118. See p. 78. The Resolution indicates that nothing can count as an authorization of the use of our armed forces in combat unless it "states that it is intended to constitute specific statutory authorization within the meaning of this joint resolution": Thus to count, the authorization has to mention the War Powers Resolution by name. See, e.g., note 17 supra (Desert Storm Resolution). Admittedly it feels a little weird to suggest that *this* provision could end up ultimately controlling a suit brought not "under" the Resolution but rather on the theory that the Constitution has been offended because the war in question hasn't been authorized, but I'm unable to understand why that doesn't logically follow. The constitutional question here is whether congressional authorization has been given, and—in what seems a plainly constitutional provision—Congress has told us what (until repeal) it does and doesn't mean to count as authorization.

119. See, e.g., *Dellums*, 752 F. Supp. at 1146; Mitchell v. Laird, 488 F.2d 611, 614 (D.C. Cir. 1973).

120. U.S. Const. art. I, § 8, cl. 11.

121. E.g., J. Story, supra note 78, §§ 1164–71; Lofgren, "War-Making Under the Constitution: The Original Understanding," 81 Yale L.J. 672, 679–80, 695–97, 699–700 (1972); 21 The Papers of Alexander Hamilton 461–62 (H. Syrett ed. 1974) ("anything beyond [repelling force with force] must fall under the idea of reprisals and requires the sanction of that Department which is to declare war").

122. I am aware that in many respects the Court has become considerably more conservative of late. But given its historical lineage, this is a "liberal-conservative" squabble in only the most transient sense. Also bear in mind that the immediate question here is whether a congressional statute should be invalidated, a course toward which "conservatives" are by no means automatically predisposed, and that the case for the constitutionality of its central mechanism is overwhelming, a condition justices of all persuasions have throughout our history most often been reliable in recognizing.

123. My proposed revision would reduce the free period to twenty days at most, and eliminate it altogether where there is time to obtain authorization in advance.

124. Even in a suit brought strictly under the Constitution, the executive branch now has available the response that whatever the Constitution would otherwise permit, Congress by the Resolution has effectively delegated it ninety free days to wage any war it likes. It seems unlikely to do so (lest it thereby legitimate the

Resolution) but the possibility makes all the more imperative adoption of the two changes mentioned in the preceding note.

125. See p. 53.

126. One might legitimately wonder whether, given their recent record of avoiding the issue, there is any greater chance of the *courts'* responding to my suggestion and getting seriously into the business of prodding Congress to do its constitutional duty. (For me personally this takes on something of an existential character: Why write this book if the courts are no more likely to change than the president and Congress?) The personal question is the easier one: We all do what we can. The courts are the constituency I am accustomed to addressing (both directly and indirectly through other scholars), and on occasion they have listened. Concerning the larger question I would make a few additional observations: (1) Throughout the first century of our nation's existence courts routinely entertained the very question I am suggesting they should now entertain. (Admittedly that one is mitigated by the fact that as regards questions of war and peace the other branches pretty much behaved as the Constitution intended them to during that period too.) (2) *Dellums*, and the positive academic reaction it has generated, might just represent a harbinger of a return to this tradition. (3) Though government officials generally are disinclined to take note of serious discussions except to the extent they can be cited in support of positions already reached, judges seem more often than others actually to read things on the theory they might be educated by them. (Stepping out for the evening with lobbyists and groupies is frowned upon.) (4) Most important, perhaps, whereas one can readily understand why the president wishes to retain his effective unilateral decision authority, and Congress equally wishes not to rock its "nonaccountability" boat, it is difficult to identify any comparable self-interest that should discourage judges from prodding Congress to do the job the Constitution assigns it. (It is of course that comparative lack of political self-interest that has generally made the American institution of judicial review one of history's most successful governmental innovations.)

127. For example, compare Ex Parte Endo, 323 U.S. 283 (1944), with Korematsu v. United States, 323 U.S. 214 (1944), and Ex Parte Milligan, 71 U.S. (4 Wall.) 2 (1866), with Ex Parte Vallandigham, 68 U.S. (1 Wall.) 243 (1863).

CHAPTER 4
THE (UNENFORCEABLE) UNCONSTITUTIONALITY OF THE
"SECRET WAR" IN LAOS, 1962–1969

1. Quoted in Hearings before the Subcomm. to Investigate Problems Connected with Refugees and Escapees of the Senate Comm. on the Judiciary, 92d Cong., 1st Sess. 100 (1971) (App. II).

2. Quoted in Sharpe, "The Real Cause of Irangate," 68 Foreign Pol'y 19, 31–32 (1987).

3. Throughout most of the war, the North Vietnamese denied the existence of the trail, and many Americans believed them.

4. Having said that, perhaps I should add—so you'll know (as we said during the period under discussion) "where I'm coming from"—that I believe just as fervently that if we had to pick a side, we were on the right one in Laos (and, God knows,

Cambodia). Vietnam is substantially less clear in this regard, though that's the war that was constitutional: I seem to be fated to spend my life pointing out that these are not the same thing.

5. Quoted in C. Robbins, The Ravens 339 (1987). (Buell ran the AID mission at Sam Thong.) As of this writing, *The Ravens* is probably the most comprehensive and responsible treatment of America's role in the war in Laos, often, for example, considerably more conservative in its estimates of American-inflicted carnage than even other apparently nonhysterical accounts.

6. 28 Cong. Q. Weekly Rep. 1243 (1970).

7. U.S. News & World Rep., Jan. 5, 1970, at 29; C. Robbins, Air America 94 ("updated" Avon ed. 1990). (Yes, this is the book on which the Mel Gibson movie of the same name was based, but it is a serious work, albeit in large measure a less comprehensive precursor of the author's *The Ravens,* supra note 5.)

8. A. Isaacs, G. Hardy & MacA. Brown, Pawns of War: Cambodia and Laos 72 (1987). "Books by men who worked with the Green Berets suggest that there was no major pause in activity because of Geneva." C. Stevenson, The End of Nowhere: American Policy Toward Laos Since 1954, at 186–87 (1972).

9. Air America, supra note 7, at 94.

10. Haney, "The Pentagon Papers and the United States Involvement in Laos," in 5 The Pentagon Papers 248, 273 (Sen. Gravel ed. 1972), breaks it down further:

> Two of the "wars" were fought by American war planes, STEEL TIGER in southern Laos, and BARREL ROLL in northern Laos. A third and less secret "war" was conducted by the Laotian *Forces Armée Royale* (FAR) . . . . The fourth war was that conducted by the irregular forces variously known as the Secret Army, the CIA Army, the Special Guerrilla Units (SGU) or the *Bataillon Guerriers* (BGS).

11. The Secret Army has been characterized as a guerrilla force, Vang Pao as a virtually independent warlord. M. Stuart-Fox, Laos: Politics, Economics, and Society 46–47 (1986). Although officially an officer (and regional commander) of the Royal Laotian Armed Forces, J. Prados, Presidents' Secret Wars: CIA and Pentagon Operations Since World War II, at 273 (1986), Vang Pao once reportedly declined to follow Premier Souvanna Phouma's order that he defend Luang Prabang. Haney, supra note 10, at 273.

12. N.Y. Times, Oct. 26, 1969, at 1, 24; The Ravens, supra note 5, at 108. General Secord reports that the "CIA eventually had over 80,000 troops, mostly Meo tribesmen, on the ground in Laos . . . ." R. Secord (with J. Wurts), Honored and Betrayed: Irangate, Covert Affairs, and the Secret War in Laos 57 (1992). "Meo" is indeed the more common usage, but will not be employed in this book, because it is not the term the Hmongs use but rather a somewhat derogatory Chinese term (essentially meaning "savage").

13. A. Isaacs et al., supra note 8, at 103; The Ravens, supra note 5, at 236.

14. N.Y. Times, Oct. 26, 1969, at 24. Cf. J. Ranelagh, The Agency: The Rise and Decline of the CIA 425 (1986).

15. Hearings on Fiscal Year 1972 Authorization for Military Procurement, Research and Development before the Senate Comm. on Armed Services, 92d Cong. 1st Sess. 4293 (1971); see also V. Marchetti & J. Marks, The CIA and the Cult of Intelligence 31 (1974).

16. Abrams, "The Once-Hidden War," New Leader, Feb. 16, 1970, at 8, 10.

17. Id. at 10.

18. N.Y. Times, Oct. 26, 1969, at 24; Branfman, "Presidential War in Laos, 1964–1970," in Laos: War and Revolution 265 (N. Adams and A. McCoy eds. 1970); C. Stevenson, supra note 8, at 4; R. Secord, supra note 12, at 68.

19. D. Kirk, Wider War: The Struggle for Cambodia, Thailand, and Laos 236 (1971). Thus "the Ravens," actually forward air controllers whose function was to direct fighter-bombers onto targets from smaller spotter planes, were officially classified as forest rangers working for AID. The Ravens, supra note 5, at 30.

20.

Continental was owned by the domestic United States airline of the same name and its Laotian service had been set up in cooperation with the CIA. Ostensibly it was flying for AID, under lucrative contracts, but in actuality it was with the CIA, and its top officers had been given special security clearances by the agency.

Air America, on the other hand, was a fully owned and operated subsidiary of the CIA—called a "proprietary."

M. Halperin, J. Berman, R, Borosage & C. Marwick, The Lawless State: The Crimes of the U.S. Intelligence Agencies 43 (1976) (footnote omitted). See also Air America, supra note 7, at 296–97. Apparently some of the business was thrown to Continental for fear that an antitrust investigation of Air America would reveal who owned it and what it was up to. J. Prados, supra note 11, at 277.

21. N.Y. Times, Sept. 18, 1970, at 10; N.Y. Times, Oct. 26, 1969, at 1, 24.

22. Halloran, "Air America's Civilian Facade Gives It Latitude in East Asia," N. Y. Times, Apr. 5, 1970, at 1, 22. This process was known as "sheep-dipping."

Sheep-dipped: A complex process in which someone serving in the military seemingly went through all the official motions of resigning from the service. The man's records would be pulled from the personnel files and transferred to a special Top Secret intelligence file. A cover story would be concocted to explain the resignation, and the man would become a civilian. At the same time, his ghostly paper existence within the intelligence file would continue to pursue his Air Force career: when his contemporaries were promoted, he would be promoted, and so on. Sheep-dipped personnel posed extremely tricky problems when they were killed or captured. There would be all sorts of pension and insurance problems, which was one of the reasons the CIA found it necessary to set up its own insurance company.

The Ravens, supra note 5, at 49 n.*. (General Secord's definition suggests less punctiliousness: "what the USAF called 'sheep dipped'—U.S. Servicemen with critical skills posing as civilian contractors on a volunteer basis." R. Secord, supra note 12, at 76.) Though I'm not aware that the term was applied here, it seems airplanes were sometimes "sheep-dipped" too:

The Air Force would deliver the planes, which were painted completely differently from their usual official coloring and had screw-on Air Force insignia and Scotch tape markings. (In fact, the 3M company had a contract to manufacture these kits.) It took about two hours to convert one of these planes so that when it was stripped down it would be non-attributable. The result was what the CIA referred to as a "sanitized" aircraft.

Air America, supra note 7, at 102–3.

23. N.Y. Times, Oct. 26, 1969, at 1, 24.

24. Id. at 24.

25. J. Orman, Presidential Secrecy and Deception 102–3 (1980) (footnote omitted).

26. Szulc, "Mum's the War," New Republic, Aug. 18 & 25, 1973, at 19, 20; N.Y. Times, Oct. 26, 1969, at 1, 24.

27. J. Prados, supra note 11, at 280.

28. F. Wormuth & E. Firmage, To Chain the Dog of War: The War Power of Congress in History and Law 260 (2d ed. 1989). There remain an estimated 533 Americans classified as "missing in action" in Laos. Sesser, "Forgotten Country," New Yorker, Aug. 20, 1990, at 39, 66.

29. For this entire chronology, see Paul, "Laos: Anatomy of an American Involvement," 49 Foreign Affs. 533, 536 (1971). Initially our planes flew reconnaissance in support of Laotian government troops. When one of our reconnaissance planes was shot down, we began sending fighter escorts. By the logic of war, strafing began, and bombing soon followed.

30.
[O]n March 31, 1968, President Johnson announced a partial bombing halt over North Vietnam. The day before the announcement the State Department sent out a cable to [certain U.S.] Ambassadors . . . . The cable revealed that

> In view of weather limitations, bombing north of the 20th parallel will be limited for the next four weeks or so . . . . Hence, we are not giving up anything really serious in this time frame. Moreover, air power now used north of the 20th can probably be used in Laos (where no policy change is planned) and in SVN.

The next day, President Johnson announced the partial bombing halt as "the first step to de-escalate the conflict." He added, "We are reducing—substantially reducing—the present level of hostilities."

Haney, supra note 10, at 275 (emphasis deleted). On the other bombing halts, see, e.g., 28 Cong. Q. Weekly Rep. 1243, 1245, (1970); The Ravens, supra note 5, at 46, 75; A. Isaacs et al., supra note 8, at 82: "Johnson's bombing halt had dramatic consequences for the war in Laos . . . . When a complete bombing halt over North Vietnam was announced at the end of October [1968], bombings in Laos took another jump, to a staggering 600 strikes per day."

31. D. Kirk, supra note 19, at 238.

32. A. Isaacs et al., supra note 8, at 82 (quoting unnamed U.S. official).

33. Id. at 74. Moreover, precisely because the war in Laos was secret, it was less restrained in terms of killing civilians. "While as in any war, atrocities were not uncommon, the military did exercise caution in conducting ground and air operations [in Vietnam] in order to minimize civilian casualties. The difference can be seen in the 'gloves off' bombing in Laos where the cameras were not watching." L. Gelb & R. Betts, The Irony of Vietnam: The System Worked 266 (1979).

34. The Ravens, supra note 5, at 195–96 (300 sorties); N.Y. Times, Sept. 23, 1969, at 9 (500).

35. Sesser, supra note 28, at 40.

36. Id.; The Ravens, supra note 5, at 332. Even the lower figure would have averaged out at seventeen tons of bombs for every square mile of the country, 6/10 of a bomb for every man, woman, and child living there. Id. Probably because villages are easier to find and hit, many more civilian villagers than Communist soldiers were killed by our bombs. See Note, "Present-Day Effects of United States Bombing of Laos During the Vietnam War: Can Injured Laotians Recover Under the Federal Tort Claims Act?" 13 Loy. L.A. Int'l & Comp. L.J. 133, 134–35, 148 (1990).

37. J. Prados, supra note 11, at 279; Branfman, "The President's Secret Army: A Case Study—The CIA in Laos, 1962–1972," in The CIA File 46, 48, 77 (R. Borosage & J. Marks eds. 1976). If for some bizarre reason you need to monetize this, the cost of bombing Laos was about $7.2 billion, or $2 million a day. Cf. 28 Cong. Q. Weekly Rep. 1243, 1246 (1979) (estimate of $1.6 million a day, based on earlier and more conservative assumptions regarding number of sorties). "That [$2 million] daily figure is almost exactly the amount that Laos—a nation where life expectancy is forty-five . . . —received in all of 1988 from other countries, United Nations programs, and private relief groups . . . ." Sesser, supra note 28, at 40. See also id. at 41 ("Only in 1982 did the United States confirm charges that . . . that it had dumped two hundred thousand gallons of herbicides on Laos in 1965 and 1966").

It has been estimated, perhaps somewhat extravagantly, that approximately 48,000 American personnel, most of them located outside Laos, were involved on a daily basis in the bombing there. Branfman, supra, at 78 (table). Cf. 28 Cong. Q. Weekly Rep. 1243, 1245–46 (1970). To this day people are being killed or maimed by previously unexploded antipersonnel cluster bombs. See Note, supra note 36, at 149–50 (Laos); Lewis, "Make a Mistake and You're Dead," N.Y. Times, May 4, 1992, at A15 (Cambodia).

The total cost of our war in Laos was obviously many billions of dollars. Senator Symington, in a secret 1971 hearing that was later declassified, put it this way:

> The only figure the people of the U.S. know we are putting into Laos is some fifty million dollars in economic aid; but when you add up the figures . . . exclusive of the bombing of southern Laos and the Ho Chi Minh Trail, you get nearly half a billion dollars, of which a large part is for the Thais that we are financing and training in Laos. If you add to that the bombing of the Ho Chi Minh Trail cost, over a billion, it is over a billion and a half dollars annually that we are spending, one way or the other, in Laos.

Branfman, supra, at 75. See also 28 Cong Q. Weekly Rep. 1243, 1246 (1970); U.S. News & World Rep., Jan. 5, 1970, at 29.

38. J. Smith, George Bush's War 9 (1992).

39. N.Y. Times, Sept. 18, 1969, at 1, 10.

40. N.Y. Times, Sept. 19, 1969, at 1.

41. N.Y. Times, Feb. 26, 1970, at 1, 6 (Sen. Mansfield); Cong. Q. Weekly Rep. 1243, 1246 (1970) (Sen. Fulbright). The parallelism is unsurprising, as the *Times'* stories apparently were based on leaks from the Symington Subcommittee.

J. Lehman, The Executive, Congress, and Foreign Policy: Studies of the Nixon Administration 128 (1974). They have not been significantly controverted during the ensuing twenty-four years.

42. One should never say that a given argument would never be made, because someone somewhere is likely to have made it. Note the last sentence from the passage of General Counsel Houston's memorandum quoted in note 44 infra: "We have no combatants as such, although the Air Force's pilots doing the bombing come close . . . ." Darned close, I'd say: General Counsel of the CIA must be a strange job.

43. So far as "covert" military obligations executed other than by official members of our armed forces are concerned, post-Vietnam legislation may appear to have substituted a simple obligation to report to the Senate and House Intelligence Committees for the Constitution's ordinary requirement of authorization by the entire Congress. See p. 105. I shall briefly discuss these laws in chapter 6, but also note that they cannot constitutionally be applied in situations where there exists no compelling military justification for keeping such operations secret. We shall see that no such justification existed in Laos; thus the new laws would not have applied to Laos even had they been on the books at the time.

44. See Memorandum from CIA General Counsel Lawrence R. Houston to Director of Central Intelligence Concerning Symington Subcommittee Hearings (Oct. 30, 1969), reprinted in Documents 50 (C. Macy & S. Kaplan eds. 1980): "If Senator Fulbright were right in saying that we are 'waging war' in Laos, we would indeed have a constitutional question . . . . I know of no definition, however, which would consider our activities in Laos as "waging war" except Senator Fulbright's. We have no combatants as such, although the Air Force pilots doing the bombing come close . . . ."

45. Cf. Joint Hearings before the House Select Comm. to Investigate Covert Arms Transactions with Iran and Senate Select Comm. on Secret Military Assistance to Iran and the Nicaraguan Opposition, 100th Cong., 1st Sess. 4 (1987) (testimony of former national security adviser Robert McFarlane to the effect the president and his advisers "turned to covert actions [in Nicaragua] because they thought they could not get Congressional support for more overt activities"). But see pp. 113–14, suggesting that War Powers Resolution be altered accordingly.

46. Senate Hearings, supra note 15, at 4289. Of course the statement that we had no combat forces stationed in Laos was misleading at best.

47. W. Burchett, The Second Indochina War 6 (1970).

48. E.g., Letter from Thomas Jefferson to James Madison (Sept. 6, 1789), in 5 The Writings of Thomas Jefferson 123 (P. Ford ed. 1895) ("We have already given . . . one effectual check to the dog of war, by transferring the power of letting him loose from the Executive to the Legislative body, from those who are to spend to those who are to pay."

49. Reveley, "Presidential War-Making: Constitutional Prerogative or Usurpation?" 55 Va. L. Rev. 1243, 1288–89 (1969); see also Note, "Congress, the President, and the Power to Commit Forces to Combat," 81 Harv. L. Rev. 1771, 1795–96 (1968); note 4 to chapter 1.

50. This is hardly a wild fantasy. The CIA has historically consisted "of 'staff,' or regular career officers, 'contract' civilians with critical skills who free-lance for the Agency from time to time; and detailees." "[A] detailee is anyone from another

governmental service assigned to fulfill a specific CIA need for which the Agency itself is not normally staffed, *such as air combat.*" R. Secord, supra note 12, at 53 (emphasis supplied). General Secord himself, while running our air war in Laos, had been detailed from the Air Force to the CIA.

51. N.Y. Times, Feb. 26, 1970, at 6.

52. Kohn, "The Constitution and National Security: The Intent of the Framers," in The United States Military Under the Constitution of the United States, 1789–1989, at 61, 74 (R. Kohn ed. 1991).

53. See sources cited note 121 to chapter 3. Earlier letters of marque and reprisal had been used primarily to authorize the settlement of private claims, but this use was essentially obsolete at the time of the Constitution, such letters by then instead being used mainly to authorize private acts in support of national military aims. Lofgren, "War-Making Under the Constitution: The Original Understanding," 81 Yale L.J. 672, 694 (1972).

54. Cf. Declaration of Independence para. 27 ("He [George III] is, at this time, transporting large armies of foreign Mercenaries to compleat the works of death, desolation, and tyranny . . . .").

55. For reasons never lucidly explained, hornbook law seems generally to be that programs unauthorized at the time can constitutionally be authorized retroactively by Congress, nunc pro tunc (thus rendering them legal not simply "from now on" but "from the outset" as well). E.g., Swayne & Hoyt, Ltd. v. United States, 300 U.S. 297 (1937). However, such retroactive authorization plainly requires knowledge on the part of the "authorizing" Congress of the existence of the prior program in issue. E.g., Ex Parte Endo, 323 U.S. 283, 303 n.24 (1944). When it passed the Tonkin Gulf Resolution Congress was patently not on anything resembling adequate notice of what our government had previously been up to in Laos.

56. E.g., L. Crovitz, A Presidential Strategy for Repealing the War Powers Resolution 4, 13, 19 (Heritage Soc. Backgrounder 1989); E. Rostow, President, Prime Minister, or Constitutional Monarch? 22 (1989); Panel, "The President's Powers as Commander-in-Chief versus Congress' War Power and Appropriations Power," 43 U. Miami L. Rev. 17, 42 (1988) (remarks of Assistant Attorney General William Bradford Reynolds); Nomination of Robert H. Bork to be Associate Justice of the Supreme Court of the United States, 100th Cong., 1st Sess., pt. 1, at 337 (Judge Bork). For once the "originalists" (Rostow does not claim to be such) agree with the originals, as the founders explicitly contemplated that wars could be ended by congressional withdrawal of funding. Note 188 to chapter 2.

Though the proposition that Congress can end *any* executive program by a denial of funds is often overenthusiastically asserted, it seems to me there are certain functions the Constitution so clearly assigns exclusively to the president that Congress could not constitutionally abort them even by withholding funds: It could not, for example, refuse "to appropriate funds for the President to receive foreign ambassadors or to make treaties," Stith, "Congress' Power of the Purse," 97 Yale L.J. 1343, 1351 (1988), or to prepare and deliver the State of the Union Address. Accord, L. Henkin, Constitutionalism, Democracy, and Foreign Affairs 31–32 (1990). Making war is manifestly not in that small category, and no one argues it is. There may also be certain battlefield decisions the Commander in Chief Clause precludes Congress from tampering with, even by withholding appropriations, cf. note 22 to chapter 1, but the decision thus entirely to end a war is always within the authority of the legislature (though it may necessitate a veto override, see pp. 44–45), a fact that transparently requires that Congress be kept informed of the war's progress, save arguably where military necessity requires otherwise, a claim respecting Laos we are about to consider.

57. A number of my students have argued—my fall 1991 National Security class bid fair to become an extended debate of this proposition alone, the crafty weasels—that Congress can constitutionally include in its authorization of a war further authorizations to the president (a) to keep the facts regarding the war's progress secret from them, and even (b) to lie to them about those facts, even when there is no compelling military justification for doing so. (Some distinguish (b) from (a).) I can understand the argument that Congress might sometimes wish it had passed such an authorization: In terms of responsibility-avoidance, it might seem a dream come true. I cannot, however, agree that it could be constitutional. The near-death of the delegation doctrine is justifiable, if at all (I think it isn't), only if Congress reserves for itself authority to repeal the authorized program (possibly over a veto) should the delegation run amok: Authorization (a), not to mention (b), is inconsistent with this reservation. (The argument is relevant not only to the instant issue but also to Congress's acquiescence in the facially unconstitutional practice of hiding the CIA's and other aspects of the defense budget (even from most of the Congress) in various innocuous-sounding appropriations for other agencies. Compare U.S. Const. art. I, § 9, cl. 7 ("No money shall be drawn from the Treasury, but in Consequence of Appropriations made by Law; and a regular Statement and Account of the Receipts and Expenditures of all public Money shall be published from time to time"), with, e.g., T. Weiner, Blank Check: The Pentagon's Black Budget (1990). See also United States v. Richardson, 418 U.S. 166 (1974) (refusing to decide the issue); Note, "The CIA's Secret Funding and the Constitution," 84 Yale L.J. 608 (1975) (a strong and balanced argument in support of the view the practice is unconstitutional).)

At all events it seems unlikely that Congress would enact a combat authorization that could reasonably be construed thus. Certainly the Tonkin Gulf Resolution did not even arguably contain any such authorization to conceal, let alone lie.

58. One might also point to statements of certain of the founders to the effect that wars could not be entered into in a clandestine fashion. However, their rhetoric generally stressed the unmanliness of such a beginning, as opposed to its unconstitutionality. See, e.g., Robertson, "Francisco de Miranda and the Revolutionizing of Spanish America," in 1 Ann. Rep. Am. Hist. A. 264 (1908) (statement of James Madison), reprinted in 1 H.R. Doc. No. 1282, 60th Cong., 2d Sess. (1909).

59. See note 32 to chapter 1.

60. A defense of the American war in Laos on the ground that it was really just a campaign in the American war in Vietnam would be substantially complicated by the fact that the former began before the latter. Under the analysis suggested here, however, the question whether the campaign in question constitutes a separate war is not dispositive. Significant clandestine campaigns within an ongoing and fully authorized war are unconstitutional unless there is a compelling military justification for keeping them secret.

61. Pp. 6–7.

62. This is not to say that it would not be a good idea for the president in such a case to seek the advice of the congressional leadership (which we might define functionally as those who can get on national television without leaking something). See further pp. 113–14.

63. One excuse the administration didn't have the gall to throw at us about Laos was that by keeping the United States' role secret from Congress and the American people they were somehow springing a military surprise on the North Vietnamese and Pathet Lao. (When someone has been dropping bombs on you for years, it is not likely to take you by great surprise when he does so again tomorrow.) However, in his 1977 interview with David Frost, President Nixon ventured just such a desperate justification for thirteen months of secret bombing of Cambodia (plus three more years of cover-up). See note 36 to chapter 5.

64. See also p. 81 (suggesting that "military excuses" that are capable of articulation in every imaginable situation—as all of those adduced by the administration in this case turned out to be—should not be entertained).

65. Paul, supra note 29, at 545.

66. At least not unless the agreement takes the form of a treaty approved by 2/3 of the Senate. Compare pp. 14–15 (treaties arguably sufficient to authorize wars) with p. 35 (executive agreements plainly insufficient to do so).

67. C. Stevenson, supra note 8, at 3 (quoted p. 112); Air America, supra note 7, at 101. See also, e.g., J. Orman, supra note 25, at 100 (the Soviets, Chinese, and some U.S. allies knew); Hearings on Kingdom of Laos before the Subcomm. on United States Security Agreements and Commitments Abroad of the Senate Comm. on Foreign Relations, 91st Cong., 1st Sess., pt. 2, at 536 (1969) [hereinafter Symington Hearings] (testimony of Assistant Secretary of State William H. Sullivan) (admitting Soviet knowledge); id. at 592–93 (transcript of Pathet Lao broadcast detailing U.S. Air Force bombing in Laos).

68. Staff of Subcomm. on U.S. Security Agreements and Commitments Abroad, Senate Comm. on Foreign Relations, 91st Cong., 2d Sess., Security Agreements and Commitments Abroad 27 (1970) [hereinafter Symington Report].

69. D. Kirk, supra note 19, at 238.

70. H. Kissinger, White House Years 251–52, 254 (1979) (argument made in specific context of Cambodia).

71.
The Pentagon Papers make clear . . . that U.S. officials considered it desirable, but by no means essential, to keep Souvanna informed on U.S. actions. A cable from Dean Rusk to the U.S. embassies in Saigon, Vientiane and Bangkok dated August 9, 1964, reported "Meeting today approved in principle early initiation air and limited ground operations in Laos . . ." Rusk suggested a meeting between the respective Ambassadors to "clarify scope and timing [of] possible operations." As one of the crucial issues to be discussed at the meeting he questioned "whether we should inform Souvanna before undertaking or go ahead without him."

Haney, supra note 10, at 268.

72. Hindsight strongly suggests that prior to the removal of our troops from Indochina Congress would *not* have forced the administration to stop bombing the Ho Chi Minh trail (or just about anything else it wanted to bomb). I do think it's

believable, however, that the administration might genuinely have feared Congress would do so.

73. Later we shall see that the same claim was made, again ambiguously, about Cambodia's Prince Sihanouk. See pp. 99–100.

74. Compare, e.g., J. Lehman, supra note 41, at 147 ("[Secretary of Defense Melvin] Laird pointed out that the publication of numbers and costs of our bombing in Laos would immediately be used by administration enemies on the Hill to pressure for legislation to cease all bombing") with id. at 150–51 ("Laird . . . adamantly refused to allow the release of the cost and number of sorties flown over Laos . . . since all of these would be of material assistance to the North Vietnamese").

75. Nixon, "Scope of the U.S. Involvement in Laos," 62 Dep't St. Bull. 405, 408 (1970).

76. Symington Hearings, supra note 67, at 542.

77. Paul, supra note 29, at 546.

78. Id.

79. H. Kissinger, supra note 70, at 454–55; see also Symington Report, supra note 68, at 27 ("If the United States so acknowledged, the International Controls Commission would be forced to make an inquiry and thereupon find the United States in violation of the Geneva Accords"). You will not be surprised to learn that when we finally did acknowledge the bombing, there was no International Controls Commission inquiry. Id.

80. Paul, supra note 29, at 545.

81. C. Stevenson, supra note 8, at 3.

82. D. Kirk, supra note 19, at 250. See also id. at 250–51 (Soviet government statements condemning U.S. activities in Laos); Symington Hearings, supra note 67, at 590.

83. See id. at 399 (testimony of Deputy Assistant Secretary Sullivan); Paul, supra note 29, at 545–46. Such suggestions, we shall see for good reason, are invariably vague. E.g., Forum, "Should the U.S. Fight Secret Wars?" Harper's Mag., Sept. 1984, at 33, 45 (statement of Leslie Gelb) ("such overt aid [to the Mujaheddin] would make relations even more difficult with the Soviet Union").

84. It has been suggested that the use of proxies and covert intervention allowed us and the Soviets to pursue our competition behind "a facade of deniability" that minimized the risk of direct confrontation. J. Gaddis, The Long Peace: Inquiries Into the History of the Cold War 240 (1987). Such considerations might reasonably have led one to conclude that means of complying with the constitutional requirement of congressional authorization less dramatic and confrontational than the traditional "declaration of war" should be preferred. Cf. p. 25. But it is difficult to imagine that they could reasonably have supported a move to repeal the authorization requirement altogether. Indeed, it was precisely (a nonobsolete) part of the point of requiring open congressional debate and approval to make wars difficult to become involved in. In any event Gaddis grants that the possibility of such a confrontation over neighboring Vietnam (where our participation was, to put it mildly, open) was remote. J. Gaddis, supra, at 240. On the "don't goad the bear" rationale generally (and in particular its relevance post–Cold War), see further p. 112.

85. Symington Hearings, supra note 67, at 590 (testimony of Deputy Assistant Secretary Sullivan).

86. Id. at 592 (Sen. Symington).

87. Symington Report, supra note 68, at 27. See also H. Kissinger, supra note 70, at 455 (1970 memorandum from Kissinger to Nixon arguing that release of Symington transcript would "make it more difficult for the Soviets to preserve their present relatively friendly posture toward the RLG [Royal Laotian Government]").

88. D. Kirk, supra note 19, at 250.

89. As does a desire to protect Americans traveling elsewhere from Soviet-bloc reprisals (one I'm not aware the administration actually invoked in this context) and doubtless many others they could have come up with.

90. Staff of Subcomm. on U.S. Security Agreements and Commitments Abroad, Senate Comm. on Foreign Relations, 92d Cong., 1st Sess., Laos: April 1971, at 4 (1972).

91. S. Rep. No. 755, 94th Cong., 2d Sess., book I at 157 (1976) (emphasis added). Kissinger's testimony was critical of the use of the CIA in Laos: Covert activities, he suggested, should not "be used simply for the convenience of the executive branch and its accountability." Id. We have also noted that the CIA appears to have been used because the presence of armed forces was illegal under the 1962 Geneva Accords. P. 70.

92. See, e.g., Time, Oct. 17, 1969, at 39 (quoting unnamed U.S. official in Vientiane): "If we [acknowledged bombing Laos] . . . every dove in the U.S. would hit us over the head with it like they did with Johnson and the bombing of North Viet Nam. The North Vietnamese don't admit the presence of their 47,000 troops. Why should we give them the advantage of admitting the bombing?" (On the "they do it, so we have to" inference generally, see pp. 104, 109.) The position that the American people had to be kept in the dark appears to have been taken more often by high officials than by our actual fighting men, who, anecdotal evidence suggests, understandably tended more to the position that if an informed American public wouldn't support the war, we should go home. See, e.g., The Ravens, supra note 5, at 159.

93. N. Sheehan, H. Smith, E. Kenworthy & F. Butterfield, The Pentagon Papers as Published by The New York Times 385 (1971); J. Orman, supra note 25, at 104.

94. E.g., J. Lehman, supra note 41, at 164.

95. Wash. Post, Oct. 30, 1969, at A1. The quotation is ambiguous on just when it is Congress was supposed to have found out. See note 124 infra.

96. E.g., Abrams, supra note 16, at 9.

97. Symington Hearings, supra note 67, at 673.

98. See p. 23.

99. J. Orman, supra note 25, at 103. See also, e.g., N.Y. Times, Sept. 18, 1969, at 1, 11 ("[Senator John Sherman Cooper] noted that neither the Pentagon nor the State Department had ever told Congressional committees that American troops were engaged in combat in Laos . . . .").

100. Branfman, supra note 18, at 215 (footnote omitted). At least prior to the publication of the Church Committee report in 1976, congressional oversight of the CIA was virtually nonexistent. E.g., L. Johnson, A Season of Inquiry: The Senate Intelligence Investigation 6–9 (1985).

101. Branfman, supra note 37, at 71. 50 U.S.C. § 403j(b) (1982) provides that

CIA funds may be spent without regard to the usual regulations governing expenditures. This section was enacted in 1949 and was in effect during the war in Laos.

In 1982 Congress again omitted the CIA from the purview of Comptroller General audits, providing that the president may exempt financial transactions relating to "sensitive foreign intelligence" from audit. 31 U.S.C. § 3524(c) (1982). The same law provides, however, that transactions exempt under 31 U.S.C. § 3524(c) and 50 U.S.C. § 403j(b) may be reviewed by the House and Senate intelligence oversight committees. 31 U.S.C. § 3524(e) (1982).

We shall see that there was a swearing contest over whether the CIA subcommittee of the Senate Appropriations Committee was in fact briefed about what was going on in Laos. Pp. 84–85.

102. J. Orman, supra note 25, at 103.

103. Symington Report, supra note 68, at 17.

104. See, e.g., Wicker, "The (Not Quite) Open Society," N.Y. Times, Apr. 21, 1970, at 42; Symington Hearings, supra note 67, at 545–46. This continued even into the Symington hearings themselves: "The executive branch continued to distort the more sensitive questions of American involvement in Laos throughout the hearings, even in the portion without deletions which has been made public." Branfman, supra note 18, at 271 (giving examples).

Former CIA Director Richard Helms stated in 1978: "I don't know of any director, at least during my time, who fiddle-faddled with Congress . . . . We presented a budget every year that had all the details. There were no secret wars in Laos and all that nonsense. That's part of the mythology of Washington . . . ." Louisville Courier-Journal, May 17, 1978, at A6. Fiddle-faddling there certainly was; "all the details" there certainly weren't; whether there was flat-out lying is more questionable. But cf. L. Johnson, supra note 100, at 37 (quoting various CIA directors and officials for the proposition that lying to Congress is often a patriotic duty).

105. Symington Hearings, supra note 67, at 544–47.

106. Id. at 547 (emphasis added).

107. Id. at 544.

108. N.Y. Times, Oct. 26, 1969, at 24. Accord, Air America, supra note 7, at 117. Sam Thong was officially referred to as Site 20, Long Cheng as 20 Alternate. Despite the fact that "the Alternate" dwarfed Site 20—in fact we built it into the second largest city in Laos—"[t]he idea was that any visiting dignitary, or prying journalist, would naturally assume that Site 20 was the bigger operation, and Alternate merely a secondary emergency landing strip." The Ravens, supra note 5, at 36.

109. Branfman, supra note 18, at 270.

110. Hersh, "How We Ran the Secret Air War in Laos," N.Y. Times, Oct. 29, 1972, § 6 (Magazine) at 96.

111. For example, Branfman, "The Secret Wars of the CIA," in Uncloaking the CIA 92 (H. Frazier ed. 1978), somewhat cryptically indicates that an AID official "exposed the CIA secret army in 1968 to Senator Kennedy's subcommittee on refugees." By 1968 significant parts of the story had begun to come out in other ways as well. See Wash. Post, Oct. 30, 1969, at A14 (quoting Senator Mansfield to the effect that he didn't learn much from the Symington hearings that he didn't already know).

This is undoubtedly explained in part by the fact that Mansfield was a southeast Asia specialist, perhaps more by his position in the "club," but it also suggests that the entire Congress wasn't as "surprised" as some members would have had us believe. Although it seems unreasonable to expect "the American people" to locate and run down allegations of American military activity in Laos appearing in, say, *The Far Eastern Economic Review*, we might expect something approaching that reaction from, say, the staff of the Senate Foreign Relations Committee.

112. 117 Cong. Rec. 42,929 (1971) (emphasis added).

113. Cf. R. McGehee, Deadly Deceits 82 (1983) (remarking on Colby's ability to lie while appearing sincere); note 118 infra.

114. W. Colby (with P. Forbath), Honorable Men: My Life in the CIA 202 (1978).

115. Hearings on Nomination of William E. Colby to be Director of Central Intelligence before the Senate Comm. on Armed Services, 93d Cong., 1st Sess. 152–53 (1973).

116. See, e.g., The Ravens, supra note 5, at 121 (footnote omitted):

In October 1967 . . . Symington personally invited Ted Shackley, whose houseguest he had been on a trip to Laos, to testify before the House Armed Services Committee. At the end of it the Senator praised the Laotian program as a suitable way to fight a war . . . . (Later, he was to reverse his view and express "surprise, shock, and anger" over the CIA's secret war, even though he had been thoroughly briefed on Vang Pao's . . . army since September 1966, and had also personally witnessed bombers leaving Udorn on missions to Laos).

To the same effect, see id. at 242–43; T. Powers, The Man Who Kept the Secrets: Richard Helms and the CIA 178–79 (1979); R. Secord, supra note 12, at 61; Cong. Q. Weekly Rep. 1243, 1254 (1970).

117. Though even his critics grant that along with everyone else he probably was unaware of the *extent* of the war in Laos. E.g., R. Jeffreys-Jones, The CIA and American Democracy 179 (1989).

118. Thus Ralph McGehee, a lapsed CIA agent plainly without interest in establishing the legality of the agency's various activities, relates a 1964 briefing of one of Congress's CIA subcommittees at which Colby (whom McGehee had briefed) not only described the CIA's training and support of Vang Pao's forces but even exaggerated their extent, so as to justify the budget request before the committee. R. McGehee, supra note 113, at 82–83. Indeed, after the Laos story broke in 1969 the CIA allegedly claimed it had briefed as many as sixty-seven senators on the "secret war" since 1963. J. Lehman, supra note 41, at 129. By now, however, we should be skeptical of just what these "briefings" comprised. See also Forum, supra note 83, at 43 (statement of Ralph McGehee): "While I was in the CIA I . . . helped prepare briefings for Congress for Mr. Colby, and it is a fact that those briefings had nothing to do with reality . . . . Very few of the facts in these briefings were true."

119. Symington Hearings, supra note 67, at 547.

120. Symington Report, supra note 68, at 5.

121. Wash. Post, Oct. 29, 1969, at A22.

Because various United States military programs undertaken in Laos were handled by different agencies, and because these programs varied in the secrecy with which they were conducted, any understanding of Laos military operations in Washington was far less than in Vientiane, where the United States Ambassador coordinated all elements of these operations. The North Vietnamese, however, along with their allies and supporters, had a clear view of all these combined United States activities.

Symington Report, supra note 68, at 6. (In a way this makes both points, that "Congress" probably didn't really know what was going on in Laos, and that it could have found out had it really wanted to.)

122. J. Orman, supra note 25, at 105 (quoting Symington Report, supra note 68, at 5). See also id. at 177–78; N.Y. Times, Sept. 21, 1969, at 14E (editorial) ("The only American operations in Laos of which most of the Congress and the country have been aware are the bombing attacks against supplies moving along the Ho Chi Minh Trail into South Vietnam").

123. C. Stevenson, supra note 8, at 209. See also M. Halperin et al., supra note 20, at 42–43.

124. H. Kissinger, supra note 70, at 454; see also id. at 451. Moreover, having testified before the Symington Subcommittee that he "had thought" that "Congress was familiar with the developments in Laos," see p. 82, Secretary of State Rogers added, "Certainly they are familiar with them now." Wash. Post, Oct. 30, 1969, at A1.

125. See also Pollak, "The Constitution as an Experiment," 123 U.Pa. L. Rev. 1318, 1336 (1975). This point is buttressed by the fact that the membership of the relevant committees, such as the Armed Services Committees, may not faithfully mirror the views of the entire Congress on issues of how readily we should get involved in wars.

126. See chapter 6.

127. Ely, "The American War in Indochina, Part II: The Unconstitutionality of the War They Didn't Tell Us About," 42 Stan L. Rev. 1093, 1123 (1990).

128. See generally We the People: Foundations (1991).

129. I believe it unlikely to inspire rebuttal to suggest that given the ratification of the Seventeenth Amendment and other changes in our Constitution over the past 200 years, cf. J. Ely, Democracy and Distrust: A Theory of Judicial Review 6 (1980), this is the remaining relevant core of *Federalist* 63.

130. Ely, "Another Such Victory: Constitutional Theory and Practice in a World Where Courts are no Different from Legislatures," 77 Va. L. Rev. 833, 855–63 (1991).

131. Cf. C. Arnson, Crossroads: Congress, the Reagan Administration, and Central America 155 (1989) ("What we have now is a contradictory public record [concerning the Nicaraguan mining operation], with CIA officials claiming that they complied with an obligation to inform Congress just as vigorously as members of the Senate insist that they did not").

132. The most concerted attempts to conceal facts have been made regarding the air war (above all the systematic bombing of towns and villages), American

ground combat involvement, CIA direction of the Armée Clandestine, American military escalation, and American subsidizing of the Thai and other foreign Asians to fight in Laos.

Branfman, supra note 18, at 265.

133. Id. at 268.

134. Id.

135. "From June 1964 to March 1970, the U.S. government never acknowledged conducting anything more than 'armed reconnaissance' flights in Northern Laos." Haney, supra note 10, at 268 (footnote omitted). Government spokespersons may have privately rationalized their statements on the theory that "armed reconnaissance" was a term of art at least sometimes understood by insiders to denote "attack sort[ies] flown in search of targets of opportunity"—in other words bombing missions. Air War Study Group, Cornell University, The Air War in Indochina 77 n.4 (R. Littauer & N. Uphoff eds. 1972); The Ravens, supra note 5, at 120. Plainly, though, the public wasn't meant to (and didn't) understand it that way—it was, for one thing, generally coupled with a denial that we were flying bombing missions—but rather to construe the words in accord with their ordinary language meaning (denoting a reconnaissance flight armed to defend itself or accompanied by jet fighters).

136. E.g., N.Y. Times, July 26, 1969, at 1; N.Y. Times, Sept. 23, 1969, at 9. This account may be a little unfair to Souvanna, who may have been taught to lie by an incident earlier in 1969, when he had told the truth, that U.S. planes were bombing Laos, only to have the American embassy quickly "correct" the story to indicate that he had actually said "our" planes, intending to refer to the Royal Laotian Air Force. The Ravens, supra note 5, at 148.

137. C. Stevenson, supra note 8, at 209–10 (footnote omitted).

138. President Nixon's "come-clean" news conference of March 6, 1970, see also note 144 infra—which actually was a good deal more forthcoming than anything Johnson or Kennedy had ever issued concerning Laos—asserted that "[n]o American stationed in Laos has ever been killed in ground combat operations." As reporters began to nose around, however—the facts by now were beginning to come out—another statement was issued admitting that Americans had fought in Laos:

> Three days later a State Department spokesman asserted that American war deaths in Laos totaled 25 contractor personnel and 1 dependent. A reporter then wrote of a military fatality, Army Captain Joseph Bush, killed at Muong Soui on February 10, 1969. In rapid succession the press revealed several other incidents where Americans had been killed, including the radar station battle at Phu Pha Thi. The Nixon administration countered with a new statement, after a search of the records, that 200 Americans had died and 193 were missing.

J. Prados, supra note 11, at 291. (Charles Stevenson states that "[f]rom 1964 through 1970, over 400 Americans died in the fighting in Laos and another 230 men were listed as missing." C. Stevenson, supra note 8, at 3 [footnote omitted].) At the very least this episode provides another example of the administration's use of technical terms to skirt the truth:

The White House belatedly admitted [Captain Bush's] death, but maintained that Bush had died not in combat, but as a result of "hostile action." This sort of deceptive semantic distinction provided the rationale for Nixon's omission of the fact that in reality hundreds of Americans had died in the war in Laos. The President had carefully limited his assertion to Americans "stationed in Laos" and who were killed in "ground combat." The phrases were crucial to Nixon's assertion because many American servicemen in Laos are technically not stationed there. They are in Laos only on "temporary duty." Also, the majority of Americans involved in the war in Laos never set foot on Lao soil. They fight the war from airplanes flying out of Thailand or from aircraft carriers in the Gulf of Tonkin.

Haney, supra note 10, at 277–78 (footnotes omitted). The administration's series of rationalizations ran as follows:

The special-operations people did not count because they "were not stationed in Laos"; the CIA contract people did not count because they were secret; the Ravens did not count because "technically" they were stationed in Thailand; Air Commandos and Air Force ground personnel were also classified Top Secret; Air America and Continental Air Services did not count because they posed as civilians.

The Ravens, supra note 5, at 228–29. "Even so, when the draft statement went over to the Pentagon it was returned with the line referring to no American combat deaths struck through *twice*. Kissinger allowed the statement to stand." Id. at 229. Dr. Kissinger's memoirs report that the misstatements resulted from "misunderstandings and a failure of communication" and gave him "a lesson in the perils of being too categorical." H. Kissinger, supra note 70, at 456.

139. See also, e.g., note 20 supra (efforts to hide the identity and role of Air America).

140. D. Kirk, supra note 19, at 234; Branfman, supra note 18, at 267–68.

141. Id. at 268.

142. Hersh, supra note 110, at 99.

143. J. Prados, supra note 11, at 290–91. Vang Pao went so far as to order the three reporters killed (in a way that could be attributed to enemy action) but was dissuaded by his CIA advisers. The Ravens, supra note 5, at 240.

144. N.Y. Times, Dec. 9, 1969, at 16; N.Y. Times, Jan. 31, 1970, at 14. Even Nixon's statement of March 6, 1970, in which he finally admitted we were flying "combat support missions" in the north on request of the Royal Laotian Government and promised to "continue to give the American people the fullest possible information on our involvement," was riddled with misstatements. Compare Nixon, supra note 75, at 409, with Haney, supra note 10, at 277–78, and Branfman, supra note 18, at 268–70. Also flagrantly untrue were the official briefings given reporters in Laos as late as February 1970. Id. at 271.

145. 28 Cong. Q. Weekly Rep. 1243, 1245 (1970). At times, it is true, the censorship did provide amusement value:

MR. KNAUR: Mr. Chairman, may I say [deleted].
SENATOR SYMINGTON: Have you been sworn?

Symington Hearings, supra note 67, at 480. A 1971 follow-up report on Laos from the same subcommittee elaborated: "We were told that the Embassy wanted to [deleted] the [deleted] with [deleted] because the [deleted] were more mobile and thus 'could do things the others could not do.' As for the future, [deleted]." 1972 Laos Report, supra note 90, at 16. Fun and games aside, what was censored out by agreement with the administration was anything but peripheral.

146. 28 Cong. Q. Weekly Rep. 1245 (1970).

147. Shaplen, "Our Involvement in Laos," 48 Foreign Affs. 478, 482 (1970).

148. H. Kissinger, supra note 70, at 450–51.

149. Mr. Shaplen was *The New Yorker*'s Far Eastern correspondent, based in Hong Kong, from 1962 to 1978. Hesitate as one must to criticize the writing of a *New Yorker* staffer, the syntactic confusion—"[t]hroughout Asia, let alone in the United States"—masked a non sequitur. That something was known where it was happening hardly implies that it was known in a nation halfway around the world whose government was trying to hide it.

Surprisingly in light of his 1970 assertion, Shaplen's own lengthy "Letter from Laos," New Yorker, May 4, 1968, at 136–62, was relatively unforthcoming about the American military role in Laos. It did report (as we shall see a number of others had by this time) that we were bombing the Ho Chi Minh trail, id. at 146, 152, but (other than allusions signaling that he knew more than he was letting on) that was about it.

There were two tantalizing references, one to "supposedly covert military assistance to Laos," id. at 136, the other to "unpublicized military and semi-military assistance, much of which stems from the Central Intelligence Agency," id. at 151, but no details followed. (The only other mention of the CIA was historical. Id. at 157.) There was also an allusion to "air support [the United States] has been rendering to General Vang Pao in the north," but here the article was most ambiguous. It is perhaps most naturally read to imply that what was involved was *equipment* support, as it immediately indicated that it was unlikely we would be able to provide further assistance because the number of trained Laotian pilots was about equal to the number of T-28s we had already supplied. (This was followed by an explanation of our reluctance to accede to Laotian requests for M-16 rifles, on the ground the rifles were too complex for the average Laotian soldier.) Id. at 152.

Although a good deal of attention was given to allegations that Chinese troops were fighting in Laos, id. at 142–44, no further mention was made of either the CIA role or our bombing of the north. The bombing halt in Vietnam was mentioned, but not the consequent massive escalation of our bombing of Laos; on the contrary, the "halt" was reported as having generated in Laos a feeling of "gloom" arising from an inference that it meant the United States was preparing to "pull up stakes" in Indochina altogether. Id. at 136. The author described the showcase headquarters at Sam Thong, id. at 140, but did not mention the real one at Long Cheng. Air America and Continental were not mentioned at all. And a major stress of the piece was on the plight of the Hmongs and how we weren't supporting them adequately. Id. at 140–42. To the same effect, see "On-Scene in Laos and Thailand," Newsweek, Apr. 22, 1968, at 46–48.

The brief allusions to the CIA and air support are enough to suggest that Shaplen suspected more than he reported in 1968, and that indeed he probably was not as surprised as the rest of us by the revelations in the *Times* and before the Symington Subcommittee in 1969. But whatever the state of his own knowledge when he wrote "Letter from Laos," it is unlikely that that piece was one of the articles to which he meant to be referring when he assured us two years later that the United States' military role had been well covered in the media all along, "common knowledge" to anyone willing to read "with a modicum of care."

In any event "Letter from Laos" appeared in 1968, by which time other periodicals were beginning to surface some new details and the dam was about to burst. Shaplen's earlier "Both Banks of the Mekong," New Yorker, Jan. 16, 1965, at 78, was substantially less helpful concerning the American military role in Laos and thus even less likely to have been one of the articles to which he meant to be adverting in his 1970 argument.

150. See also, e.g., Sesser, supra note 28, at 40 ("Although the CIA managed to recruit a mercenary army of thirty thousand Hmong . . . and although several hundred American fliers lost their lives in Laos, news of the operation had been successfully hidden from the American people for most of the time between 1964 and 1973").

151. Air America, supra note 7, at 172.

152. The Ravens, supra note 5, at 237.

153. The beginning of the bombing in 1964 *was* news, and on June 14 and 15 *The Washington Post* conspicuously featured UPI reports of a New China News Service allegation (identified as such) that the Plain of Jars had been bombed by American planes for three days. Wash. Post, June 14, 1964, at A1; Wash. Post, June 15, 1964, at A1. Two days later, paragraph 6 of a story headlined and principally about American civilian pilots in the Congo reported confirmation by a source within the government. Wash. Post, June 17, 1964, at A1. That same day the *Post* exasperatedly editorialized: "What in heaven's name does the United States think it is doing by trying to keep these strikes secret? Does the Government really have the naiveté to believe that its hand in these operations can be concealed?" Wash. Post, June 17, 1964, at A18. Reasonable on the surface, you might suppose, but the "naiveté" turned out to be the editorial's. The administration denied the substance of the report, taking the position it was to maintain until 1970—that we were not bombing northern Laos but rather flying only occasional "armed reconnaissance missions" as requested. Souvanna Phouma backed us up on this lie, e.g., Wash. Post, June 16, 1964, at A14, and as a media item the story was dead. See also Haney, supra note 10, at 268. Those Americans who believed it—and probably most did not, given that it was our government's word against the Chinese—very likely soon concluded, in light of the lack of follow-up, that this had been an isolated incident. (Indeed, the bombing of Laos *was* comparatively light in 1964, and events in Vietnam beginning in August of that year soon overpowered Laos as a news story.)

154. See, e.g., Time, May 29, 1964, at 25–26; Time, Oct. 30, 1964, at 40; Time, Nov. 27, 1964, at 36–37 (ironic in that the fact the planes were over Laos—"strictly reconnaissance," of course—was used as a defense to the charge we were violating *North Vietnamese* air space); Time, June 11, 1965, at 35; Time, Dec. 17, 1965, at 28–29; U.S. News & World Rep., Jan. 24, 1966, at 37–39; Time, May 19, 1967, at 34–35; Bus. Week, Jan. 6, 1968, at 20–21. Neither were more "serious" U.S. periodicals generally that far ahead. See, e.g., Pace, "Laos: Continuing Crisis," 43 Foreign

Affs. 64 (1964); Tran, "Laos: The Fiction of Neutrality," New Republic, Feb. 24, 1968, at 27–29; note 149 supra (Shaplen articles); but cf. sources cited note 156 infra.

155. Time, Jan. 26, 1968, at 30–31.

156. E.g., Newsweek, Mar. 31, 1969, at 23. U.S. News & World Rep., July 4, 1966, at 24–25, was ahead of its time, indicating (without mention of the CIA or other details) that "American civilians" were helping the Hmongs; but see U.S. News & World Rep., May 28, 1969, at 8–9 (adverting only to action on and over the Ho Chi Minh trail). Also "early" were certain reports in other hardly obscure but nonetheless comparatively low-circulation magazines. See Grant, "Report from Laos: The Hidden War," New Republic, May 20, 1968, at 17–19 (American involvement run by CIA); Braestrup, "Laos," 220 Atlantic Monthly 10, 12–13 (1967) (bombing of north); Warner, "Our Secret War in Laos," The Reporter, Apr. 22, 1965, at 23–26 (same).

157. Once again, cf. note 153 supra, events elsewhere in Indochina overtook Laos as a subject of much interest in the United States. Prince Sihanouk was deposed in March 1970 and President Nixon openly sent American troops into Cambodia the next month, just ten days after the issuance of the Symington Subcommittee's (uninformative) report on Laos.

158. I'm not saying it necessarily *is* all that different, but that's part of the point.

159. The bombing of the Ho Chi Minh trail was mentioned from time to time—the only thing Congress really knew about and the rest of us at least suspected—as was the possibility that we were airdropping supplies to Vang Pao. In April 1969, several months before the *Times'* series, a piece in *The Economist* alluded in a phrase to Long Cheng and some "special forces that officially aren't there." Economist, Apr. 5, 1969, at 27. There was, however, no mention prior to 1968 of either the CIA's on-the-ground support of Vang Pao's Secret Army or our bombing of the north—although there were several stories whose context would have demanded such mention. See, e.g., Economist, Jan. 6, 1968, at 16–17. But see Economist, Jan. 27, 1968, at 25; Economist, Feb. 1, 1969, at 25–26 (both discussing bombing).

160. See Jones, "In Harm's Way," Far E. Econ. Rev., Jan. 13, 1966, at 57–59; Munthe-Kaas, "Laos: The Still Centre," Far E. Econ. Rev., Apr. 21, 1966, at 150–53; Hannoteaux, "The Savage Peace," Far E. Econ. Rev., Nov. 21, 1968, at 405–7.

161. Jones, supra note 160, at 57.

162. Ono, "Breathing Space in Laos," Far E. Econ. Rev., June 19, 1965, at 517 (suggesting the U.S. was bombing the north but insisting it had had no role in training Laotian troops since the Geneva agreement).

163. Shchedrov, "Laos: Anxieties and Hopes," New Times (Moscow), Nov. 18, 1964, at 18–20; Yurtsev, "Tension Returns to Laos," New Times (Moscow), Jan. 25, 1967, at 13–14. Cf. Montagu, "The Other War—Laos," Labour Monthly, July 1966, at 322–27. Like other articles ahead of the American media, Montagu's was understandably imprecise, but it was quite perceptive about how much effect such writings could be expected to have on Western opinion leaders: "Few people are aware that alongside the big war in Vietnam that hits the headlines, another bloody conflict of intervention is being waged, equally ruthless, equally in violation of solemn international obligations, and has been going on for almost as long [*sic*], in Laos. Few people, that is, except the Laos." Id. at 322.

164. The timing on this score was exquisite. See notes 153 and 157 supra.

165. Compare in this regard the Nazis' assurances to the German people that the Jews, sometimes beloved acquaintances of people left on the scene, were merely being relocated, or the Chinese government's 1989 assurances to its people that only a few "gangsters" were killed by government troops in Tiananmen Square, right in the middle of Beijing.

166. See Ely, "About the Evidence," N.Y. Times, Oct. 30, 1975, at 39 (discussing my feelings, as a former Warren Commission staff member, of incredulity and betrayal at revelations that the CIA and FBI had lied to the Commission).

167. Cf. Symington Report, supra note 68, at 27:

> In March 1970 the President acknowledged the bombing; and in April 1970 the Laos transcript of the Subcommittee added further details. Not one of the [military or diplomatic] events viewed with apprehension by some of the Administration witnesses has occurred.
>
> On the contrary, the primary issue that developed as a result of this disclosure was within the United States, where the public was given its first reliable insight about the activities of its own government in Laos.

168. —State regards the release of the Symington Subcommittee testimony as being the simplest way to do this. We might kill two birds with one stone: placate Symington, Fulbright, et al., *and show the public what we are really doing.*
—On the other hand, it is doubtful whether the release of the sensitive parts of the testimony will placate the Senators. They know what is going on in Laos, and why. *The executive sessions have given them all this . . . .*

H. Kissinger, supra note 70, at 454 (quoting 1970 memorandum) (emphasis added). In fact the Symington Subcommittee transcript was so heavily censored (at the executive branch's insistence) before it came out that the *Times'* earlier series remains a substantially better source.

169. Quoted in W. Shawcross, Sideshow: Kissinger, Nixon, and the Destruction of Cambodia 307 (rev. ed. 1981). Of course, Dr. Kissinger was joking.

170. The basic fact is that the CIA will not tell a Senator Symington when it decides to deploy agents in the field in Cambodia. Should Symington find out about it from a newspaper report, he has no independent means of checking the CIA's answer that the men are just "intelligence-gathering"; any questions he asks, given the fact that he has no independent evidence, are essentially pointless; and, in the end, he must let it pass, with the weak admonition, "I do not want to get into any dogfight about it. My advice would be to cut it out."

Branfman, supra note 37, at 74.

171. Of course Congress could threaten to impeach the president, or other relevant executive officials, if the facts concerning the war were not forthcoming and convincing. But that's even more attenuated. In the case of Laos, and in this regard it's likely to be typical, there were not prior to 1969 sufficient facts even "in the air" to embolden Congress to think about impeachment.

172. U.S. Const. art. II, § 4; see C. Black, Impeachment: A Handbook 28, 33–37, 39–40 (1974); R. Berger, Impeachment: The Constitutional Problems 70 (1973).

173. 83 Stat. 469, 487 (1969).

174. And indeed, all these programs continued apace. See 1972 Laos Report, supra note 90.

175. 115 Cong. Rec. 39169 (1969).

176. Charles Black makes the same point about the secret bombing of Cambodia:

> [T]he question ... whether the long-secret 1973 Cambodian bombing could amount to an impeachable offense is complicated by the fact that, on its being revealed, Congress, by postponing until August 15, 1973, the deadline for its ending, would seem to have come close to ratifying it. One is sailing very close to the wind when one says, "You may do it till August 15, but it is an impeachable offense."

C. Black, supra note 172, at 35. However, the point does not comfortably fit the Cambodian situation, as there was a three-year gap between the secret bombing of Cambodia (which actually took place in 1969–70) and Congress's finding out about it in 1973, during which three-year period (following our public 1970 ground incursion into Cambodia) Congress had authorized the continuous bombing of Cambodia. Thus in 1973 Congress was not, as Black suggests, in the position of extending a secret campaign about which it had just learned, but rather of extending (for three months) a campaign it had authorized for the prior three years (though it had just learned that the program had existed an additional year before its initial authorization). But if Black's statement of the facts suggests some confusion here, his analysis appears to fit the *Laotian* situation like a glove.

177. On this point, the March 6 "come-clean" statement was vintage Nixon: "It would, of course, have posed no political problem for me to have disclosed in greater detail those military support activities which had been initiated by two previous administrations and which have been continued by this administration." Nixon, supra note 75, at 408. It is also true, of course, that many officials of the previous administrations "became preening doves as soon as their responsibility ended." W. Isaacson, Kissinger: A Biography 489 (1992).

178. See, e.g., Berger, "War-Making by the President," 121 U. Pa. L. Rev. 29, 65 (1972).

179. Of course such things are mixed bags: By 1973, Americans were no longer dying in Vietnam, relations with the Soviet Union were improved, relations with China much improved. A motion of censure would have permitted a more discrete focus on Laos.

CHAPTER 5
THE (ENFORCEABLE) UNCONSTITUTIONALITY OF THE
SECRET BOMBING OF CAMBODIA, 1969–1970

1. N.Y. Times, Nov. 4, 1969, at 16.

2. Sharpe, "The Real Cause of Irangate," 68 Foreign Pol'y 19, 24 (1987).

3. Statement of Information: Hearings Before the House Comm. on the Judiciary Pursuant to H. Res. 803, Book XI, Bombing of Cambodia, 93d Cong., 2d Sess. 6–7 (1974) [hereinafter Impeachment Report].; W. Shawcross, Sideshow: Kissinger, Nixon, and the Destruction of Cambodia 30–31, 289–90 (rev. ed. 1981).

4. Impeachment Report, supra note 3, at 307 n.154; S. Karnow, Vietnam: A History 592 (1983); W. Isaacson, Kissinger: A Biography 176 (1992). The Cambodia desk officers at the U.S. embassy in Saigon also were not told. Sharpe, supra note 2, at 24. Relevant inaccurate testimony by administration officials before congressional committees is detailed at Impeachment Report, supra, at 10–23; inaccurate statements to the public are reported in id. at 28–50.

5. W. Isaacson, supra note 4, at 173. But cf. note 10 infra.

6. Deputy Secretary of Defense William P. Clements testified in 1973 that "he had been told" that Senators Russell, Dirksen, and Stennis, and Congressman Mahon had been informed. Impeachment Report, supra note 3, at 61–62. A week earlier, a Defense Department response to a House inquiry had named Senators Russell, Dirksen, Stennis, and Congressmen Arends, Rivers, and Ford. Id. at 63. Dr. Kissinger's memoirs also mention those six—only those six—by name. H. Kissinger, White House Years 253 (1979). In 1973 President Nixon cited Congressman Hébert as having known, 31 Cong. Q. Weekly Rep. 2299 (1973); however, Nixon's memoirs recall that "[i]n order to preserve the secrecy of the bombing, we informed only Richard Russell and John Stennis." R. Nixon, RN: The Memoirs of Richard Nixon 382 (1978). Secretary of Defense Laird later recalled that he had told Ford, Mahon, Rivers, and Hébert. W. Isaacson, supra note 4, at 179. William Shawcross states that the Cambodia impeachment article wasn't voted in part because "a full inquiry would have demonstrated that Senator Mike Mansfield, the Senate Majority leader and other Democrats had known about the secret bombing at the time it was taking place." W. Shawcross, supra note 3, at 330. However, Mansfield's name appears on none of the lists I have cited, and Kissinger specifically denies that Mansfield knew. H. Kissinger, supra, at 251 n.*.

7. E.g., W. Shawcross, supra note 3, at 413 (Stennis); Debate on Articles of Impeachment: Hearings of the House Comm. on the Judiciary to Investigate Whether Sufficient Grounds Exist for the House of Representatives to Exercise Its Constitutional Power to Impeach Richard M. Nixon, President of the United States of America, 93d Cong., 2d Sess. 498 (1974) [hereinafter Impeachment Debate] (Stennis, Arends).

8. W. Isaacson, supra note 4, at 177. Over roughly the same period, and often coordinated with the bombing, American forces conducted "cross-border patrols into Cambodia just like those into Laos." J. Prados, Presidents' Secret Wars: CIA and Pentagon Covert Operations Since World War II 300 (1986). "There were four hundred operations into [Cambodia] in 1967–1968, and over a thousand during the next two years." Id.; see also W. Isaacson, supra, at 175; Szulc, "Mum's the War," New Republic, Aug. 18 & 25, 1973, at 19. In July 1973 the Defense Department "announced that 121 US servicemen, officially reported as having been killed in Vietnam, actually died in the two adjoining countries." Id. at 20. (A Mauldin cartoon of the time depicted an army officer on a young widow's front porch tipping his hat and advising her, "Your husband's death in Vietnam is inoperative. He died in Cambodia.") I will not focus on the ground operations, but they seem as unconstitutional as the bombings.

9. On May 9, 1969, The New York Times reported that "American B-52 bombers in recent weeks have raided several Vietcong and North Vietnamese supply dumps in Cambodia for the first time, according to Nixon Administration sources." N.Y.

Times, May 9, 1969, at 1. The story also got nine lines in *The Wall Street Journal* a week later, Wall St. J., May 16, 1968, at 1, two sentences at the end of a *Washington Post* story (on the shelling of a *U.S.* base) two days after that, Wash. Post, May 18, 1969, at A14, and a remarkably well-informed four sentences (including the fact that "high-ranking Air Force generals" had not been informed) in *Newsweek* for June 2, 1969, at 19. Obviously there had been a leak. However, the report was not officially confirmed; it was never reported on television, D. Hallin, The "Uncensored War": The Media and Vietnam 190 (1986); and "[t]here was no press follow-up," W. Shawcross, supra note 3, at 34, not even in the *Times*. It is thus no great surprise that "no members of the Senate Foreign Relations Committee or the Appropriations committees voiced concern," id., and the story died, not to surface again until Mr. Knight blew the whistle in 1973. See also W. Isaacson, supra note 4, at 212–13. Presumably those who had read it concluded in time that it either was mistaken or had referred to a few isolated incidents. (Indeed, the *Post* item made it sound as if the bombing was essentially on the Vietnam/Cambodia border.)

But if the leak accomplished nothing in calling the attention of Congress or the public to the bombing, it did cause hysteria in the White House, resulting in taps being placed on the phones of certain key aides—one of the first steps down the road to the plumbers and Watergate. W. Shawcross, supra, at 34–35; H. Kissinger, supra note 6, at 252–53; R. Nixon, supra note 6, at 388.

10. 31 Cong. Q. Weekly Rep. 2299 (1973). The newspeak proliferated; consider the testimony of General George S. Brown before the Senate Armed Services Committee, also in 1973: "I do not believe it is correct to characterize reports under special security precautions directed by higher authority as 'false.' So long as the reports met in every detail the requirements imposed, they were not intended to deceive those with a security 'need to know.'" Hearings on Bombing in Cambodia before the Senate Comm. on Armed Services, 93d Cong., 1st Sess. 17 (1973).

Doonesbury © 1974 G. B. Trudeau. Reprinted with permission of Universal Press Syndicate. All rights reserved.

11. N.Y. Times, July 22, 1973, § 4, at 3. See also W. Shawcross, supra note 3, at 152 ("Knight, who was still burning the true records of the continuing Menu missions, was appalled [in 1970] at the President's assertion that until now the United States had respected Cambodia's neutrality").

12. 9 Weekly Comp. Pres. Doc. 1011 (Aug. 27, 1973).

13. Hearings before the Senate Comm. on Foreign Relations, 93d Cong., 1st Sess. 33 (1973).

14. Sihanouk's general line has been that he did not invite the B-52 raids of 1969–1970, N.Y. Times, July 25, 1973 (or even know about them! W. Shawcross, supra note 3, at 390). However, he certainly was not entirely happy with the presence of North Vietnamese sanctuaries in Cambodia (though he had "acquiesced" in them too) and also had no wish to annoy the United States. Thus while his principal aim was to keep the war from spreading to his country, he was trying to get along with everybody, to the point of allowing each of us to "violate" Cambodia a little. He apparently had indicated on at least two occasions that he would not be altogether unhappy if, in "hot pursuit," we were to track North Vietnamese troops into otherwise unpopulated areas of Cambodia. S. Karnow, supra note 4, at 590; H. Kissinger, supra note 6, at 250. (Kissinger has the advantage of being able to quote "verbatim" from sources that are still classified without supplying the context; Karnow provides corroboration here from a separate interview.) But see W. Shawcross, supra, at 68–71, 438–39. And a 1973 letter to Senator Thurmond from Um Sin, the Lon Nol government's Ambassador to the United States, recalled that Sihanouk had chosen not to make an issue of American bombing either, so long as it was secret and did not affect areas inhabited by Cambodians. Impeachment Report, supra note 3, at 276 n.132. No one quotes Sihanouk as having invited a bombing campaign of the magnitude that transpired.

However, and this is really all it should take to establish this link of the administration's version, it appears he *did* acquiesce in the bombing once it had begun, or at least he did not protest very strenuously. E.g., W. Shawcross, supra, at 92. In fact diplomatic relations with the United States, which Sihanouk had broken off in May 1965, were reestablished in July 1969, four months after the bombing campaign began, D. Kirk, Wider War: The Struggle for Cambodia, Thailand, and Laos 32 (1971), and during the bombing Sihanouk "very warmly" invited Nixon to make a state visit. Nixon, VFW speech, supra note 12, at 1011. It is true that American officials remained in a state of uncertainty about just how much Sihanouk would put up with—preparations for the raids invariably included preparations for the contingency that Sihanouk would object, W. Shawcross, supra, at 94, and it is no coincidence that our ground incursion was held until Sihanouk was overthrown, id. at 117—but that may more testify to his mercurial nature than undercut the claim of acquiescence. Even in retrospect "[p]inning down exactly what Sihanouk truly felt at any point is a task beyond most historians." W. Isaacson, supra note 4, at 178.

15. Nixon wanted to avoid criticism, and the North Vietnamese could not protest without essentially admitting what they were otherwise denying, that they had troops in Cambodia; thus no government had an interest in blowing the whistle. Cf. p. 77 (secrecy in Laos served interests of Laotian and American governments). The bombing of Cambodia was minor compared to that of Laos, the secret much better kept.

16. For example, despite administration apoplexy over the "likelihood" that the May 9 *New York Times* story, note 9 supra, would trigger a protest from Sihanouk, H. Kissinger, supra note 6, at 252, it didn't.

17. See also A. Isaacs, G. Hardy & MacA. Brown, Pawns of War 89 (1987); D. Hallin, supra note 9, at 211.

18. See p. 31.

19. See also D. Hallin, supra note 9, at 211.

20. R. Nixon, supra note 6, at 382.

21. H. Kissinger, supra note 6, at 249.

22. Id. at 254; see also W. Isaacson, supra note 4, at 173.

23. H. Kissinger, supra note 6, at 252, 254.

24. Another of Kissinger's suggestions is that we did not publicize the Cambodian bombing because of feared "North Vietnamese retaliation (since how could they fail to react if we had announced we were doing it?)." Id. at 252. Six pages earlier, however, he had related a memo he had written before the bombing was undertaken: "The risks [of bombing] ranged from a pro forma Cambodian protest to a strong Soviet reaction; from serious Cambodian opposition to explicit North Vietnamese retaliation—though it was hard to imagine what escalation Hanoi could undertake beyond what it was already doing." Id. at 246. The unsettling analysis of our National Security Council thus apparently was that there wasn't anything further the North Vietnamese could do in response to our bombing Cambodia, but they would probably devise some novel retaliation were the president to tell *Congress* we were bombing Cambodia! Dr. Kissinger may come closest to candor when he writes that the administration "saw no sense" in admitting it was bombing. Id. at 251–52.

25. E.g., Szulc, supra note 8, at 21; R. McGehee, Deadly Deceits 58 (1983); Hing, "The CIA Against Cambodia," in Uncloaking the CIA 82–85 (H. Frazier ed. 1978); N. Sihanouk, My War with the CIA (1973) (as tendentious as it sounds).

26. It had long been no secret that our government found the Sihanouk regime less than helpful to our interests. Prom Thos, who was Lon Nol's Minister of Industry, has pointed out that it really doesn't matter whether Lon Nol received explicit promises of support: "We all just knew that the United States would help us; there had been many stories of CIA approaches and offers before then." W. Shawcross, supra note 3, at 122. A number of U.S. agencies were in touch with Lon Nol and his people at the time of the coup, and General Abrams' deputy has confirmed that various U.S. commanders were advised of it several days in advance. J. Prados, supra note 8, at 303. (Dr. Kissinger apparently sent President Nixon a memorandum outlining Lon Nol's plans for expanding the Cambodian army the day before the coup. Id.) Moreover, the CIA was quite likely involved at least to the extent of putting out "disinformation" to help make sure the coup succeeded—for example, persuading Sihanouk's mother to advise him that the gathering threat was not so serious as to require his return, W. Shawcross, supra, at 120, and later suggesting to Sihanouk that there was no chance that if he did return he could possibly reseize power, id. at 122. Also probative is the lightning speed with which our government recognized Lon Nol after the coup. Afterward, Secretary of Defense Laird announced that he had no "direct knowledge" that "the approval of Sihanouk's overthrow was made," and Kissinger (much later) assured the press that there was no United States involvement in the coup, "at least not at the top level." Id.

27. Compare Impeachment Report, supra note 3, at 57–58, with id. at 59, 71. See also W. Shawcross, supra note 3, at 289; Impeachment Report, supra, at 55–56 (Gen. Wheeler's testimony that Nixon directed him to congratulate those responsible on the high degree of secrecy that had been maintained).

28. See also W. Issacson, supra note 4, at 178.

29. See W. Shawcross, supra note 3, at 146.

David Frost asked Kissinger about Nixon's lie. Kissinger replied: "That statement should not have been made."

> FROST: Why did he make it?
> KISSINGER: Because he was given to hyperbole.
> FROST: Why did you make the same statement in your background briefing to the press on the same day?
> KISSINGER (*looking angry*): Because I suppose to us this bombing had become so much part of the landscape that we did not really focus on that. But that was not a correct statement.
>
>   . . .

> Kissinger fails to note in his book that the lie was made not just once but over and over again. Nixon repeated it in his report to the nation [two months later] . . . ; this report was written by Kissinger. It was repeated again in the President's Foreign Policy Report to Congress on February 25, 1971; that report too was written by Kissinger. Countless other reports, briefings, computer printouts sent to Congress through 1970, 1971, 1972 and early 1973 reiterated it . . . . But for Knight, there is no reason to suppose that Kissinger or any other administration official would have told any of the truth.

Id. at 413–14. But see note 30 infra (Kissinger's assertion that the inaccurate reports sent to Congress were merely a "bureaucratic blunder").

30. E.g., N.Y. Times, July 22, 1973, § 4, at 3; Impeachment Report, supra note 3, at 23. But see H. Kissinger, supra note 6, at 253 n.*:

> The Pentagon's double-bookkeeping had a motivation much less sinister than that described in revisionist folklore. To preserve the secrecy of the original (originally intended as the only) raid, Pentagon instructions were kept out of normal channels. The purpose was not to deceive Congress (where key leaders were informed) but to keep the attack from being routinely briefed to the Saigon press. The procedure was continued by rote when bombing became more frequent two months later. When Congressional committees asked for data four years later, new Pentagon officials, unaware of the two reporting channels, unwittingly furnished data from the regular files. This was a bureaucratic blunder, not deliberate design.

But see W. Shawcross, supra note 3, at 94–95:

> Even after 1970 when [the secret bombing operation] had ended and Sihanouk, exiled, no longer needed protection, Nixon, Kissinger, Rogers, Laird, Elliot L. Richardson and other public officials all continued to assure Congress, press and public, without equivocation, that the United States had scrupulously declined to attack Communist positions in Cambodia before spring 1970.

31. W. Isaacson, supra note 4, at 176–77.

32. N.Y. Times, July 17, 1973, at 1, 4; W. Shawcross, supra note 3, at 287.

33. Id. at 32; see also Cambodia Hearings, supra note 10, at 9 (testimony of Hal Knight).

34. Impeachment Debate, supra note 7, at 509–10; see also Impeachment Report, supra note 3, at 59; W. Shawcross, supra note 3, at 277 (interview with Ambassador Emory Swank).

35. M. Kalb & B. Kalb, Kissinger 132 (1974).

36. R. Nixon, supra note 6, at 382. It is true that in his 1977 interview with David Frost, Nixon attempted a military justification for the secrecy which was neither "Sihanouk" explanation but rather an entirely new one. He said that the records were falsified "in order to protect the security of the operation." W. Shawcross, supra note 3, at 290. "[I]n war there are times when you have to, in dealing with the enemy, in order to mislead them, you may not be able to level with your friends, or even with your own people." Id. He went on to compare the situation with our misleading of the Germans about the site of the Normandy landings. Id. This is evidently preposterous as a justification for keeping bombing raids secret from Congress four years after they happened; the fact that Nixon came up with it in 1977 further suggests (as if we needed more) that neither Sihanouk explanation was the real one.

37. News Release, Office of Ass't Secretary of Defense for Public Affairs, Feb. 27, 1984, at 4–5.

38. Impeachment Debate, supra note 7, at 489–90. Conyers' proposed article was derived from an earlier motion proposed by Congressman Robert Drinan in July 1973 when the cover-up was first revealed. W. Shawcross, supra note 3, at 152, 330.

39. It may be that the Democratic leadership was unwilling to support it because a full inquiry would have demonstrated that a (very) few prominent members of their party had known about the secret bombing at the time. See W. Shawcross, supra note 3, at 330; but cf. note 6 supra. My conclusion that President Nixon should have been impeached for secretly bombing Cambodia does not necessarily carry with it the conclusion that these people should have been comparably punished. The impeachable offense was making war unconstitutionally; the most that knowledgeable members of Congress were guilty of was "misprision of" (i.e., not blowing the whistle on) that offense. Misprision of a felony is not even a crime in most jurisdictions, and even where it is, it is one respecting which grand juries actually sometimes refuse prosecutorial requests for indictment. That doesn't mean we should reelect such people to public office, however.

40. Note that a coherent defense would need one explanation for the cover-up at the time, another for maintaining it three years after Sihanouk was replaced by Lon Nol. I suppose it's possible, but I'd sure like to conduct the cross-examination.

41. "Thanks to elaborate records falsification, Operation Menu continued for fourteen months in absolute secrecy from the American public." A. Isaacs et al., supra note 17, at 89. That the secret held until 1973 is corroborated by the fact that the "exposés" of the early 1970s—ranging from the most carefully researched to the most radical "America-can-do-no-right" sort—did not so much as hint at the existence of the Cambodian bombing campaign. E.g., D. Kirk, supra note 14; W. Burchett, The Second Indochina War (1970). See also, e.g., U.S. News & World Rep., Apr. 28, 1969, at 8 ("Improved relations between the U.S. and Cambodia, diplomats indicate, almost certainly mean there will be no B-52 strikes or sizable American ground forays into Cambodia").

42. It is true that this case shares with Laos the characteristic that Congress subsequently authorized a continuation of the combat activity that had previously been hidden from it. They are different, however, in that in this case the question presented to Congress was not whether to authorize a program that had until then been carried on without its knowledge or authorization, but whether (because of years-old history it had just learned about) to discontinue a program it had been authorizing for some years. See note 176 to chapter 4. If the fact of subsequent congressional authorization is permitted invariably to bar impeachment, it is unlikely, given the momentum of wartime situations, that we will ever find an effective deterrent to presidential wars that are begun covertly in order to shield them from scrutiny.

43. "Richard Nixon won many great victories, but he was not a likeable man, and in the end he was chased out of Washington like some kind of poison troll." H. Thompson, Generation of Swine 128 (1988).

44. W. Shawcross, supra note 3, at 331.

CHAPTER 6
"COVERT" WAR TODAY

1. Report of the Special Study Group on the Covert Activities of the Central Intelligence Agency, Sept. 30, 1954 (declassified 1976), quoted in 1 Senate Select Comm. to Study Governmental Operations with Respect to Intelligence Activities, Final Report: Foreign and Military Intelligence, S. Rep No. 755, 94th Cong., 2d Sess. 50 (1976) [hereinafter Church Committee Report].

2. Quoted in J. Persico, Casey: From the OSS to the CIA 538 (1990).

3. The Intelligence Act of 1991, 105 Stat. 441 (codified at 50 U.S.C.A. §§ 413–413b (Supp. 1992)), currently controls. It provides that the president may not authorize a covert action unless he determines it to be "necessary to support identifiable foreign policy objectives of the United States" and "important to the national security of the United States." Such findings are to be reported to the two intelligence committees "as soon as possible" after approval and before the commencement of the covert action involved, unless the president "determines that it is essential to limit access to the finding to meet extraordinary circumstances affecting vital interests of the United States," in which case he can report it to only the so-called "gang of eight" (the chairs and ranking minority members of the two committees, the Speaker and minority leader of the House, and the majority and minority leaders of the Senate). On unspecified occasions even a prior report to the gang of eight can be omitted, however, as the Act goes on to provide that when neither the committees nor the gang of eight have been given prior notice, "the President shall fully inform the . . . committees in a timely fashion and shall provide a statement of the reasons for not giving prior notice." (An effort by Senators Cohen and Boren to require that notice of all findings be given to at least a few legislators within forty-eight hours of their approval passed the Senate overwhelmingly in 1988 but died in the 100th Congress and was not reintroduced in the 101st. See B. Blechman, The Politics of National Security: Congress and U.S. Defense Policy 161–63 (1990).) Like its predecessors, the 1991 Act is explicit that the *approval* of neither the intelligence committees nor the gang of eight is required.

4. The quotation is from a reader's report for a press other than Princeton on my proposal for this book (which included a version of the Laos chapter but nothing on the subsequent development of covert action law). I do not know the commentator's identity but assume him (or her) to be knowledgeable, because (1) I don't submit my work to low-rent outfits, (2) he (or she) refers to me more often as "John," raising the possibility that we are acquainted, and (3) that press also accepted the book.

5. Also the Green Beret border crossings, of course, as well as similar moves into Cambodia and our bombing of that country.

6. 199 Cong. Rec. 25,079 (1973).

7. Id. at 25,092. See T. Eagleton, War and Presidential Power: A Chronicle of Congressional Surrender 186–96 (1974).

8. The first statute we should mention, however, is a much earlier one, the Neutrality Act of 1794, 1 Stat. 381, which is still on the books and in its present form provides:

> Whoever, within the United States, knowingly begins or sets on foot or provides or prepares a means for or furnishes the money for, or takes part in, any military or naval expedition or enterprise to be carried on from thence against the territory or dominion of any foreign prince or state, or of any colony, district, or people with whom the United States is at peace, shall be fined not more than $3,000 or imprisoned not more than three years, or both.

18 U.S.C. § 960 (1988). From the beginning the Neutrality Act was judicially interpreted to apply to executive-sponsored as well as private ventures. United States v. Smith, 27 F. Cas. 1192 (C.C.N.Y. 1807) (No. 16,342) (Paterson, J.). See generally Lobel, "The Rise and Decline of the Neutrality Act: Sovereignty and Congressional War Power in United States Foreign Policy," 24 Harv. Int'l L.J. 1 (1983). This reading fit the framers' intentions like a glove (which is hardly surprising, given that Paterson had been a delegate to the constitutional convention)—whether or not we were "at peace" with a given nation being a decision to be made *by Congress*. Thus unless the Neutrality Act has been implicitly repealed at least in part by the post-Vietnam legislation—Dellums v. Smith, 577 F. Supp. 1449 (N.D. Cal. 1984), rev'd on other grounds, 797 F.2d 817 (9th Cir. 1986), held that it was not—"covert wars" not approved by Congress are not simply beyond the authority of the executive branch, they are criminal.

I shall conclude below that none of the recent statutes can responsibly be read to have delegated to the executive authority to wage covert war. In setting up a reporting scheme for covert wars, however, such laws clearly take cognizance of the fact that the president (presumably on his own constitutional authority) regularly engages in them, an act of recognition it seems to me must serve to repeal the earlier imposition of criminal liability on persons participating in them at his direction (unless the war in question has been statutorily outlawed, in which case the Neutrality Act should not be read as having been repealed with respect to it, though it effectively has been so read by certain courts. E.g., United States v. Terrell, 731 F. Supp. 473 (S.D. Fla. 1989)).

9. Actually it is difficult to understand why section 102(d)(4), empowering the CIA "to perform, for the benefit of the existing intelligence agencies, such additional services of common concern as the National Security Council determines can be

more efficiently accomplished centrally," should not be equally or more useful, but for some reason it is not the one that has been seized upon. (I merely note the phenomenon and do not suggest that subsection (4) should be read thus: The legislative purpose and constitutional arguments precluding such a reading of subsection (5) preclude it of subsection (4) as well.)

10. 50 U.S.C. § 403(d)(5) (1988).

11. J. Ranelagh, The Agency: The Rise and Decline of the CIA 115 (1986).

12. E.g., Borosage, "Para-Legal Authority and Its Perils," 40 Law & Contemp. Probs. 166, 175–77 (1976); T. Weiner, Blank Check: The Pentagon's Black Budget 116 (1990).

13. Quoted in 1 Church Committee Report, supra note 1, at 478. Houston was essentially ordered to reverse this opinion by Hillenkoetter and Secretary of Defense Forrestal, and did so. J. Ranelagh, supra note 11, at 115; T. Weiner, supra note 12, at 117. This reversal is relegated to an endnote for two reasons.

First, it was a nakedly political overrule of a reasoned legal conclusion. The CIA's attitude toward law, at least at the time in question, could not be more disarmingly summed up than it was by G.J.A. O'Toole's recent sympathetic history of the agency and account of the incident: "Hillenkoetter resisted the bureaucratic temptation to use Houston's finding as the basis for a safe and negative response to Forrestal's request. Instead, he told the secretary of defense the CIA was ready to take on the job. Once again, in the space of a few weeks, the role of the agency had been enlarged." G. O'Toole, Honorable Treachery: A History of U.S. Intelligence, Espionage, and Covert Action from the American Revolution to the CIA 436 (1991). (That's more like it: a can-do kind of outfit undeterred by such "bureaucratic" considerations and "safe" exits as illegality.)

Second, the opinion as reversed no longer prevails, even within the CIA General Counsel's office, which in 1962 concluded:

[I]n order for the National Security Act to provide authority for the conduct of the wide range of covert action engaged in by the CIA, Section 102(d)(5) would have to read, "perform such other functions and duties related to the national security" as the NSC might from time to time direct, and not "perform such other functions and duties related to intelligence affecting the national security."

1 Church Committee Report, supra, at 479 (footnote omitted). After this later interpretation was given by the General Counsel, no attempt was made by the executive branch to have the National Security Act amended.

14. 88 Stat. 1795, 1804 (1974) (superceded by Intelligence Act of 1991, 105 Stat. 441).

15. See note 3 supra for a more complete summary of current statutory requirements.

16. 1 Church Committee Report, supra note 1, at 135.

17. I hope you can forgive my noting one last time that when Congress acts to allow presidential acts of war it prefers to do so backhandedly—this time not by saying covert actions are lawful but rather by setting up a procedural system that makes sense only on the assumption that they are. The yen for "plausible deniability," see note 23 infra, is not limited to the executive branch.

18. P. 26.

19. Pp. 76–77. I had previously argued that the emergency being responded to need not actually constitute an attack on U.S. territory, but could encompass other serious threats to our national security. If you disagree with me about that, as I indicated a number of responsible commentators do, the current discussion should end here for you, as there surely is no need *covertly* to respond to actual attacks on the United States.

20. "Critical flaws that would be apparent in the light of day do not appear; no debate occurs within the government generally." F. Wormuth & E. Firmage, To Chain the Dog of War: The War Power of Congress in History and Law 264 (2d ed. 1989). It is particularly important that the president get the advice of some people who don't work for him, lest the "discussion" actually become a disguised monologue "in which one man is getting reflections of what he sends out." Hearings on S. 1125 before the Subcomm. on Separation of Powers of the Senate Comm. on the Judiciary, 92d Cong., 1st Sess. 465–66 (1971) (testimony of George Reedy, special assistant and press secretary to President Johnson). Secretary Vance also reports being "struck" by "how seldom," left to their own devices, "the President, or even his closest advisors, were exposed to the views of experienced outsiders who owed no special deference to the President," Vance, "Striking the Balance: Congress and the President Under the War Powers Resolution," 133 U. Pa. L. Rev. 79, 91 (1984), and the final chapter of Robert Kennedy's book on the Cuban missile crisis, Thirteen Days (1969), waxing eloquent about the importance of broadly consulting as many executive officials and departments as possible, astonishingly never mentions Congress (of which he was at least titularly a member when he completed the book) as a possible source of advice. Possibly most chilling, however—though here at least the author appears to have gotten the point—is President Ford's rendition of the National Security Council meeting on the *Mayaguez* crisis, which David Kennerly, the White House *photographer*, interrupted to ask, "Has anyone considered that this might be the act of a local Cambodian commander who has just taken it into his own hands to halt any ship that comes by? Has anyone stopped to think that he might not have gotten his orders from Phnom Penh? If that's what has happened, you know, you can blow the whole place away and it's not gonna make any difference." G. Ford, A Time to Heal 279 (1979). (And to think that when I was in the Ford Administration, I used to regard Mr. Kennerly as an indefensible waste of the taxpayers' money—obviously aside from the rare occasion on which I happened to be standing next to someone important at the right time.)

In addition to outside input on covert wars, we forfeit the pause, the chance for a sober second thought that can itself preclude our plunging ahead with a half-baked scheme, and we suffer as well a likely diminution in public (to say nothing of congressional) support once the war has begun. As former National Security Adviser Robert McFarlane had learned by 1987, "it is virtually impossible, almost as a matter of definition, to rally public support behind a policy that you can't even talk about." Joint Hearings before the House Select Comm. to Investigate Covert Arms Transactions with Iran and Senate Select Comm. on Secret Military Assistance to Iran and the Nicaraguan Opposition, 100th Cong., 1st Sess. 4 (1987).

As for the loss of *presidential* control, see note 23 infra.

21. I have in mind here more than the tragicomic hash our fabled "Delta Force" made of the attempt to rescue the hostages in Iran. I hope, for example, that in

focusing on the unconstitutionality of our covert wars in Laos and Cambodia, I didn't cause you to forget how unsuccessful they were militarily. See also C. Robbins, The Ravens: The Men Who Flew in America's Secret War in Laos 134 (1987) ("Intelligence gathered in Laos by the CIA throughout the conflict was good . . . . The military planning of the CIA was less impressive—little more than a series of reactions to enemy initiatives."). More generally:

> The U.S. Army was unprepared to fight these wars [against guerrillas and terrorists]. Its tanks and bombs and armored personnel carriers were useless against kidnappers and saboteurs. Force was no match for terror. It was the wrong weapon for Third World political intrigues . . . .
>
> The CIA wasn't much good at waging these battles either. It could hire private armies, but they often proved corrupt and ineffectual . . . . It couldn't free American hostages or even find them. It could tell you the gross national product of Lebanon, but it couldn't draw up a detailed street map of Beirut, not one that showed the back alleys and basements in bombed-out southern slums where the Shiite kidnappers kept their hostages in chains.

T. Weiner, supra note 12, at 173. Thus in 1987 former Secretary of Defense Clark Clifford testified that "on balance covert activities have harmed this country more than they have helped us," because of the "repeated instances of embarrassing failure—where the goals of the operations themselves were not fulfilled and unforeseen setbacks occurred instead." Hearings on S. 1721 and S. 1818 before the Senate Select Comm. on Intelligence, 100th Cong., 2d Sess. 225 (1987). The judgment of President Reagan's Secretary of the Navy, John Lehman, is similar: "One cannot escape the conclusion, upon reviewing 215 years of American covert operations, that we haven't conducted them very well and that we might have been better off not to have tried." J. Lehman, Making War: The 200-Year-Old Battle Between the President and Congress over How America Goes to War 202 (1992).

At this point the answer is sometimes given that we hear only of our covert failures, that "naturally" our covert successes go unsung. Actually this doesn't make sense even a priori: There is little reason to suppose our failures would be harder to hide than our successes, and the motive of those responsible to reveal the latter is much stronger. Thus we saw in our study of Laos how our clear "covert" accomplishments, even those so transiently significant as the annual retaking of the Plain of Jars, seemed to find their way into the papers from government sources. See also C. Robbins, supra, at 121 (CIA "was rather smug about Laos and boasted [at least to a few selected visitors such as Senator Symington] about its success there"). CIA director Allen Dulles also leaked the Agency's involvement in the overthrows of Mosssedegh and Arbenz to *The Saturday Evening Post*.

But the point is more general. We have all become aware, albeit necessarily in retrospect, of the CIA's various covert "accomplishments": the 1953 overthrow of the populist nationalist Prime Minister Mohammed Mossedegh of Iran; the 1954 toppling of the democratically elected land-reformer President Jacobo Arbenz Guzman of Guatemala; the attempted overthrow and assassination of Prime Minister Patrice Lumumba of the Belgian Congo in 1960 and 1961 (which can't be counted a full-fledged victory, as Joseph Mobutu killed him before the CIA could); helping with the overthrow (though probably not in any more direct sense with the subsequent killing) of Chilean President Salvador Allende Gossens in 1973. I needn't go on to list the CIA's various "failures," as my mission here was to rebut the argument that we never learn of its "successes." (You will not have missed my subtle secondary mission—the quotation marks are a big clue to this one—to question whether the list is so rich in long-range success as to justify the covert action function generally. It is true Mobutu remains in power and pro-American, though his country, now called Zaire, remains—despite the world's richest copper mines—one of Africa's poorest. Allende's overthrow ended a century of democratic tradition in Chile, Arbenz's ushered in an era of brutal military rule in Guatemala that persists today, and Mossedegh's hardly had the long-term effect of stabilizing Iran. Our arming and training of the Afghani Mujaheddin is conventionally regarded as a success, but if so that only proves my point: Our activities in Afghanistan were from the outset fully authorized, even at times aggressively pushed, by Congress. See, e.g., B. Blechman, supra note 3, at 137–38; cf. note 38 infra.)

22. It was around the time of President Kennedy that someone decided—legend has it it was the man himself—that we should get into the business of fighting guerrillas, and that the way to do that was to learn the techniques of guerrilla warfare. This was not the soundest inference in our history. "The reason minor powers choose to engage in terrorism, quasi- or irregular warfare against us is they have no other choice. For us to oppose such countries, however, in a similarly piecemeal, hasty or irregular fashion is neither necessary or advantageous. It only allows them a chance to compete, perhaps to win." R. Christian Peel, "The Real National Security Myths in a Country Defended by Invisible Bombers, Poseidon, Trident and the President," Dec. 1991, at 27 (student paper). Our military advantages as a nation hardly lie in our ability to blend into and live off unfamiliar land, but quite the contrary in our wealth, natural resources, technological superiority, and (when the American people can be mobilized behind a war) a tenacity rooted in a historical sense of special moral mission. Thus while we are not at all suited to wars fought either hit-and-run or half-heartedly, our advantages are such—since the death of the Soviet Union more clearly than ever before in our (or arguably any nation's) history—that we can almost certainly win decisively any war to which we are prepared to commit unequivocally. Congressionally unauthorized "covert" wars do not fit this description. Those that do are wars begun the way the Constitution provides, wars sufficiently supported by the people that they can garner the authorization of both houses of Congress as well as the president.

> What we do well is fight military crusades, all-out efforts where our slowly but fully aroused power can overcome any foreseeable opposition. To insist on the constitutional warmaking procedures with full congressional participation is to better insure that we fight only these kinds of wars for which we are suited. [This argument encompasses] both the so-called "lessons of Vietnam." For it acknowledges on the one hand that there are wars . . . we are not equipped to fight . . . . Yet at the same time, it insists that when we do fight, we must fight to win, all-out in a united effort . . . . [T]he best way to heed both lessons is to only fight wars which Congress, undoubtedly with public support, has seen fit to declare or authorize.

Peel, supra, at 27–28. (You will have noted that I have quoted several student papers in this book. Lest you think me some sort of ventriloquist's dummy, I would hasten to note that each of their authors had taken my course in National Security Law, though admittedly that leaves open the question of who was teaching whom.) The message here seems to be getting through, at least for now, at least among our top military leaders, whose "school" was Indochina, if not entirely among their civilian bosses, who skipped that grade. See, e.g., J. Smith, George Bush's War 85, 178, 224–25 (1992). Prior to the Cold War we pretty much "eschewed foreign adventures except when national survival was at stake." Id. at 257. It is no coincidence that the change in this regard has come hand in hand with the executive's assumption of effective authority to decide when we go to war.

23. On the battlefield, as General Secord has granted, "nasty, undeclared wars tend to breed nasty, indefensible atrocities." R. Secord (with J. Wurts), Honored and Betrayed: Irangate, Covert Affairs, and the Secret War in Laos 177 (1992); see also note 33 to chapter 4. At home, "covert action with its emphasis on secrecy breeds contempt and distrust for the democratic decision-making process." F. Wormuth & E. Firmage, supra note 20, at 263–64. The law of covert war today is hardly demanding: It requires only notice to a couple of congressional committees, with a good deal of discretion vested in the president as to when that notice need be given. Note 3 supra. But even this has been deemed within the executive to require evasion—if you don't have to tell the entire Congress, let alone the American people, why should you have to tell anybody?—and a variety of techniques for evasion have been developed. They need not be elaborated here—they are in M. Glennon, Constitutional Diplomacy 297–300 (1990)—as the mere mention of Iran-Contra should be sufficient to make the point. "In part, such a scandal was predictable by the very nature of covert action." F. Wormuth & E. Firmage, supra, at 264. As Secretary of the Army John O. Marsh, Jr., testified before the Iran-Contra Committee, there had developed a belief (from the top of the chain of command to the bottom) that "if it's secret it's legal," an axiom pursuant to which "all existing regulations and laws and norms and customs very frequently fall by the wayside." Report of the Congressional Committees Investigating the Iran-Contra Affair, H.R. Rep. No. 433, S. Rep. No. 216, 100th Cong., 1st Sess., App. B, Vol. 17, at 803–4 (1987). Colonel North put it with characteristic economy: "We operated from the premise that everything we did do was legal." 2 Iran-Contra Hearings, supra note 20, at 43.

The next logical step along this road is a loss of *presidential* control: If you feel you don't have to tell Congress or even its statutorily designated committees about covert wars, it begins to become unclear why you should have to tell *anybody*. In fact a failure to tell the president has been converted into a *virtue* by the invention and twisted extension of the concept of "plausible deniability":

> Traditionally, plausible denial was a practice designed to give the President and the United States the ability to deny responsibility for covert activities if for some reason their involvement in the covert operations is suspected or questioned by another foreign government. However, in the Iran-Contra affair, officers of the National Security Council used deniability to protect the President from domestic uproar following disclosure of the illegal arms sales and fund diversion to Congress and the American public.

F. Wormuth & E. Firmage, supra, at 266. Thus the logic of plausible deniability: (1) lie to the world (to protect the United States from foreign criticism), and because that's okay (2) lie to Congress and the American public (to protect the president from domestic criticism). But as if that weren't enough, there was an all-too-easy third application as well: (3) If you really want to protect the president from possible criticism, don't tell *him* what you're doing, let alone seek his permission. (Of course Hughes-Ryan's requirement of a presidential finding was designed to preclude this final extension, but at least according to the testimony of presidential subordinates, it hasn't worked.)

Thus former CIA Director Richard Helms testified before the Church Committee that the plot to assassinate Fidel Castro had not been revealed to President Kennedy because "I just think we all had the feeling that we're hired to keep those things out of the Oval Office," S. Rep. No. 465, 94th Cong., 1st Sess. 149 (1975) (interim report), and former National Security Adviser John Poindexter testified similarly before the Iran-Contra Committee that he had made "a very deliberate decision not to ask the President" for permission to divert the Iranian arms sale proceeds to the Nicaraguan Contras in order to "insulate [him] from the decision and provide some future deniability for the President if it ever leaked out." Iran-Contra Report, supra, at 271. (I'm certainly not vouching for the truth of the assertion that either President Kennedy or President Reagan actually was kept in the dark, merely quoting the inference used to justify doing so, which inference surely might be acted on on some occasions, whether it was in fact on either of these.) It's undeniably true that removing the president from the decision process is likely to make his future denial more credible: Unfortunately it's also true that it eliminates the input of any elected official whatever in the decision to eliminate a foreign leader or otherwise wage war on foreign nations.

Separation of powers issues aside, the general attitude of lawlessness essential to the successful pursuit of covert actions can be turned against our own citizens as well. "Surely at this point in time it is not necessary to remind ourselves of the certainty that the techniques that we apply to others will inevitably be turned on the American people by our own intelligence services." 1 Church Committee Report, supra note 1, at 522 (testimony of Morton S. Halperin. Cf. Borosage, supra note 12, at 168: "Para-legal justification may thus represent a transitional form between the rule of law and the reign of a leader"). That testimony was given in the mid-1970s, after the disclosure of widespread domestic intelligence-gathering by the CIA, and in this regard we seem to have been doing somewhat better of late: I suppose, therefore, this is one of the times it *is* "necessary to remind ourselves."

24. A third error is that the war in Laos was far from adequately reported even to the relevant committees.

25. Thus insofar as the 1991 Act's definition of "covert action" to include "activities of the United States Government to influence political, economic, or military conditions abroad, where it is intended that the role of the United States Government will not be apparent or acknowledged publicly," 50 U.S.C.A. § 413b(e) (Supp. 1992), is read to relieve acts of war from the requirement of advance congressional authorization whenever the executive simply thinks it advisable not to acknowledge them publicly, it is unconstitutional, and consequently should not be so read. (The statutory definition is obviously recklessly broad.) For reasons we canvassed in chapter 2, Congress generally cannot delegate away its constitutional obligation to decide who our enemies will be. P. 26.

26. Cf. J. Persico, supra note 2, at 273 ("The operation would have to be covert, Casey knew. The American people, the Congress, even elements in the Reagan administration would balk at open U.S. involvement in Nicaragua"); R. Secord, supra note 23, at 42, 49.

27. Damrosch, "Covert Operations," 83 Am. J. Int'l L. 795, 799 (1989).

28. Id. at 799 n.25.

29. N.Y. Times, Jan. 19, 1992, at 1.

30. Id. This might not be a bad way to proceed, but it provides an additional reason for following the Constitution and taking the contemplated military action to Congress as opposed to calling it "covert" and not seeking authorization. Cf. J. Smith, supra note 22, at 118 ("Ike's caution [in seeking congressional authorization when he wished to stage military shows of force] was well served. Perhaps because he had the support of Congress, American forces were not challenged. Hostilities did not ensue").

31. N.Y. Times, Jan. 19, 1992, at 6.

32. Geralyn Smitherman, "Private Affairs," Dec. 17, 1991, at 39 (student paper).

33. Forum, "Should the U.S. Fight Secret Wars?" Harper's Mag., Sept. 1984, at 33, 35 (Daniel Patrick Moynihan). Accord, id. (William Colby); id. at 41 (Ray S. Cline).

34. We even boasted of our efforts in Laos to our South Vietnamese allies. P. 82.

35. C. Stevenson, The End of Nowhere: American Policy Toward Laos Since 1954, at 3 (1972). See also sources cited note 67 to chapter 4; Forum, supra note 33, at 44–45 (Morton S. Halperin) ("What is in fact covert about these interventions . . . is that they are kept secret from the American people and the political process, sometimes for a very long time").

36. Of course no civilian can be certain of the number, but it has been responsibly estimated that fifty-seven U.S. planes and helicopters were lost in Operation Desert Storm. J. Smith, supra note 22, at 9.

37. See note 84 to chapter 4. Cf. G. Treverton, Covert Action: The Limits of Intervention in the Postwar World 13 (1987) (American war in Laos "not so much secret as unacknowledged"); but cf. pp. 77, 82 (actually unacknowledged to our enemies but secret from us, a combination that tells us much about the administration's motivations).

38. As they can on any nonverifiable argument, infinite variations can be run on this one—here, for example, that although everyone knows we're involved in a certain war, we can't make it public lest an *ally* refuse to cooperate. Aside from Laos and Cambodia (with respect to each of which the assertion's fraudulence has already been demonstrated, pp. 77–79, 100) the most commonly adduced recent example is Pakistan, which, it is sometimes asserted, would have refused to act as our conduit to the Afghan war had its role been made public. E.g., Forum, supra note 33, at 45 (Leslie Gelb). That one doesn't work either: In fact it's an example that cuts strongly the other way. There is no reason whatever that Congress can't authorize a military effort without going on to list the other countries that will be helping us. See also Halperin, "Lawful Wars," 72 Foreign Pol'y 173, 182–85 (1988). In fact that's exactly what happened in the case of Afghanistan: In October 1984 Congress passed a resolution deploring the Soviet invasion and authorizing support for the Afghan rebels. Of course everyone involved knew about Pakistan's role. (How

could they not?) But Congress didn't declare it publicly. (Why would it, even if it hadn't been asked not to?) That omission obviously provided all the deniability the Pakistanis felt they needed. (Assuming there was any truth at all to the report they wouldn't cooperate if they didn't get it: I have to confess the more of these justifications for excluding Congress one examines in detail, only to find there is literally nothing there, the more cynical one gets about the bona fides of the justificatory apparatus.) Cf. Forum, supra, at 46 (Angelo Codevilla):

> Is Pakistan's acquiescence in serving as a conduit for arms and other assistance for the Mujaheddin based on the fact that the Soviet Union does not know that such assistance is flowing through Pakistan? That seems unlikely. Rather, the Pakistanis cooperate because they are confident the United States will come to their aid should they be attacked by the Soviet Union. Since the Russians know this, they refrain from attacking.

I am aware that it is possible that the Soviets were behind the death of Pakistani President Zia (and U.S. Ambassador Raphel) but if that is so it is obviously because the Soviets could see perfectly well that Pakistan (and the U.S.) were assisting a war against them. No one, however zealous, could plausibly attribute the assassination, assuming that's what it was, to any action of Congress (which, I repeat, did *not* mention Pakistan in its authorization).

39. In any event there are relatively nonconfrontational ways of obtaining congressional authorization, and the more routine and recognized as constitutional necessities they become, the less such authorizations are likely to be seen as gauntlets.

40. The fact that CIA employees are often "detailees" from the armed forces, see note 50 to chapter 4, further reinforces Eagleton's point.

41. But see, e.g., M. Glennon, supra note 23, at 117.

42. I also suggest there should be *no* free period where there does not exist a compelling reason to dispense with the ordinary constitutional requirement of advance authorization, but for the moment I mean to be discussing operations whose advance disclosure the president genuinely believes will put our troops at serious additional risk. (Systematically degraded as the language has been in this area, I cling to the faith that the claim will occasionally be true.) Under my proposed statute the sort of "overt-covert" operation discussed above, where no serious attempt at secrecy is essential or for that matter even made, would require authorization in advance.

43. One Senate study concluded that 136 of 148 news stories containing classified information cited executive officials as the source. Boston Globe, July 17, 1987, at 9.

44. A Congress less trustful of itself than I (and with a lower estimate of the acuity of those being strafed by the newly arrived American forces) could always consider—with what degree of responsibility I leave them to judge—retaining the forty-eight hour reporting lag (rather than requiring a request for authorization simultaneous with the commencement of hostilities) in cases where advance authorization is not required because—the language is from my section 4(a)—"keeping the pendency of the United States's response . . . secret prior to its initiation is clearly essential to its military effectiveness." (Though I can imagine no excuse for retaining it in cases where advance authorization wasn't obtained because there wasn't

time to do so: If there's time to send the troops to some trouble spot, there's time to send an Under Secretary to Capitol Hill.) Anything beyond that, however, would seem pretty clearly another version of the unconstitutional routine of letting the president start the wars and the Congress wait and see how they're playing (or at least retaining for itself the rationalization that the war was so well under way it didn't really have any choice but to go along).

APPENDIX
TOWARD A WAR POWERS (COMBAT AUTHORIZATION)
ACT THAT WORKS

1. E.g., A. Thomas & A. Thomas, The War Making Powers of the President 141 (1982).

2. A joint resolution, like a statute, is subject to the requirement of presentation to the president and thus must be signed by him or passed over his veto to become law. A concurrent resolution is not presented to the president and thus resembles more a declaration of congressional opinion.

3. See note 111 to chapter 3.

4. Pp. 119–20.

5. Should Congress (benightedly) decide to reenact the statute without reducing the sixty-day free period, it should eliminate existing section 8(d)(1) but keep existing 8(d)(2). See pp. 137–38.

6. Essentially this line is taken in Legal Opinion of Lloyd Cutler, Counsel to President Carter, War Powers Consultation Relative to the Iran Rescue Mission (May 9, 1980), and Statement of Abraham D. Sofaer, State Department Legal Adviser (Apr. 29, 1986).

7. That the section's function is confusing is understandable—if you need to be further confused, see Biden & Ritch, "The War Powers Resolution at a Constitutional Impasse: A 'Joint Decision' Solution," 77 Geo. L.J. 367, 386–88 (1988)—given that at least as ultimately enacted it was intended to be hortatory only. Syntactically, three constructions seem possible: (1) the one suggested in the text, that the only presidential military actions that are lawful without advance congressional authorization are responses to attacks on U.S. territory or troops, though such responses must be reported immediately and approved within sixty days; (2) that responses to such attacks at *no* point require either a report or congressional authorization, but other threats to the national security can be militarily met by the president subject to the 4(a)/5(b) requirements of an immediate report and congressional authorization within sixty days; and (3) that responses to attacks on U.S. territory or troops never require either a report or congressional authorization, and other threats to the national security cannot be militarily met by the president without authorization in advance (that is, the 4(a)/5(b) system will not suffice with respect to them). We shall see that construction (1) is subject to the objection that it too narrowly restricts the occasions on which the president can respond without advance authorization. Construction (2) would mean that an attack on American troops (recall what was passed off as such in connection with our invasion of Panama and the bombing of Libya) would enable the president to wage war in response as long as he wished

(or what would functionally be the same, until Congress summoned the will to pass over his veto a statute stopping him). Construction (3) is subject to both those objections (and in addition would seem to leave no function whatever for section 4(a) and 5(b)). Thus all three are seriously objectionable, though the objection to (1) seems considerably the weakest, which makes it no surprise that the ensuing debate over how 2(c) might be amended can be rendered coherent (or something approximating it) only on the assumption that (1) is the correct construction of the existing provision.

8. Sources cited note 11 infra.

9. See, e.g., sources cited Note, "A Defense of the War Powers Resolution," 93 Yale L.J. 1330, 1335 n.31 (1984); J. Sundquist, The Decline and Resurgence of Congress 258 n.56 (1981).

10. E.g., Franck, "After the Fall: The New Procedural Framework for Congressional Control Over the War Power," 71 Am. J. Int'l L. 605, 639 (1977); Glennon, "The War Powers Resolution Ten Years Later: More Politics Than Law," 78 Am. J. Int'l L. 571, 580 (1984); M. Glennon, Constitutional Diplomacy 332, 336 (1990) (proposed Use of Force Act, making revised § 2(c) judicially enforceable).

11. E.g., Scigliano, "The War Powers Resolution and the War Powers," in The Presidency in the Constitutional Order 122 (J. Bessette & J. Tulis eds. 1981); Glennon, "The War Powers Resolution: Sad Record, Dismal Promise," 17 Loy. L.A. L. Rev. 657, 662 (1984). It would be a mistake to infer, however, that the omission was inadvertent. Katzmann, "War Powers: Toward a New Accommodation," in A Question of Balance: The President, the Congress, and Foreign Policy 50 (T. Mann ed. 1990). Senator Eagleton's bill to remedy this never got anywhere. L. Fisher, Constitutional Conflicts Between Congress and the President 299 (1985).

12. Hearings on War Powers before the Subcomm. on Internal Security and Scientific Affairs of the House Comm. on International Relations, 94th Cong., 1st Sess. 90–91 (1975). See also Note, supra note 9, at 1333–34 and sources cited therein.

13. Indeed, forestalling an imminent attack, which even moderate commentators think should be included, e.g., Biden & Ritch, supra note 7, at 386, is omitted from Leigh's list.

14. M. Glennon, supra note 10, at 332.

15. There would also seem to be inescapable *"Chadha* problems," as Congress would undeniably be second-guessing a presidential interpretation of a delegation it had extended him. Cf. p. 124.

16. See note 86 to chapter 3.

17. There is of course the possibility that although Congress would never enforce such limits prospectively, it would do so retroactively, by impeaching the president. That is an approach deserving of little respect, as it constitutes yet another method whereby Congress can refuse to take responsibility for decisions of war and peace, wait to see how the war in question goes, and then jump the president if it goes badly. Impeaching the president for failing to follow the Resolution's (and the Constitution's) "procedural" mandate that he obtain advance congressional authorization when there had been time to do so would be a responsible course of action. Doing so over a disagreement about whether the national security was "really" implicated seems a highly dangerous procedure, one the language of the Resolution should not encourage.

18. Once the hostilities in question have received "specific statutory authorization," 5(c) no longer applies. Cf. note 25 infra.

19. 462 U.S. 919 (1983).

20. Justice White's dissent scored some powerful points. *Chadha* is also helpfully analyzed in Strauss, "Was There a Baby in the Bathwater? A Comment on the Supreme Court's Legislative Veto Decision," 1983 Duke L.J. 789.

21. Others have attempted such a distinction. Professor Casper has correctly observed that accepting *Chadha*'s logic would mean that the president, "supported only by one-third plus one of the membership of *either* house," could start and sustain a war (at least until the clock has run). Casper, "Constitutional Constraints on the Conduct of Foreign and Defense Policy: A Nonjudicial Model," 43 U. Chi. L. Rev. 463, 484–85 (1976). However, this is a universal result of *Chadha*—if Congress cannot veto the president's exercise of a delegation, it takes a repeal to stop him—which brings us back to the question whether the sixty/ninety-day "free period" is truly a delegation. Professor Carter's (explicitly hesitant) argument that *Chadha*'s presentment requirement cannot be applicable because under the Constitution declarations of war (and other combat authorizations) are not vetoable by the president in the first place, Carter, "The Constitutionality of the War Powers Resolution," 70 Va. L. Rev. 101, 129–32 (1984), displays no failure of logic: It is the premise that is questionable. Carter's source for the proposition that "scholars are divided" on the question whether declarations of war are vetoable is L. Henkin, Foreign Affairs and the Constitution 295 n.5 (1972), but Henkin, who does not endorse the Carter premise himself, cites only an 1896 speech on the Senate floor, by one Senator Morgan of Alabama, in support of it. But see C. Berdahl, War Powers of the Executive in the United States 95 (1921); Baldwin, "The Share of the President of the United States in a Declaration of War," 12 Am. J. Int'l L. 1 (1918); U.S. Const. art. I, § 7, cl. 3:

> Every Order, Resolution, or Vote to which the Concurrence of the Senate and House of Representatives shall be necessary (except on a question of Adjournment) shall be presented to the President of the United States; and before the Same shall take Effect, shall be approved by him, or being disapproved by him, shall be re-passed by two thirds of the Senate and House of Representatives, according to the Rules and Limitations prescribed in the Case of a Bill.

Every declaration of war in our history—perhaps most notably including that voted just twenty-three years after the ratification of the Constitution—has been signed by the president. See sources cited in Lungren & Krotoski, "The War Powers Resolution After the *Chadha* Decision," 17 Loy. L.A. L. Rev. 767, 786 n.84 (1984). Apparently President Cleveland threatened to veto a declaration of war against Spain, thereby forestalling said declaration until the administration of President McKinley, who resisted but did not veto. C. Rossiter, The Supreme Court and the Commander in Chief 66 n.1 (expanded ed. 1966).

22. Ides, "Congress, Congressional Responsibility and the War Power," 17 Loy. L.A. L. Rev. 599, 630 n.101 (1984).

23. Justices Powell and White both indicated that they read the Court's opinion as invalidating all legislative veto provisions, 462 U.S. at 959, 974, and Justice White specifically referred to section 5(c), id. at 970–71. Subsequent judicial deci-

sions have read *Chadha* in this spirit. L. Tribe, American Constitutional Law § 4–3, at 217 (2d ed. 1988).

24. A quite contrary reason it has been suggested that we need not be too upset over the probable unconstitutionality of 5(c) is that constitutional or not, the president would likely heed a concurrent resolution calling for an end to hostilities. It's true he might well, but *Chadha* is likely to give Congress yet another rationale for not passing such a resolution.

25. Should Congress decide to keep 5(c)—perhaps (fat chance) in order to pass a concurrent resolution and thus force a test case—other problems should be considered. Professor Glennon, writing before *Chadha*, suggested that 5(c) be "amended to apply the concurrent resolution termination procedure to situations in which the armed forces are used pursuant to specific statutory authority." Glennon, "Strengthening the War Powers Resolution: The Case for Purse-Strings Restrictions," 60 Minn. L. Rev. 1, 37 (1975). However, such an extension manifestly could not be defended on the theory elaborated in the text (that 5(c) is but one part of a package defining a "reasonable opportunity" for congressional consideration); indeed there is a danger that by blurring the rationale for 5(c) it could serve to sink the entire provision (although it is probably sunk anyway). Section 5(c) also does not apply in 4(a)(2) or 4(a)(3) situations or, indeed, in 4(a)(1) situations where there are not actual hostilities but only the imminent likelihood thereof. This last surely should be remedied if 5(c) is retained. I shall recommend elimination of 4(a)(2) and 4(a)(3). Were they, and 5(c), retained, however, their relation too would be a candidate for repair.

26. See generally B. Blechman, The Politics of National Security: Congress and U.S. Defense Policy 173–77 (1990). More specifically, see R. Turner, The War Powers Resolution: Its Implementation in Theory and Practice (1983), at 54–57 (Phnom Penh, Saigon), 59–64 (*Mayaguez*), 69–73 (Iran); T. Franck & E. Weisband, Foreign Policy by Congress 72–74 (1979) (*Mayaguez*, Iran); Vance, "Striking the Balance: Congress and the President Under the War Powers Resolution," 133 U. Pa. L. Rev. 79, 88–90 (1984) (*Mayaguez*, Iran, Grenada); Rubner, "The Reagan Administration, the 1973 War Powers Resolution, and the Invasion of Grenada," 100 Pol. Sci. Q. 627, 630–36 (1986); Hearings on War Powers, Libya, and State-Sponsored Terrorism before the Subcomm. on Arms Control, International Security and Science of the House Comm. on Foreign Affairs, 99th Cong., 2d Sess. 117 (1986) (statement of Professor Archibald Cox) (Tripoli).

27. Senator Eagleton's proposed amendment to this effect, *see* N.Y. Times, May 22, 1975, at 1, never got anywhere.

28. See W. Reveley, War Powers of the President and Congress: Who Holds the Arrows and the Olive Branch? 254–55 (1981); P. Holt, The War Powers Resolution: The Role of Congress in U.S. Armed Intervention 34 (1978).

29. Congress has yet generally to organize itself to play a consultative role, even by rule. L. Fisher, supra note 11, at 311. It has, however, on at least one particular occasion, and the executive responded derisively:

[A]t the end of October 1990 Congress set up a committee of 18 senior members from both houses that was to be consulted with in case hostilities [in Kuwait] were contemplated by the executive. The Bush White House responded that it "didn't recognize" the group because it would lead to deciding war "by committee." Reflecting the administration's view, Secretary of Defense Dick Cheney said it might be "an advantage that Congress was out of town."

Nathan, "Revising the War Powers Act," 17 Armed Forces & Soc. 513, 527 (1991) (footnote omitted). (The administration was right about one thing: War isn't supposed to be decided "by committee." It is supposed to be decided by Congress.)

30. See note 114 to chapter 3.

31. If sections 4(a)(2) and 4(a)(3) are retained, but cf. p. 124, the consultation requirement should probably be made applicable to them too.

32. A few commentators have slid from the conclusion that 5(c) appears to be unconstitutional under *Chadha* to the conclusion that 5(b) is as well. E.g., Lungren & Krotoski, supra note 21; Moore, "Do We Have an Imperial Congress?" 43 U. Miami L. Rev. 139, 152 (1988); Rostow, "Learning 'Lessons' from Vietnam," in Congress, the President, and Foreign Policy 102 (J. Moore & R. Turner eds. 1984). This is a mistake. *Chadha* expressly stated that "other means of control, such as durational limits on authorizations and formal reporting requirements, lie well within Congress' constitutional power." 462 U.S. at 955 n.19. As Professor Carter has pointed out, rather than constituting a legislative veto, section 5(b) is a sort of "sunset law," the functional equivalent of a statute providing that troops simply may not be unilaterally committed to combat for more than sixty days (unless the statute is amended). Carter, supra note 21, at 133.

33. E.g., Glennon, supra note 25; Vance, supra note 26, at 93.

34. See note 56 to chapter 4. That all admit it is constitutional does not necessarily mean that all will obey it, as the Reagan Administration's failure to comply with the Boland Amendment demonstrates. It does, however, improve the odds.

35. The word *hostilities* was substituted for the phrase *armed conflict* during the subcommittee drafting process because it was considered to be somewhat broader in scope. In addition to a situation in which fighting actually has begun, *hostilities* also encompasses a state of confrontation in which no shots have been fired but where there is a clear and present danger of armed conflict. "*Imminent hostilities*" denotes a situation in which there is a clear potential either for such a state of confrontation or for actual armed conflict.

H.R. Rep. No. 287, 93d Cong., 1st Sess. 7 (1973) (emphasis in original). See also id. at 5, 9; 119 Cong. Rec. 33859 (daily ed. Oct. 12, 1973) (statement of Rep. Zablocki). I wouldn't recommend that any revision build on the quoted language, however: A clear potential of a clear and present danger is a little hard to get your mind around.

36. E.g., Huguez v. United States, 406 F.2d 366, 374–79 (9th Cir. 1968).

37. Multinational Force in Lebanon Resolution, 97 Stat. 805, § 2(b) (1983).

38. Emphasis supplied.

39. In some instances there may be a risk that publicly announcing that there is an imminent danger of hostilities will increase the likelihood of bringing them about. Cf. R. Turner, supra note 26, at 90. (Though on more occasions it would probably have the opposite effect.) However, this too is an argument not against the War Powers Resolution specifically but against the Constitution more generally:

However the process is structured, going to Congress for authorization will alert the world to the fact that the president thinks the situation is serious. Indeed, making the standard less demanding should lessen the crisis atmosphere to the same degree.

40. This was probably another reason the War Powers Resolution claim was raised by the private, as opposed to the congressional, plaintiffs. See note 116 to chapter 3.

41. Note 24 to chapter 3.

42. E.g., Zablocki, "War Powers Resolution: Its Past Record and Future Promise," 17 Loy. L.A. L. Rev. 579, 598 (1984); M. Glennon, supra note 10, at 103; Rubner, supra note 26, at 646.

43. R. Turner, supra note 26, at 111–12.

44. Not much would be lost by eliminating sections 4(a)(2) and 4(a)(3). Apparently they have roots in the desire of Senator Mansfield, like Senator Taft and others before him, to establish a congressional role in deciding whether the president should be permitted to augment, say, our NATO forces. A reporting requirement covering such commitments may slightly symbolize the thought that Congress also has a role in such decisions, but it doesn't mean anything operationally. Moreover, given that such troop movements generally are not (and could not be) kept secret, Congress doesn't really need to have them reported. In theory sections 4(a)(2) and 4(a)(3) might make a difference in the case of a *classified* troop movement, but in such a situation the president would probably tell the leaders of Congress anyhow. If he wouldn't, we would presumably be talking about the movement of troops to a staging area for a surprise strike. Recall, however, that the existing requirement is that the report be filed within forty-eight hours of the reported-upon event. By that time we probably would have passed beyond the staging-area phase (and almost certainly beyond the point at which the troops' presence would remain secret) and into a situation that would plainly require a 4(a)(1) report.

If 4(a)(2) and 4(a)(3) are retained, the reference to equipment should probably be eliminated, and it should be made explicit that the president is to report under the "highest" applicable subsection.

45. Note, "The Future of the War Powers Resolution," 36 Stan. L. Rev. 1407, 1441 n.185 (1984).

46. The District of Columbia Circuit's "equitable discretion doctrine" was discussed in note 82 to chapter 3.

47. See notes 82 and 105 to chapter 3.

48. It is for such reasons that I have recommended simply making the ordinary time limits of the statute applicable to "covert" actions—in general, by the time those limits have been reached the operation won't be a secret any more—rather than more directly involving the courts in the questions whether secrecy still exists and is militarily necessary. P. 113.

49. But see Mitchell v. Laird, 488 F.2d 611, 613 (D.C. Cir. 1973) (holding case not moot in part because it could provide information that might prove relevant in an impeachment proceeding). My suggestion, obviously, is that this aspect of *Mitchell* was in error: Impeachment investigations should be left to Congress, as indeed they plainly seem to be by the Constitution. (It also seems to me that cases will be extremely rare in which the president's purportedly military decision to seek authorization contemporaneously rather than in advance was so clearly fraudulent

that he should be impeached for it: Here too the potential for Congress's retroactively punishing a war or a president it has decided it doesn't like seems dangerously great. Cf. note 17 supra. This book surely does not lack examples of behavior for which presidents *should* be impeached, notably fighting entire wars without ever seeking authorization. No one—not the courts and not the Congress either—needs to get into the business of second-guessing presidential judgments that military considerations required the request for authorization to be contemporaneous. We'll have come a long way if we can move the president even that far.)

50. That the period bears no rational relation to its only legitimate rationale comes as no surprise, given that the sixty/ninety arrangement was a compromise between the Senate version's thirty days and the House's 120. A few members of Congress, notably Senator Eagleton, voted against the Resolution substantially on the ground that it gave the president ninety days to wage war at will, but others voted for it despite such scruples, regarding this as an opportunity to weaken President Nixon. Representative Abzug switched her vote in the belief that an override could "accelerate the demand for the impeachment of the President," and Senator Nelson confided to Eagleton, "I heard your argument. I agree with you. I love the Constitution, but I hate Nixon more." T. Eagleton, War and Presidential Power 215, 220 (1974); Hearings on The War Power After 200 Years before the Special Subcomm. on War Powers of the Senate Comm. on Foreign Relations, 100th Cong., 2d Sess. 16 (1989) (testimony of Senator Eagleton).

One alternative would be to try to write the constitutional requirement into the Resolution essentially *in haec verba*, providing that if a reasonable period for congressional response has passed and specific statutory authorization has not been forthcoming, the court should rule the hostilities illegal. I don't see how this could work, however. I see no plausible excuse for not requiring the president to *seek* congressional authorization no later than the moment he gives the order committing the troops. Note 29 to chapter 1. The rub would come in deciding on a case-by-case basis when Congress has had sufficient time to consider the matter and decide whether to authorize the war. Courts have been relatively successful in interpreting somewhat comparable commands, such as that requiring the police to obtain a search warrant when it is reasonably possible to do so. In our case, however, the facts are far less compassed. Congressional motives will be mixed, and it will be next to impossible to separate admissible problems from faintheartedness. It thus seems extremely unlikely that there would ever be a case in which a court would select a period of fewer than twenty days. Moreover, the court's remedy in such a situation would not wisely be a simple order that the president withdraw the troops. Instead, it would probably "remand" the issue to Congress for its prompt consideration, which order itself would likely require the setting of an exact time limit! A central contribution of the War Powers Resolution was to translate the Constitution's generalities into precise numbers. The numbers chosen were too generous by far, but the impulse toward precision was sound. Leaving requirements vague helps ensure that they will not be enforced.

In some cases, Congress will be comfortably able to reach a decision one way or the other in fewer than twenty days. I have therefore included in my proposed statute a provision that where it can beat the timetable, it should. An early defeat of an authorizing resolution would probably be unenforceable under *Chadha*—and thus the president would be legally entitled to his twenty free days no matter what Congress did before they expired—though in any event, given the realities of judicial timetables, such an order would almost certainly be practically unenforceable irrespective of *Chadha*. Like a concurrent resolution, however—to which it bears substantial functional similarity—there would probably be considerable *political* impact to an early negative decision. The reasons I have relegated mention of this provision to an endnote include not only its unenforceability in court but also the gross unlikelihood that Congress would ever bring to the floor and defeat an authorizing resolution significantly in advance of the twenty-day deadline. On the other hand, it might *enact* one in significantly less than twenty days, and in that event too expeditiousness seems desirable.

51. Even the longest debate on record, that leading to the declaration of the War of 1812, took only seventeen days.

52. Glennon, supra note 10, at 573–74; note 111 to chapter 3.

53. See President Nixon's Veto Message (Oct. 24, 1973), in Dep't State Bull., Nov. 26, 1973, at 663.

54. One former executive branch official opined, for example, that "the Shi'a gunmen in Lebanon carried out their attacks with one eye on the war powers' clock [established by Congress's eighteen-month extension, see p. 49]," making the Congress, in his view, responsible for the deaths of the Marines in 1983. (Obviously, this is nonsense. The terrorists involved in these incidents almost certainly never heard of the legislation, much less were familiar with its provisions, nor founded tactical decisions on the eighteen-month authorization—with the explicit possibility of renewal—provided prior to the bombing of the marines' barracks.)

B. Blechman, supra note 26, at 190. See also Senate Hearings, supra note 50, at 125:

> SENATOR PRESSLER: Now, do you believe that our adversaries have changed their military planning any because of the existence of the War Powers Act? . . .
>
> GENERAL [DAVID C.] JONES: I doubt that they have changed their plans . . . .
>
> GENERAL [JOHN W.] VESSEY: I would echo that . . . .

Generals Jones and Vessey are former Chairs of the Joint Chiefs of Staff.

The charge that the Resolution has hampered *American* military planning with tragic results is equally reckless. E.g., L. Crovitz, A Presidential Strategy for Repealing the War Powers Resolution 2, 10 (Heritage Foundation Backgrounder 1989) (attributing deaths of 220 Marines in Lebanon to "the strategy forced on the executive branch by the knowledge that the military could have only 60 days to effect its peacekeeping mission"). For one thing, the tragic attack on the Marine barracks occurred after Congress had granted the president permission to keep the Marines in Lebanon an additional eighteen months! See also Senate Hearings, supra, at 125:

> GENERAL JONES: I really do not believe that the War Powers Resolution has had any conscious [effect] on war planning at all . . . .
>
> GENERAL VESSEY: I think that's right . . . . I have looked down the list of the other 35 or so incidents that one might say have taken place where armed

forces have been deployed since the War Powers Resolution has been enacted, and I do not believe that the War Powers Resolution had any impact
on the planning for any of those.

Accord, id. at 125–26 (testimony of General, and once and future National Security
Adviser, Brent Scowcroft).

55. A related danger, against which President Nixon also warned in his veto
message, supra note 53, is that the president will be moved to escalate *our* military
effort as the deadline approaches. However, by escalating the bombing of North
Vietnam whenever he felt Congress's patience was wearing thin, Staff of House
Comm. on Foreign Affairs, 97th Cong., 2d Sess., The War Powers Resolution 103–
4 (1982), Nixon himself had demonstrated that such reactions do not necessarily
depend on any clock but rather on the need for congressional acquiescence more
generally.

56. See also, e.g., M. Glennon, supra note 10, at 102.

57. If for some bizarre reason a subsequent Congress were to make unmistakable
its intention both to authorize a war and to do so in a way that did not comply with
section 8(a)(1), I suppose that should be deemed a pro tanto repeal of that section.

58. Note 23 to chapter 2.

59. Vance, supra note 26, at 86.

60. The ripeness holding aside, Judge Greene's opinion in *Dellums v. Bush* (discussed in chapter 3) is the sort of opinion I have in mind.

61. In the event twenty days then pass and Congress does nothing to authorize
the war, the proposed statute would require the president to withdraw the troops,
and would cut off further funding for the war. (Service personnel plaintiffs would
also be released from further obligation to comply with orders to participate in the
war.) Experience and prior rhetoric suggest that the president would respect this. In
the unlikely event of defiance on the part of the president (and complicity by
everyone else associated with the budget process) impeachment would seem the
appropriate response. If, however, Congress chose not to respond to such flagrant
illegality, the case might well end up back in court, which would then appropriately
issue a declaratory judgment somewhat different from the earlier one, in that it
would provide that the president is *now* conducting a war in violation of the Constitution (and perhaps an injunction against his continuing to do so, though it is
unclear what that would add operationally). Should the president persist at this point
in his disobedience and Congress in its refusal to act, we will all be in very
deep water, and certainly will have passed the point where judicial action is very
relevant.

This catechism, however, has taken on the aspect of responding to a child who
keeps asking, "But what if they don't?" Nothing useful in legal analysis is accomplished by discussions of gross improbabilities, cf. J. Ely, Democracy and Distrust:
A Theory of Judicial Review 182–83 (1980), or by trying to design a judicial fix for
Armageddon. It is hardly an indictment of the statute suggested here (or any other)
that it doesn't provide a foolproof recipe for a situation where the president of the
United States is prepared openly to defy both congressional statute and judicial
order, and the Congress of the United States refuses to do anything about it. (Obviously we should try to minimize the chances of such an impasse's developing, but
that's what the discussion of remedy in note 86 to chapter 3 was about.)

I certainly do not mean here to have described the way the system typically should work. If it is always or even often necessary to go to court to get the president and Congress to do their jobs, we will have failed. What is contemplated, instead, is an educational process. Once everyone gets the idea that the courts stand ready to start the clock, it should follow that the president will begin doing so without the need of a lawsuit, and that Congress will then readily assume its constitutional duty to decide on war and peace. If overzealous police officers, and even racial bigots, can be conditioned by the rule of law to operate within fetters they initially condemned as impossibly constricting, can't we expect as much of the president and Congress?

Index

The endnotes accompanying the listed pages of text should also be consulted.

Printed in the United States
67496LVS00001B/96

War and Responsibility

CONSTITUTIONAL LESSONS OF
VIETNAM AND ITS AFTERMATH

John Hart Ely

PRINCETON UNIVERSITY PRESS

PRINCETON, NEW JERSEY

Copyright © 1993 by Princeton University Press
Published by Princeton University Press, 41 William Street,
Princeton, New Jersey 08540
In the United Kingdom: Princeton University Press,
Chichester, West Sussex

Cover photograph © 1993 James Pipkin

Library of Congress Cataloging-in-Publication Data

Ely, John Hart, 1938–
War and responsibility : constitutional lessons of Vietnam and its
aftermath / John Hart Ely.
p. cm.
Includes bibliographical references and index.
1. War and emergency powers—United States—History. 2. War
Declaration of—United States—History. 3. Vietnamese conflict,
1961–1975—United States. I. Title.
KF5060.E58 1993 342.73'0412—dc20 [347.302412] 92-45769

ISBN 0-691-08643-5
ISBN 0-691-02552-5 (pbk.)

This book has been composed in Adobe Times Roman

Princeton University Press books are printed on acid-free paper
and meet the guidelines for permanence and durability of the
Committee on Production Guidelines for Book Longevity of the
Council on Library Resources

Fourth printing, and first paperback printing, 1995

Printed in the United States of America

10 9 8 7 6 5 4